The Organizational Aspects of
Corporate and Organizational Crime

The Organizational Aspects of Corporate and Organizational Crime

Special Issue Editor

Judith van Erp

MDPI • Basel • Beijing • Wuhan • Barcelona • Belgrade

MDPI

Special Issue Editor
Judith van Erp
University Utrecht
Netherlands

Editorial Office
MDPI
St. Alban-Anlage 66
Basel, Switzerland

This is a reprint of articles from the Special Issue published online in the open access journal *Administrative Sciences* (ISSN 2076-3387) in 2018 (available at: http://www.mdpi.com/journal/admsci/special_issues/Organizational_Crime)

For citation purposes, cite each article independently as indicated on the article page online and as indicated below:

LastName, A.A.; LastName, B.B.; LastName, C.C. Article Title. *Journal Name* **Year**, *Article Number*, Page Range.

ISBN 978-3-03897-258-7 (Pbk)
ISBN 978-3-03897-259-4 (PDF)

Contents

About the Special Issue Editor

Judith van Erp is professor of Public Institutions at the Utrecht School of Governance, Utrecht University, the Netherlands. She studies corporate crimes and offenses, and legal and extralegal reactions to it.

administrative
sciences

MDPI

Editorial

The Organization of Corporate Crime: Introduction to Special Issue of Administrative Sciences

Judith van Erp

Utrecht School of Governance, Utrecht University, Bijlhouwerstraat 6, 3511 ZC Utrecht, The Netherlands;
J.G.vanErp@uu.nl

Received: 12 July 2018; Accepted: 12 July 2018; Published: 19 July 2018

Corporate crimes seem endemic to modern society. Newspapers are filled on a daily basis with examples of financial manipulation, accounting fraud, food fraud, cartels, bribery, toxic spills and environmental harms, corporate human rights violations, insider trading, privacy violations, discrimination, corporate manslaughter or violence, and, recently, software manipulation. Clearly, the problem of corporate crime transcends the micro level of the individual 'rotten apple' (Ashforth et al. 2008; Monahan and Quinn 2006); although corporate crimes are ultimately committed by individual members of an organization, they have more structural roots, as the enabling and justifying organizational context in which they take place plays a defining role. Accounts of corporate fraud, misrepresentation, or deception that foreground individual offender's motivations and characteristics, often fail to acknowledge that organizational decisions are more than the aggregation of individual choices and actions, and that organizations are more than simply the environment in which individual action takes place (Huising and Silbey 2018). "Corporate crime is organizational crime, and its explanation calls for an organizational level of analysis" (Kramer 1982, p. 79).

Organization studies have therefore become increasingly preoccupied with explaining organizational dysfunctional and antisocial behavior, misconduct, and deviancy (Greve et al. 2010), known as "the dark side of organization" (Linstead et al. 2014), and also has an important contribution to make to our understanding of corporate crime and its prevention. On the other hand, administrative and organization sciences studying the administration, management, leadership, cultures, and governance institutions of organizations, as well as their interactions with the behavior within these organizations, should address corporate crimes as an object of study, as failures and rogue processes can inform organization theory.

The multiple aspects and causes of corporate crime call for a multidisciplinary and interdisciplinary approach and a variety of perspectives. Corporate crime has been predominantly studied in criminology, economics, and law. In addition, insights from psychology, sociology, anthropology, business ethics and political science, high reliability and safety science, and information and technological sciences are highly relevant. Many of these have links with organization science. In criminology, Edwin Sutherland (1949) is usually named the "founding father" of corporate and white-collar crime scholarship, introducing the notion that crime happens not just in the streets, but also "in the suites", in his Presidential Address to the American Sociological Association in 1939; although corporate crime scholarship dates back much further and has European roots (Hebberecht 2015; Huisman et al. 2015). Criminology, "the body of knowledge regarding crime as a social phenomenon [including] ... processes of making laws, of breaking laws, and of reacting towards the breaking of laws" (Sutherland and Cressey 1960, p. 3), studies white-collar crime, "crimes of the powerful", elite crime, and corporate and organizational crimes. Within this spectrum, we define corporate or organizational crimes as illegal or harmful acts, committed by legitimate organizations or their members, primarily for the benefit of these organizations (Van Erp and Huisman 2017). This broad conceptualization parallels Greve et al.'s (Greve et al. 2010, p. 56) definition of organizational misconduct, as "behavior in or by an organization that a social-control agent judges to transgress a line separating right from wrong; where such a line can separate legal, ethical, and socially responsible behavior from their antitheses", in the sense that it encompasses formally criminalized acts as well as a range of harmful acts that use creative compliance and exploit legal loopholes, particularly in the global economy. Corporate crimes may also incur individual gain, but the term corporate crime is usually reserved for crimes in which this is only a secondary motive or outcome, as opposed to white-collar crime, namely, "crime committed by a person of respectability and a high social status in the course of his occupation" (Friedrichs 2010), primarily for the benefit individuals. As the concept of corporate crime better grasps the organizational and structural aspects of these forms of misconduct than the more individually-oriented term white-collar crime, 'corporate and organizational crime' has been chosen as the primary perspective for this special issue.

Organization studies have a long tradition of studying misconduct and deviance in organizational contexts (Linstead et al. 2014). This scholarship initially addressed misconduct at the workplace. Numerous crimes or unethical acts may be committed within organizations by its employees, such as theft, aggression, falsely calling in sick, falsifying reports, or other kinds of fraud or unethical behavior at the workplace (Biron 2010). These forms of deviance have frequently been addressed in organization science as the "dark side" of organizations (Linstead et al. 2014). In analogy, criminologists analytically distinguish workplace and occupational crimes—crimes with organizational members as victims or misconduct by employees against the organization—from corporate crime, which tends to focus on acts harmful to victims outside of the organization (Clinard and Quinney 1973; Van Erp and Huisman 2017).

In organization psychology, misconduct in organizations tends to be approached form an individualist rotten apple perspective (Linstead et al. 2014), although some research has started to explain individual misconduct at the workplace from more structural causes, such as the negative reciprocity that employees may display towards abusive management (Biron 2010), and the influence of 'toxic leadership' (Lipman-Blumen 2005; Pelletier 2011). Following numerous revelations and corporate scandals, organization studies have shifted their attention from rotten apples, towards studying 'rotten barrels' and 'rotten orchards' (Scholten and Ellemers 2016; Zyglidopoulos and Fleming 2016); and have provided accounts of the social organization of institutionalized deviance (Vaughan 1999; Gray 2013). The sociology of deviance acknowledges the difference between individual deviance in an organizational context, and organizational deviance rooted in the system itself (Vaughan 1999), by addressing the institutional structures and power relations that may generate unethical organizational behavior. What criminologists call corporate crime, however, such as industrial hazards (Vaughan 1999, 2002; Perrow 1984), workplace unsafety or corporate manslaughter (Gray 2013; Almond and Gray 2017), and labor exploitation and modern slavery (Crane 2013), is sometimes seen as outside the realm of organization studies, which have not been particularly preoccupied with the victims of organizational deviance. The obvious organizational aspect in these harms and the fact that they clearly surpass individual intentionality warrants more attention in organization science.

This special issue of Administrative Sciences focuses on the organizational and administrative aspects of a broad spectrum of corporate and organizational crimes. In addition to the macro-level factors (such as regulation, enforcement, and market conditions) and the micro-level factors (such as CEO's narcissistic traits or individual greed) as motives for white-collar crime, meso-level factors related to organizations and their administration (such as organizational structure, culture, and management and leadership) play a major role in the explanations for corporate crime. Organizations provide individuals with positions, incentives, networks, rules, routines, perceptions, and beliefs, which structure opportunities for crime. Thus, organizational factors can explain how misconduct in organizations is defined, perceived, normalized, organized, and facilitated on the one hand, and controlled and prevented on the other hand. In parallel, this introduction discusses the relation between organizations and corporate crime along three lines, the role of the organization as 'cause' of corporate crime, its role as 'cure' for corporate crime, and, lastly, the 'organization of' the crime, referring to the instrumental and social means that organizations offer (cf. Rosoff 2007; Punch 2000, 2003; Wheeler and Rothman 1982).

1. The Organization as Cause

Following the idea that crime is not only a matter of bad apples but also bad barrels, criminologists have embraced the study of organizational factors as causes of corporate crime (Zyglidopoulos and Fleming 2016; Huisman 2016). Corporate organizations form the institutional context for corporate offenses, as organizations provide the motives, opportunities, and means for corporate crime (Punch 2000, 2003). Thus, an organizational perspective is an important part of the explanatory theories of corporate crime. Although some critical criminologists argue that all corporations are inherently and 'pathologically' dispositioned towards bending the law in the interest of profit maximization (Tombs and Whyte 2015; Gross 1978), it is widely accepted that some organizations are more crime-prone than others; organizations have 'criminogenic' features related to specific characteristics of the organizational strategy, structure, and culture (Huisman 2016).

Organizational strategies provide employees with incentives to perform, which can turn into motivations for fraud in firms prioritizing short term profit over long term profit and imposing unrealistic growth targets on personnel. Unattainable targets are often associated with strain (Merton 1938; Agnew et al. 2009), due to the perception that legitimate means are insufficient to meet economic goals, and that illegal means are the only option to realize ambitious targets (Huisman 2016). Strain is often experienced at the middle-management level, when middle managers are pressurized to realize goals set by top management, without providing appropriate means. Many studies find positive relations between economic strain and corporate crime (see [Huisman 2016] for an overview). The Volkswagen Diesel fraud is a recent and grave example of corporate fraud stemming from the combination of Volkswagen's extreme growth targets and its inability to develop the technological innovations required for meeting sustainability standards in ways that would still satisfy consumers (Ewing 2017).

Organizational 'structures' and 'information' and 'decision-making' procedures may result in irrationalities, group think, flawed risk perceptions, or secrecy with regard to misconduct (Vaughan 1999; Mills and Koliba 2015; Van De Bunt 2010), in various ways. Firstly, the complexity of an organization is seen as a potential contributing factor to misconduct and fraud. Complex organizations are, in general, more difficult to control and generate a diffusion of responsibilities, which may create ambiguity with regard to desired behavior or opportunities for offenses. Complexity may regard the geographical dispersion of firms with many production sites, firms with many layers of hierarchy, a specialized division of labor, or with more interdependent subunits working on pieces of a larger and more complex task. In highly decentralized multinationals, local units may feel detached from the mother corporation and feel justified to engage in local corruption to satisfy specific local needs or to adapt to local practices. These forms of complexity offer more autonomy to subunits and complicate control, which is also being more costly than in less complex organizational structures. Both Nick Leeson's fraud at Barings Bank, and more recently, the Libor fraud, are examples of corporate frauds where geographic and cultural distances between the Hong Kong and the London headquarters in the case of Barings, and between the Rabobank headquarters in the Netherlands and the 'rogue' Rabobank traders in the London City in the Libor case, contributed to the fraud.

With regard to information processing, scholars have also addressed limitations in the organizational capacity and professionality as explanations for corporate crime. Corporate crime can stem from incompetence, omission, negligence, mismanagement, failed risk awareness, or group think (Huisman and Van Erp 2013; Huisman 2016). Important parallels exist between the criminological scholarship addressing these failures and the scholarship on mistakes, accidents, and disasters in organization sociology and the sociology of deviance (Vaughan 1999, 2002; Gray and Silbey 2014; Palmer 2012; Perrow 1984).

In addition to the structure of the firm itself, the structure of the firm's environment is a relevant organizational aspect that matters for the explanation of corporate crime, such as the degree of competitiveness, the growth or decline of the industry; the regulations and professional norms of the industry; and the informal social control in the industry, including opportunities for reporting by external witnesses (Van Erp and Loyens 2018). Also, the potential facilitating roles of professional consultants, such as lawyers, accountants, tax advisers, and banks in facilitating corporate crime, is an area of research in which organizational studies of professions can provide important insight.

Organizational hierarchies are related to corporate crime in several ways. Firstly, there are opportunities and flaws inherent to the leadership position itself, related to the status of top managers and the narcissistic character elements attributed to leaders. High-status positions may induce feelings of invulnerability, entitlement, overconfidence, hubris, and excessive optimism about risk (Graffin et al. 2013; Chatterjee and Hambrick 2007). Leadership research has drawn attention to the risks related to 'heroic' and 'celebrity' CEO's, the leaders who perceive rules as 'for other people', as they see themselves as innovators of rules rather than subjected to rules; parallel to the saying that "managers do things right, but leaders to the right things" (Arnulf and Gottschalk 2013). Arnulf and Gottschalk argue that the recognition of heroic leadership status in the general public may have a stimulating effect on the psychological traits that could increase the likelihood of engaging in white-collar crime; an observation shared in criminology, where media have been found 'cheerleading' offending firms (Rosoff 2007). Media attention may increase success and admiration, which may strengthen the sense of importance and entitlement already inherent in leadership positions, and may bring narcissistic personality traits to the fore. In fact, 'superstar' CEO's are found to engage significantly more often than less celebrity CEO's to encounter criminal prosecutions or dismissal by shareholders (Graffin et al. 2013). These factors not only explain individual behavior of corporate leaders, but also apply to corporations themselves, as high-status manufacturing firms are more likely to commit corporate crimes than low-status firms (Mishina et al. 2010).

Narcissistic personality traits in corporate leaders have also been empirically associated with corporate and white-collar crime. As narcissistic leaders display overconfidence and a risk-appetite, as well as a lack of empathy and social responsibility, they may set impossible goals or engage in illegal practices when the legal practices to realize goals are insufficient (Ouimet 2010; Piquero et al. 2005). Narcissistic leaders may also perceive the organization as an extension of themselves—organizational identification that may lead managers to dismiss contradiction and search for competitive, risk-taking, winner-mentality employees (Galvin et al. 2015). Lastly, high status can induce status anxiety, namely the fear of falling and loosing what has been achieved, which can motivate offenses (Weisburd et al. 1991). Thus, high status and heroic leaders may degrade into destructive or toxic leadership that may stimulate the breach of ethical or legal norms through the exploitation of vertical relationships in organizations. (Aguilera and Vadera 2008).

Success and heroic status may also create opportunities by advancing trust in a leader and putting someone beyond doubt, as is most vividly illustrated in the case of Bernie Madoff (Van De Bunt 2010), but also in other research, which points to unethical business leaders as role-models for their peers (Mishina et al. 2010; Bichler et al. 2015).

Organizational hierarchy also involves authority, control, and obedience. Authority plays a key role in influencing individuals to engage in organizational crime, as it may disengage people from social responsibilities and result in what are seen as crimes of obedience or crimes of loyalty. Haslam and Reicher (2017) argue that rather than blind obedience, organizational deviance stemming from authority should be understood as 'engaged followership', in which people are prepared to harm others because they identify with their leaders' cause and believe their actions to be virtuous. Thus, employee over-identification with an organization may result in organizational exploitative behavior, in which the relationship between the individual and the organization turns toxic, in the sense that the organization's identity subsumes and completely defines the self (Ouimet 2010; Biron 2010), and independent decision-making is compromised, as the individual blindly, narrowly, and single-mindedly pursues what he or she perceives to be in the organization's interest. Central to this are the neutralization techniques (Sykes and Matza 1957; Stadler and Benson 2012) adopted by individuals to justify unlawful or unthical behavior and at the same time, maintain positive self-concept's (Trahan 2011). Neutralizations may include 'appeals to higher loyalties'—collectivistic business cultures may stimulate individuals to put the interests of the organization or subgroup within the organization above their own values or norms (Aguilera and Vadera 2008). Neutralizations may also result in the denial of the legitimacy of the law and enforcement or a conviction that offending is justified as 'everyone else is doing it.'. The organization may also place a cognitive barrier between the individuals responsible for, and the victims of organizational misconduct. The study of these neutralizations is an important part of organizational behavioral ethics, the empirical branch of ethics that addresses how organizations socialize individuals to adopt motives and goals, as well as norms, beliefs, and identities (Kaptein 2013). Behavioral ethics research can sometimes explain how even well-intentioned people can behave unethically in organizations when situational and social factors stimulate them to do so (Haugh 2017a, 2017b; Kaptein 2013; Feldman 2018). Even in organizations with ethical codes and compliance programmes, toxic leadership by managers may overpower the normative pressure exercised by formal organizational ethics (Biron 2010; Mitchell and Ambrose 2007). When employers preach, but not practice ethical behavior, and employees feel that they are not treated ethically, the employees are less likely to conform to the organization's ethical values (Biron 2010).

Neutralizations often institutionalize beyond individual rationalizations to become part of deeper organizational cultures, shaping beliefs, cognitive biases, and social norms within organizations. Theories on white collar crime in criminology have originated from Sutherland's study of socialization processes, providing individuals with deviant social norms through differential association (Sutherland 1949). Organizational culture can refer to "shared values and beliefs, myths, interpretations, and meanings within an organization, and actions and behaviors, including customs, practices, norms, rituals, and implementation of control systems" (Schein 2010). 'Toxic' or 'criminogenic' organizational cultures can explain why paradoxically, it is often *conformity* to organizational norms and goals that can explain corporate deviancy (Vaughan 1999).

This special issue profiles four articles dedicated to various relations between organizational cultures and corporate crimes. The paper by Van Rooij and Fine (2018) offers an elaborate overview of the elements of toxic corporate culture, presented as an analytical framework enabling assessors to conduct a 'forensic ethnography' of organizational cultures. Van Rooij and Fine apply their analytical framework to the cases of the Volkswagen Diesel Fraud, BP's drilling in the Gulf of Mexico, and Wells Fargo's misselling of financial products to customers; these are three high profile and recent cases of corporate crime that highlight that toxic cultures were deeply embedded even in the most high-profile and high-regarded corporations—both Volkswagen and BP had reputations for corporate social responsibility. In addition to deconstructing the toxic cultural elements in these organizations, Van Rooij and Fine also pay attention to 'detoxing' corporate cultures; the steps necessary to increase ethical decision-making within organizations. These insights are not limited to ostensibly offending corporations, but may be of value to all organizations with unethical structures, values, or practices. Van Rooij and Fine argue that, although holding executives accountable is an important element of detoxing, it certainly does not end with the replacement of the responsible leaders; changing culture requires de-neutralizing the values and organizational norms that allowed rule-breaking to start.

An organization–cultural perspective may explain why behavior that may seem antisocial or irrational from an outside perspective, is often rational from the perspective of insiders. This is the central point of argumentation in Kanti Pertiwi's (Pertiwi 2018) contribution to this special issue, which consists of a critical analysis of the literatures on corruption in organizations. Pertiwi underscores the value of an anthropological perspective, which focuses on social constructions of correct and incorrect behavior in organizations, rather than departing from a predetermined norm. Contextual analyses foreground people's situated and subjective experience of norms, practices, and role identities, and thus may help to understand corruption better than the more normative approaches that see corruption as inherently dysfunctional, she argues.

The empirical research presented by Gorsira et al. (2018) in this special issue, relates individual corruption to the ethical climate of organizations. Their findings suggest that organizational culture influences individual personal norms and social norms with regard to corruption; employees who perceive their organization's culture as less ethical, experience weaker personal and social norms to refrain from corruption. This research is at the core of administrative and organization science connecting individual motives to organizational culture.

Lastly, Sandra Schruijer's (Schruijer 2018) essay on collusion in organizations offers a psychodynamic perspective by describing the subtle and often nonconscious group decision-making processes in which organizational members' mutually supportive relations satisfy needs for approval and security and avoid rejection. Although collusion in itself is no crime, it may be part of a toxic culture that entails neglect, irresponsible, corrupt, or other criminal behavior, or may result in people collectively choosing the wrong course of action.

2. The Organization as Cure

A range of formal and informal systems of social and administrative control operate within organizations. Thus, organizations not only constitute causes of corporate crime, but also offer important opportunities for its prevention. Organizational crime can stem from an absence or poor quality of formal procedures for business conduct, as is likely in firms that put goals over means, such as firms in highly competitive markets, or newly started entrepreneurial firms that are more busy with developing and expanding the business than with risk management (Aguilera and Vadera 2008). Organization and administrative sciences as well as business ethics have extensively studied compliance, ethics, and integrity programmes and policies, identifying ingredients for successful policies and identifying compliance failures. It is not uncommon to find these failures in organizations with elaborate compliance programmes and codes of conduct—an indication that compliance systems can also be introduced as symbolic responses to external pressure, and resort to check-the-box bureaucratic ritualism and cosmetic compliance (Merton 1968; Krawiec 2003). Volkswagen and Enron are just two examples of firms that had extensive compliance programmes, yet conducted massive fraud, as these programmes did not actually curb misconduct. Methodologically, there is a knowledge gap with regard to the causality relation between formal and informal control; do formal control systems make for ethical organizations, or do ethical organizations create elaborate control systems (Apel and Paternoster 2009)?

Corporations often attribute fraud to rogue departments or individuals (Scholten and Ellemers 2016). This reaction may stem from a truly limited view on what causes misconduct as well as unawareness of the influence of organizational culture, but may also be part of the compliance 'ritual', as Parker remarks in her research on the social meaning of deterrence of cartel laws, "the corporate elite see it as their job to define anti-cartel law into risk management strategies and internal compliance programs that their senior officers can implement—boxes that they can tick off, in order to demonstrate their positive commitment to the law, and 'manage' any breaches that do occur. They might hope that their compliance systems do work to avoid non-compliance, but they are also well aware that the existence of these systems can be used to displace any responsibility for cartel conduct that does occur to 'rogue' individuals or units within the firm" (Parker 2013, p. 188). Likewise, Haugh (2017b) observes a 'criminalization' of compliance, in the sense that corporate compliance is increasingly adopting a criminal law approach, making use of surveillance, audits, criminal background checks, and internal sanctions. Haugh questions the effectiveness of such programmes, as ethical behavior should come from intrinsic motivation, not from monetary incentives. Indeed, formal internal control systems should be backed up by informal control within organizations to create a shared culture of integrity. Rather than strengthening deterrence, corporations should adopt compliance programmes that combat the psychological mechanisms behind corporate crime, reverse rationalizations of violations, and allow employees to discuss compliance and ethics dilemma's in their daily work environment.

The contribution of Clarissa Meerts (2018) to this special issue adds to the debate about the nature of corporate compliance and control systems by addressing the role of corporate security investigators, such as: private investigation firms, forensic accountancy services, or in-house security departments tasked with the identification and settlement of internal norm violations within organizations. As the equivalent of external law enforcement, Meerts finds these investigators to have a significant role in deciding upon the detection, disclosure, and settlement of organizational offenses, without having a clear legal basis or a justice focus. Moreover, they contribute to a lack of transparency of corporate crime, limit general deterrence by handling offenses within corporations behind closed doors, and tend to protect the firm, which may hinder societal retribution and redress and also disproportionly blame the individual offender. Meerts's argumentation thus adds to the scholarship debating the effectiveness of 'criminal justice'-oriented compliance not by criticizing its effectiveness, but its justice component; its lack of procedural legitimacy and contribution to societal unawareness about corporate misconduct.

Yet, the latter is only one of the factors limiting the prosecution of corporate crimes. Perhaps more importantly, the reporting of corporate offenses to authorities is often disincentivized, as employees or other witnesses face serious negative consequences of reporting. Whereas many organization and administrative science scholars have addressed whistleblowing protection and whistleblower motives (Miceli and Near 2002; Lewis et al. 2014; Roberts 2014), the institutional arrangements for whistleblowing have received much less attention. The contribution of Loyens and Vandekerckhove (2018) in this special issue fills this gap with a comparative case study of whistleblowing agencies in 11 countries. Their research indicates that countries are more frequently installing dedicated whistleblowing protection agencies, and describes the tasks, means, and organization of these agencies. The degree and nature of support to whistleblowers varies. In particular, their research raises the question whether investigative tasks and whistleblower support can effectively be combined in one organization—a question with clear practical relevance.

3. The Organization of the Crime

The question how corporate crimes are organized is classic to criminology, but is also one that fits very well in organization sciences, as organizations provide opportunities for mobilizing the specialist knowledge necessary to commit crime; for guarding secrets; disguising illegality, and generating, hiding, and spending illegal profit—all opportunities that individuals lack. Organizations can also use their resources to delay or obstruct enforcement; through litigation against enforcement authorities; the destruction of evidence about who was responsible (including shredding of documents) or delaying detection by raid procedures, or use political contacts to prevent the force of the law applying to them (Coleman 1985). Organizations can thus be perceived not only as the cause or cure, but also as the weapon for corporate crime (Wheeler and Rothman 1982; Punch 2000, 2003); not as the environment for misconduct, but its purposive instrument. Organizational scholars know relatively little about the implementation of organizational crime within firms and its coordination (Aven 2015), and have called for more empirical research in this area (Brass et al. 1998, Greve et al. 2010; Palmer and Maher 2006).

The contribution of Lord et al. (2018) to this special issue on organizing the monies for corporate crime is a fine example of how such empirical research may uncover the misuse of legitimate organizational structures for concealing illicit proceeds of corporate crimes. Through case studies of corporate bribery in international businesses and corporate tax fraud, Lord et al. reveal how the legitimacy and anonimity of corporations provides cover for illicit practices, and how third-party professionals facilitate these. Whereas Lord et al.'s paper focuses on the misuses of organizational structures, an organization perspective can also provide understandings of the social organization of corporate crimes; the interaction and communication between participants, for example, and strategies to conceal illegal acts (Baker and Faulkner 1993; Van De Bunt 2010). The involvement in criminal acts add a specific challenge to the communication between organizational members; not only must

Adm. Sci. **2018**, *8*, 36

they share information to coordinate activities, as in all areas of organizational life, they must also keep the activity secret to avoid detection. This provides a classic dilemma between security and efficiency (Morselli et al. 2007). The Madoff fraud case is particularly illustrative, as Madoff's social and professional status and reputation functioned as a cover for his criminal enterprise, and the management and physical structure of his firm—with a 'secret' department on a different floor, and a stand-alone computer to serve the Ponzi scheme—made it possible to execute his deceit (Van De Bunt 2010). Aven's study of organizational communication in accounting fraud uses archival email data of the Enron Corporation (2015) to show that participants in Enron's corrupt projects initially communicate less than participants in non-corrupt practices. Their secretive behavior diminishes over time, which can be attributed to increased trust between participants. Thus, an interest in corporate crime draws the attention of organization scientists from the large, public, and formal organizations, often studied in organization sciences to the less visible, covert, secret, and underground aspects of organizational life (Scott 2013).

As corporate crimes are often embedded within the firm's social and professional environment, organizations often collaborate to commit and conceal crime (Bertrand et al. 2014; Lord and Levi 2017; Jaspers 2017). The corporate crime literature has primarily focused on the relations between individual motives and actions, and organizational characteristics and behaviors—the vertical relationships between organizations and their members, often with a focus on hierarchy and decision making processes. Less attention has been paid to how businesses collaborate to commit crimes, and how they commit crimes collectively rather than individually (Bertrand et al. 2014). Organizational theory adds the perspective of (social) networks (Greve et al. 2010); a perspective that can be highly valid for the explanation of interorganizational illegal activities, such as cartels (Baker and Faulkner 1993) and the crimes committed in value chains involving various related actors, such as food fraud. The role of social and organizational networks and business associations in facilitating connections between elite members and deviant organizations, as well as in disseminating deviant norms and illegal practices, is a relevant point of overlap between corporate crime and organization studies (Baker and Faulkner 1993; Reeves-Latour and Morselli 2017). This includes the interpersonal relationships between the deviant (and law-abiding) members of the corporate elites, as they interact in informal social circles that may become fertile ground for criminal activities. The social network study by Bichler et al. (2015), of the interlocks between the CEO's of firms found in violation of Securities and Exchange Commission regulation and compliant firms is an excellent example of the value of such research; although they find violating CEO's to be less well-connected than compliant CEO's, their study also points to particular industries with significant interlock (pharmaceutical and financial industry); and specific business associations that connect violators and compliant firms. As social networks can provide environments for the diffusion of deviant norms and practices, such studies have specific societal relevance. This is not only the case for the networks of the corporate elites, but also networks in everyday business, where line managers and sales persons are tasked with the realization of corporate performance targets in difficult markets, and extensive social pressure is sometimes exercised (Parker 2013).

Conflicts of Interest: The author declares no conflict of interest.

References

Agnew, Robert, Nicole Leeper Piquero, and Francis T. Cullen. 2009. General strain theory and white-collar crime. In *The Criminology of White-Collar Crime*. Edited by Sally S. Simpson and David Weisburd. New York: Springer, pp. 35–60.

Aguilera, Ruth V., and Abhijeet K. Vadera. 2008. The dark side of authority: Antecedents, mechanisms, and outcomes of organizational corruption. *Journal of Business Ethics* 77: 431–49. [CrossRef]

Almond, Paul, and Garry C. Gray. 2017. Frontline Safety: Understanding the Workplace as a Site of Regulatory Engagement. *Law and Policy* 39: 5–26. [CrossRef]

Apel, Robert, and Raymond Paternoster. 2009. Understanding "criminogenic" corporate culture: What white-collar crime researchers can learn from studies of the adolescent employment–crime relationship. In *The Criminology of White-Collar Crime*. Edited by Sally S. Simpson and David Weisburd. New York: Springer, pp. 15–33.

Arnulf, Jan Ketil, and Petter Gottschalk. 2013. Heroic Leaders as White-Collar Criminals: An Empirical Study. *Journal of Investigative Psychology and Offender Profiling* 10: 96–113. [CrossRef]

Ashforth, Blake E., Dennis A. Gioia, Sandra L. Robinson, and Linda K. Treviño. 2008. Re-viewing organizational corruption. *Academy of Management Review* 33: 670–84. [CrossRef]

Aven, Brandy L. 2015. The paradox of corrupt networks: An analysis of organizational crime at Enron. *Organization Science* 26: 980–96. [CrossRef]

Baker, Wayne E., and Robert R. Faulkner. 1993. The social organization of conspiracy: Illegal networks in the heavy electrical equipment industry. *American Sociological Review*, 837–60. [CrossRef]

Bertrand, Olivier, Fabrice Lumineau, and Evgenia Fedorova. 2014. The supportive factors of firms' collusive behavior: Empirical evidence from cartels in the European Union. *Organization Studies* 35: 881–908. [CrossRef]

Bichler, Gisela, Andrea Schoepfer, and Stacy Bush. 2015. White collars and black ties: Interlocking social circles of elite corporate offenders. *Journal of Contemporary Criminal Justice* 31: 279–96. [CrossRef]

Biron, Michal. 2010. Negative reciprocity and the association between perceived organizational ethical values and organizational deviance. *Human Relations* 63: 875–97. [CrossRef]

Brass, Daniel J., Kenneth D. Butterfield, and Bruce C. Skaggs. 1998. Relationships and unethical behavior: A social network perspective. *The Academy of Management Review* 23: 14–31. [CrossRef]

Chatterjee, Arijit, and Donald C. Hambrick. 2007. It's All about Me: Narcissistic Chief Executive Officers and Their Effects on Company Strategy and Performance. *ASQ* 52: 351–86. [CrossRef]

Clinard, Marshall Barron, and Richard Quinney. 1973. *Criminal Behavior Systems: A Typology*, 2nd ed. New York: Holt, Rinehart and Winston.

Coleman, James William. 1985. Law and power: The Sherman Antitrust Act and its enforcement in the petroleum industry. *Social Problems* 32: 264–74. [CrossRef]

Crane, Andrew. 2013. Modern slavery as a management practice: Exploring the conditions and capabilities for human exploitation. *Academy of Management Review* 38: 49–69. [CrossRef]

Ewing, Jack. 2017. *Faster, Higher, Farther. The Volkswagen Scandal*. New York: Norton and Company.

Feldman, Yuval. 2018. *The Law of Good People. Challenging States' Ability to Regulate Human Behavior*. Cambridge: Cambridge University Press.

Friedrichs, David. 2010. *Trusted Criminals: White-Collar Crime in Contemporary Society*. Belmont: Wadsworth Cengage Learning.

Galvin, Benjamin M., Donald Lange, and Blake E. Ashforth. 2015. Narcissistic organizational identification: Seeing oneself as central to the organization's identity. *Academy of Management Review* 40: 163–81. [CrossRef]

Gorsira, Madelijne, Linda Steg, Adriaan Denkers, and Wim Huisman. 2018. Corruption in Organizations: Ethical Climate and Individual Motives. *Administrative Sciences* 8: 4. [CrossRef]

Graffin, Scott D., Jonathan Bundy, Joseph F. Porac, James B. Wade, and Dennis P. Quinn. 2013. Falls from grace and the hazards of high status: The 2009 British MP expense scandal and its impact on parliamentary elites. *Administrative Science Quarterly* 58: 313–45. [CrossRef]

Gray, Garry C. 2013. Insider accounts of institutional corruption: Examining the social organization of unethical behaviour. *British Journal of Criminology* 53: 533–51. [CrossRef]

Gray, Garry C., and Susan S. Silbey. 2014. Governing Inside the Organization: Interpreting Regulation and Compliance. *American Journal of Sociology* 120: 96–145. [CrossRef]

Greve, Henrich R., Donald Palmer, and Jo-Ellen Pozner. 2010. Organizations Gone Wild: The Causes, Processes, and Consequences of Organizational Misconduct. *The Academy of Management Annals* 4: 53–107. [CrossRef]

Gross, Edward. 1978. Organizations as Criminal Actors. In *Two Faces of Deviance: Crimes of the Powerless and Powerful*. Edited by Paul R. Wilson and John Braithwaite. Brisbane: University of Queensland Press, pp. 198–213.

Haslam, S. Alexander, and Stephen D. Reicher. 2017. 50 Years of "Obedience to Authority": From Blind Conformity to Engaged Followership. *Annual Review of Law and Social Science* 13: 59–78. [CrossRef]

Haugh, Todd. 2017a. The Ethics of Intracorporate Behavioral Ethics. *California Law Review Online* 8: 1–18.

Haugh, Todd. 2017b. Cadillac Compliance Breakdown. *Stanford Law Revieuw Online* 69: 198.

Hebberecht, Patrick. 2015. Willem Bonger: The Unrecognised European Pioneer of the Study of White-Collar Crime. In *The Routledge Handbook of White-Collar and Corporate Crime in Europe*. Edited by Judith van Erp, Gudrun Vande Walle and Wim Huisman. Routledge: Abingdon, pp. 125–32.

Huising, Ruthanne, and Susan Silbey. 2018. From Nudge to Culture and Back Again: Coalface Governance in the Regulated Organization. *American Review of Law and Social Sciences*, forthcoming. [CrossRef]

Huisman, Wim. 2016. Criminogenic organizational properties and dynamics. In *The Oxford Handbook of White-Collar Crime*. Edited by Shanna R. Van Slyke, Michael L. Benson and Francis T. Cullen. Oxford: Oxford University Press.

Huisman, Wim, and Judith Van Erp. 2013. Opportunities for Environmental Crime: A Test of Situational Crime Prevention Theory. *British Journal of Criminology* 53: 1178–200. [CrossRef]

Huisman, Wim, Judith van Erp, G. Vande Walle, and Joep Beckers. 2015. Criminology and White-Collar Crime in Europe. In *The Routledge Handbook of White-Collar and Corporate Crime in Europe*. Edited by Judith van Erp, Gudrun Vande Walle and Wim Huisman. Abingdon: Routledge, pp. 1–21.

Jaspers, Jelle D. 2017. Managing cartels: How cartel participants create stability in the absence of law. *European Journal on Criminal Policy and Research* 23: 319–335. [CrossRef]

Kaptein, Muel. 2013. *Workplace Morality: Behavioral Ethics in Organizations*. Bingley: Emerald.

Kramer, Ronald C. 1982. Corporate Crime: An Organizational Perspective. In *White-Collar and Economic Crime: Multidisciplinary and Cross-National Perspectives*. Edited by Peter Wickman and Timothy Dailey. Lexington: Lexington Books, pp. 75–95.

Krawiec, Kimberly D. 2003. Cosmetic Compliance and the Failure of Negotiated Governance. *Washington University Law Quarterly* 81: 487–544. [CrossRef]

Lewis, David, Alexander Jonathan Brown, and Richard E. Moberly. 2014. Whistleblowing, its importance and the state of the research. In *International Handbook on Whistleblowing Research*. Edited by Alexander Jonathan Brown, David Lewis, Richard Moberly and Wim Vandekerckhove. Cheltenham: Edward Elgar Publishing, pp. 1–34.

Linstead, Stephen, Garance Maréchal, and Ricky W. Griffin. 2014. Theorizing and researching the dark side of organization. *Organization Studies* 35: 165–88. [CrossRef]

Lipman-Blumen, Jean. 2005. Toxic leadership: a conceptual framework. In *Encyclopaedia of Executive Governance*. Edited by Frank Bournois and Jerome Duval-Hamel. Paris: European School of Managemen, pp. 182–85.

Lord, Nicholas, and Michael Levi. 2017. Organizing the finances for and the finances from transnational corporate bribery. *European Journal of Criminology* 14: 365–89. [CrossRef]

Lord, Nicholas, Karin van Wingerde, and Liz Campbell. 2018. Organising the Monies of Corporate Financial Crimes via Organisational Structures: Ostensible Legitimacy, Effective Anonymity, and Third-Party Facilitation. *Administrative Sciences* 8: 17. [CrossRef]

Loyens, Kim, and Wim Vandekerckhove. 2018. Whistleblowing from an International Perspective: A Comparative Analysis of Institutional Arrangements. *Administrative Sciences* 8: 1–16. [CrossRef]

Meerts, Clarissa Annemarie. 2018. The Organisation as the Cure for Its Own Ailments: Corporate Investigators in The Netherlands. *Administrative Sciences* 8: 1–15. [CrossRef]

Merton, Robert King. 1938. Social structure and anomie. *American Sociological Review* 3: 672–82. [CrossRef]

Merton, Robert King. 1968. *Social Theory and Social Structure*. New York: Simon and Schuster.

Miceli, Marcia P., and Janet P. Near. 2002. What makes whistle-blowers effective? Three field studies. *Human Relations* 55: 455–79. [CrossRef]

Mills, Russell W., and Christopher J. Koliba. 2015. The challenge of accountability in complex regulatory networks: The case of the Deepwater Horizon oil spill. *Regulation and Governance* 9: 77–91. [CrossRef]

Mishina, Yuri, Bernadine J. Dykes, Emily S. Block, and Timothy G. Pollock. 2010. Why "good" firms do bad things: The effects of high aspirations, high expectations, and prominence on the incidence of corporate illegality. *Academy of Management Journal* 53: 701–22. [CrossRef]

Mitchell, Marie S., and Maureen L. Ambrose. 2007. Abusive Supervision and Workplace Deviance and the Moderating Effects of Negative Reciprocity Beliefs. *Journal of Applied Psychology* 92: 1159. [CrossRef] [PubMed]

Monahan, Susanne C., and Beth A. Quinn. 2006. Beyond 'bad apples' and 'weak leaders' Toward a neo-institutional explanation of organizational deviance. *Theoretical Criminology* 10: 361–85. [CrossRef]

Morselli, Carlo, Cynthia Giguère, and Katia Petit. 2007. The efficiency/security trade-off in criminal networks. *Social Networks* 29: 143–53. [CrossRef]

Ouimet, Gérard. 2010. Dynamics of narcissistic leadership in organizations: Towards an integrated research model. *Journal of Managerial Psychology* 25: 713–26. [CrossRef]

Palmer, Donald. 2012. *Normal Organizational Wrongdoing: A Critical Analysis of Theories of Misconduct in and by Organizations*. Oxford: Oxford University Press.

Palmer, Donald, and Michael W. Maher. 2006. Developing the process model of collective corruption. *Journal of Management Inquiry* 15: 363–70. [CrossRef]

Parker, Christine. 2013. The war on cartels and the social meaning of deterrence. *Regulation and Governance* 7: 174–94. [CrossRef]

Pelletier, Katie L. 2011. Leader toxicity: An empirical investigation of toxic behavior and rhetoric. *Leadership* 6: 373–389. [CrossRef]

Perrow, Charles. 1984. *Normal Accidents: Living with High-Risk Technologies*. New York: Basic Books.

Pertiwi, Kanti. 2018. Contextualizing Corruption: A Cross-Disciplinary Approach to Studying Corruption in Organizations. *Administrative Sciences* 8: 12. [CrossRef]

Piquero, Nicole Leeper, Stephen G. Tibbetts, and Michael B. Blankenship. 2005. Examining the role of differential association and techniques of neutralization in explaining corporate crime. *Deviant Behavior* 26: 159–88. [CrossRef]

Punch, Maurice. 2000. Suite Violence: Why Managers Murder and Corporations Kill. *Crime, Law and Social Change* 33: 243–80. [CrossRef]

Punch, Maurice. 2003. Rotten Orchards: "Pestilence", Police Misconduct and System Failure. *Policing and Society* 13: 171–96. [CrossRef]

Reeves-Latour, Maxime, and Carlo Morselli. 2017. Bid-rigging networks and state-corporate crime in the construction industry. *Social Networks* 51: 158–70. [CrossRef]

Roberts, Perter. 2014. Motivations for whistleblowing: personal, private, and public interests. In *International Handbook on Whistleblowing Research*. Edited by Alexander Jonathan Brown, David Lewis, Richard Moberly and Wim Vandekerckhove. Cheltenham: Edward Elgar Publishing, pp. 207–29.

Rosoff, Stephen M. 2007. The Role of the Mass Media in the Enron Fraud. In *International Handbook of White-Collar and Corporate Crime*. Edited by Henry N. Pontell and Gilbert Geis. New York: Springer, pp. 513–22.

Schein, Edgar H. 2010. *Organizational Culture and Leadership*, 4th ed. San Francisco: Jossey-Bass.

Scholten, Wieke, and Naomi Ellemers. 2016. Bad apples or corrupting barrels? Preventing traders' misconduct. *Journal of Financial Regulation and Compliance* 24: 366–82. [CrossRef]

Schruijer, Sandra. 2018. The Role of Collusive Dynamics in the Occurrence of Organizational Crime: A Psychoanalytically Informed Social Psychological Perspective. *Administrative Sciences* 8: 1–5. [CrossRef]

Scott, Craig. 2013. *Anonymous Agencies, Backstreet Businesses, and Covert Collectives: Rethinking Organizations in the 21st Century*. Palo Alto: Stanford University Press.

Stadler, William A., and Michael L. Benson. 2012. Revisiting the Guilty Mind: The Neutralization of White-Collar Crime. *Criminal Justice Review* 37: 494–511. [CrossRef]

Sutherland, Edwin Hardin. 1949. *White-Collar Crime*. New York: Dryden Press.

Sutherland, Edwin Hardin, and Donald Ray Cressey. 1960. *Principles of Criminology*. New York: Rowman and Littlefield.

Sykes, Gresham M., and David Matza. 1957. Techniques of neutralization: A theory of delinquency. *American Sociological Review* 22: 664–70. [CrossRef]

Tombs, Steve, and David Whyte. 2015. *The Corporate Criminal: Why Corporations Must be Abolished*. London: Routledge.

Trahan, Adam. 2011. Filling in the Gaps in Culture-Based Theories of Organizational Crime. *Journal of Theoretical and Philosophical Criminology* 3: 89–109.

Van De Bunt, Henk. 2010. Walls of secrecy and silence: The Madoff case and cartels in the construction industry. *Criminology and Public Policy* 9: 435–53. [CrossRef]

Van Erp, Judith, and Wim Huisman. 2017. Corporate Crime. In *Routledge Companion to Criminological Theory and Concepts*. Edited by Avi Brisman, Eamonn Carrabine and Nigel South. Abingdon: Routledge.

Van Erp, Judith, and Kim Loyens. 2018. Why external witnesses report organizational misconduct to inspectorates: A comparative case study in three inspectorates. *Administration and Society*. [CrossRef]

Van Rooij, Benjamin, and Adam Fine. 2018. Toxic Corporate Culture: Assessing Organizational Processes of Deviancy. *Administrative Sciences* 8: 1–38. [CrossRef]

Vaughan, Diane. 1999. The dark side of organizations: Mistake, misconduct, and disaster. *Annual Review of Sociology* 25: 271–305. [CrossRef]

Vaughan, Diane. 2002. Criminology and the Sociology of Organizations: Analogy, Comparative Social Organization, and General Theory. *Crime, Law, and Social Change* 37: 117–36. [CrossRef]

Weisburd, David, Stanton Wheeler, Elin Waring, and Nancy Bode. 1991. *Crimes of the Middle Classes: White-Collar Offenders in the Federal Courts*. New Haven: Yale University Press.

Wheeler, Stanton, and Mitchell Lewis Rothman. 1982. The organization as weapon in white-collar crime. *Michigan Law Review* 80: 1403–26. [CrossRef]

Zyglidopoulos, Stelios C., and Peter Fleming. 2016. Organizational Self Restraint. In *The Oxford Handbook of White-Collar Crime*. Edited by Shanna R. Van Slyke, Michael L. Benson and Francis T. Cullen. Oxford: Oxford University Press.

administrative
sciences

MDPI

Article

Toxic Corporate Culture: Assessing Organizational Processes of Deviancy

Benjamin van Rooij [1,*] **and Adam Fine** [2]

[1] School of Law, University of California, Irvine, 401 East Peltason Drive CA 92697 and School of Law, University of Amsterdam, Nieuwe Achtergracht 166, 1018 WV Amsterdam, The Netherlands
[2] School of Criminology and Criminal Justice, Arizona State University, 411 N. Central Ave, Suite 633 Phoenix, Tempe, AZ 85004, USA; adfine@asu.edu
* Correspondence: bvanrooij@law.uci.edu

Received: 17 April 2018; Accepted: 16 June 2018; Published: 22 June 2018

Abstract: There is widespread recognition that organizational culture matters in corporations involved in systemic crime and wrongdoing. However, we know far less about how to assess and alter toxic elements within a corporate culture. The present paper draws on management science, anthropology, sociology of law, criminology, and social psychology to explain what organizational culture is and how it can sustain illegal and harmful corporate behavior. Through analyzing the corporate cultures at BP, Volkswagen, and Wells Fargo, this paper demonstrates that organizational toxicity does not just exist when corporate norms are directly opposed to legal norms, but also when: (a) it condones, neutralizes, or enables rule breaking; (b) it disables and obstructs compliance; and (c) actual practices contrast expressed compliant values. The paper concludes that detoxing corporate culture requires more than changing leadership or incentive structures. In particular, it requires addressing the structures, values, and practices that enable violations and obstruct compliance within an organization, as well as moving away from a singular focus on liability management (i.e., assigning blame and punishment) to an approach that prioritizes promoting transparency, honesty, and a responsibility to initiate and sustain actual cultural change.

Keywords: compliance; organizational culture; organizational crime; ethical climate; business ethics; social norms

1. Introduction

Following major corporate scandals, most of the attention focuses on assigning individual liability to the highest possible executive. Certainly, this practice is important as impunity should not be permitted to continue. However, to reduce corporate crime and misconduct, we must look beyond the role of high-level executives or a few rogue employees to focus on the organizational traits that stimulate rule-breaking and harmful behavior. This paper outlines how we can assess and address such toxic elements in corporate cultures. It does so by analyzing three major cases of corporate wrongdoing: BP, Volkswagen, and Wells Fargo. These recent scandals demonstrate that addressing organizational traits is vital.

On 20 April 2010, an explosion and fire at the Deepwater Horizon drilling rig resulted in a massive crude oil leak in the Gulf of Mexico. On that day, BP, the British petroleum company that operated the rig, became responsible for the largest oil spill in U.S. history (PBS 2010). In addition to causing tremendous economic, ecological, and health effects around the Gulf's coast, eleven employees died.

This was not the first time BP operations had caused a major disaster in the U.S. On 23 March 2005, an explosion at a BP refinery in Texas City killed 15 people and injured 170 more. And in March 2006, BP caused the largest spill on Alaska's North Slope, leaking 267,000 gallons of crude oil on the freezing tundra. That particular spill went undetected for five days (Barringer 2006).

In all three disasters, the accidents occurred because BP had failed to perform sufficient maintenance, had constantly cut costs, had reduced its engineering capacity, and had not responded to employee complaints about safety hazards (Steffy 2010). These incidents demonstrate that well before the massive Deepwater Horizon spill in 2010, BP had continuously suffered from safety issues and had repeatedly received information about hazards. Yet incident after incident, complaint after complaint, report after report, and promise after promise, it continued to seek ways to cut costs instead of prioritizing safety and compliance. The issues at BP were not just the product of individual decisions, but rather of broader patterns within the company. As such, these problems were endemic to the culture at BP. Indeed, William Reilly, the co-chair of the presidential investigation commission on the Gulf of Mexico oil disaster concluded that BP had been operating under a "culture of complacency" (Goldenberg 2010).

BP is not unique. In 2014, American researchers started to suspect that German carmaker Volkswagen (VW) was using a device that would lower its vehicles' emissions specifically during laboratory testing, while the nitrogen oxides (NOx) emissions under actual driving conditions would be about 40 times higher (Ewing 2017). Investigations uncovered that VW had actually installed this cheat device in over 11 million vehicles. After a West Virginia University research report first discovered the discrepancy between laboratory and real driving emissions, and California regulators later confirmed this, VW stalled the investigations, questioned the investigative methods, and even modified the cheat device to make it even more effective. Under pressure from the California Air Resource Board (CARB), which threatened to block VW from selling cars in California in 2016, the company admitted its cheating (Ewing 2017).

Just like at BP, the corporate wrongdoing in the VW case was not just the work of a single—or even a few—"bad apples." Rather, it appears to have been embedded within the company for quite some time. As Eric Schneiderman, the Attorney General of New York at the time, concluded, "Hundreds of very high-level executives and engineers knew about this. We did not find one email saying that maybe we should not be doing this, or this is against the law or put the breaks on this system. So this was a corporate culture permeated by fraud."[1] VW had first been caught using a cheating device in 1973, when it settled a case for $1,200,000 with the U.S. Environmental Protection Agency (EPA) (Ewing 2017).

Moreover, diesel emission violations have been widespread in the industry, with 97% of cars failing emissions tests according to a 2016 report (Carrington et al. 2016). And there had been major fines against car companies for using such defeat devices earlier as well. In 1998, major diesel truck manufacturers including Caterpillar Renault and Volvo came to a $1 billion settlement with the DOJ and EPA for similar violations (Department of Justice 1998).

These types of corporate misconduct are not even limited to the automotive and oil industries. Between 2009 and 2016, Wells Fargo, the California-based U.S. bank, had fraudulently opened 3.5 million accounts without authorization from their customers (Cowley 2017). Moreover, the bank had enrolled 528,000 customers for online bill payment services without their authorization. Recent evaluations suggest that the fraudulent practices had actually been occurring for about 15 years (Independent Directors of the Board of Wells Fargo 2017). However, the offenses had for a long time been treated as individual offenses of local bank employees, who if found to have created unauthorized or fake accounts would simply be fired (Colvin 2017). Yet, these sales practices had become endemic in the bank, occurring across its local branches and even in its San Francisco headquarters.

When the scandal broke in 2016, Wells Fargo blamed and fired 5300 local employees found to be involved in the practices. However, soon it became clear that these were not simply the actions of bad individuals in a particular locale, but rather the result of corporate incentives within the firm, pushing employees to continually increase their sales, and sell customers as many products as possible. In a

---

[1]   As stated in the Netflix Documentary Dirty Money, season 1 episode 1, minute 27:26.

2017 report of the Independent Directors of the Board of Wells Fargo, the bank itself came to admit that what happened was an organizational, not just an individual problem: "The root cause of sales practice failures was the distortion of the Community Bank's sales culture and performance management system, which when combined with aggressive sales management, created pressure on employees to sell unwanted or unneeded products to customers and, in some cases, to open unauthorized accounts" (Independent Directors of the Board of Wells Fargo 2017).

These three cases are intended to illustrate major, recent corporate wrongdoing. In all three cases, the conduct was not merely attributable to particular executives or particular employees. In fact, broader organizational traits initiated, stimulated, and sustained the wrongdoing and offending behaviors. White collar criminologists have long known that corporate crime is not just the product of a few bad individual corporate criminals, but is also embedded in so-called "criminogenic" traits of the corporate organization (Sutherland 1940; Needleman and Needleman 1979; Apel and Paternoster 2009; Clinard 1983; Clinard and Yeager 1980).

Recently, company boards have expressed that they must address toxic elements in their cultures. As the *Wall Street Journal* reported in October 2017, companies, including Whirlpool, Citigroup, and CACI International, recently formed board culture committees (Lubin 2017). The U.S. National Association of Corporate Directors Blue Ribbon Commission on Culture as a Corporate Asset concluded that boards should create formal oversight of company culture (National Association of Corporate Directors 2017). Companies are also hiring culture experts who have provided them with survey tools to evaluate negative elements in their corporate culture (Lubin 2017). Wells Fargo, for instance, now regularly assesses the so-called "happy to grumpy ratio" of its employees, based on the idea that when more people are happy, unethical behavior is less likely to occur (Kellaway 2015).

Consequently, there appears to be a *cultural moment* in addressing corporate crime and wrongdoing (Glazer and Rexrode 2017). With all the recent scandals, major corporations and banks now at least have started to discuss culture. It seems that they can no longer get away with just deflecting blame. It is no longer sufficient to just focus on *bad apples*, but *bad barrels* need to be addressed (cf. Scholten and Ellemers 2016; Pertiwi 2018). Of course, it is not entirely clear whether there is a true commitment to address the culture, or whether firms just discuss this to move beyond yet another crisis and reduce their future liability. However, for the sake of reducing wrongdoing, it is clear that culture matters, and it is clear that it must be addressed. What is less well understood is exactly what organizational culture is or what makes a culture toxic or come to support wrongdoing and rule breaking. Corporations do not clearly know how to measure or assess their own culture and toxic elements within it, let alone how to change and detox it (Glazer and Rexrode 2017).

Presently, it is widely agreed that changing corporate wrongdoing through external enforcement is challenging. Indeed, a recent systemic review of all available studies on corporate deterrence found that: "The evidence fails to show a consistent deterrent effect of punitive sanctions on individual offending, company level of fending, geographic-level offending, or offending among studies" (Simpson et al. 2014). It must be acknowledged that this is not just another study in the literature. This study is the most comprehensive, rigorous, and up-to-date review of all available scientific evidence about deterrence for corporate crime and misconduct across a range of corporate crimes, and it failed to find a deterrent effect.

There are several explanations for why corporate deterrence is difficult. A first reason is that just like for individual crime (Nagin 2013), certainty of punishment likely matters more for a company than the purported severity of the punishment. Further, stronger sanctions only have an effect if a tipping point of certainty is achieved (Brown 1978; Chamlin 1991). However, because of the complexity of corporate organizations and processes, detecting corporate violations in the first place is quite challenging (Gray and Silbey 2014; Pontell et al. 1994; Gray and Mendeloff 2005; Gray and Scholz 1991; Plambeck and Taylor 2015; Henriques 2011). In fact, stronger punishment threats can actually lead to more investment to prevent getting caught, resulting in a cat and mouse game (cf. Plambeck and Taylor 2015). For instance, when VW discovered that California and US regulators knew about their cheating, their initial response was to improve the software and hide their cheating through a recall (Ewing 2017).

A second reason is that deterrence is subjective (cf. Apel 2013). Oftentimes, corporate executives who are supposed to be deterred simply are not aware of the certainty and severity of punishment (Thornton et al. 2005). Or for some companies, the expected penalties are seen as the price of business and made part of the budget. VW high level engineers and executives had since 2006 looked at penalties in other cases. But as New York Attorney General Eric Schneiderman concludes: "They had concluded we can survive this type of penalty."[2]

Further, when wrongdoing is actually detected, it remains difficult to prosecute. For example, presenting complex evidence of corporate operations to lay-juries (in the U.S. context at least) is very challenging (Pontell et al. 1994). And even when it is successfully prosecuted, penalty fines often remain uncollected (Ross and Pritikin 2010). Of course, even when law enforcement would be successful to deter corporations from breaking the law, such corporations would still have to address organizational traits that had been responsible for rule-breaking and harmful behavior. Thus, corporate culture is key.

The chief aim of this paper is to show how existing scholarship can aid corporations that are willing to assess and detox their cultures. To do so, the present paper reviews existing social, behavioral, and management science literature on these questions. In addition, it illustrates their insights by looking deeper into the three cases of corporate misconduct at BP, VW, and Wells Fargo. Accordingly, this paper should be viewed not as an empirical investigation of theories through analyzing quantitative data, but rather as an illustration of how existing theories about offending and wrongdoing can be used in tandem to both assess and change toxic elements in corporate cultures.

We should note that this paper takes a broad approach to examining toxic corporate cultures. It does not merely view toxicity as violating the laws or regulations. Very often, the law provides vague and conflicting direction to organizations, and when companies and their compliance managers and lawyers interact with legal norms and regulatory agencies, these legal rules get re-interpreted (Talesh 2015, 2009; Edelman et al. 1991; Edelman and Talesh 2011; Lange 1999). In addition, with new forms of regulation, so-called *process-oriented rules* (Gilad 2010) and *management-based regulation* (Coglianese and Lazer 2003), the law often does not provide direct behavioral guidance. Especially in industries with complex technical procedures, industries themselves develop the actual standards for behavior (Mills and Koliba 2015). Thus, in this paper, toxic behavior includes both behavior that is clearly illegal, as well as corporate behavior that a reasonable person would see as clearly damaging or promotive of misbehavior.

The paper focuses on organizations with toxic cultures. These are organizations with long-term and systemic rule breaking and damaging behavior. The focus on toxic culture is different from existing studies. Toxic culture is not the same as a criminogenic organizational culture or a criminogenic organization (Sutherland 1940; Clinard 1983; Clinard and Yeager 1980). Organizations with toxic cultures do not operate to engage in crime and break the law. Toxic culture is negative and therefore different from studies that have focused on safety culture (Silbey 2009) or compliance culture (Interligi 2010).

The paper first outlines what organizational culture is, how it can become deviant, and how it can create and sustain rule-breaking behavior. It highlights how to assess elements of a toxic corporate culture through a framework for *forensic ethnography*. Then, it uses the forensic ethnography framework to analyze deviant elements of corporate culture at BP, VW, and Wells Fargo. Based on these analyses of the root cultural causes for corporate misconduct, the paper concludes by discussing their implications for addressing corporate wrongdoing and changing toxic corporate cultures.

---

[2]   As stated in the Netflix Documentary Dirty Money, season 1, episode 1, minute 27:28.

2. What Is Corporate Culture and How Does It Become Toxic?

2.1. Tangible and Intangible Corporate Culture

Cultural anthropology has long been the most important field of study to seriously ponder what culture is. Whereas earlier anthropologists defined culture in observable expressions such as art, architecture, lineage structures, and customs, since the 1970s, the leading definitions stress immaterial and less tangible aspects that are harder to capture and observe (Eriksen 2001). Most influential has been Clifford Geertz' approach (Geertz 1973). For Geertz, culture is not some essential, observable, material fact, or something that can be captured in an essential static way, as an unchanging trait of a certain society. Instead, culture is all about interpretation. Culture consists of shared interpretations within a social group (Geertz 1973).

Insights about organizational culture show a similar understanding of the complexity of both tangible and intangible interpretative elements of such organizational culture. While some commentators of the corporate scandals talk about cultural change solely by pointing to tangible aspects (e.g., changing the incentive structures; changing the leadership), there is now widespread recognition amongst management and organizational scientists that organizational culture exists at both tangible and intangible levels. Parker and Nielsen, in their review of compliance management programs, explain that organizational culture can refer to "shared values and beliefs, myths, interpretations and meanings within an organization, and actions and behaviors, including customs, practices, norms, rituals, and implementation of control systems" (Schein 2010). Certainly, this approach to culture is thus very much in line with cultural anthropological explanations (Geertz 1973).

The most widely-cited approach to organizational culture has been developed by Edgar Schein (2010). According to his approach, organizational culture exists at three levels. The first consists of what he calls "artifacts." These are the tangible aspects of an organization's culture and consist both of the "visible and feelable structures and processes" as well as of "observed behavior" (Schein 2010, p. 23). Artifacts are at the surface of an organization's culture, they are how the organization manifests its culture. They are the visible products of an organization that may include its physical environment and architecture, its technology, its creations, its style, and its stories and myths. Moreover, artifacts also include the published documents that cover the values, operations, rituals, and organizational charts (Schein 2010). The second level are what Schein calls "the espoused beliefs and values," which encompass the shared ideals, goals, values, and aspirations between individuals within an organization. These can come in the form of shared ideologies and also rationalizations for what the organization does. These espoused beliefs and values are deeper in the organization and cannot be directly observed, but must be learned by talking to organizational members (Schein 2010). The third and deepest level of an organizational culture are what Schein calls the "basic underlying assumptions." These are most deeply embedded within the organization and operate unconsciously through organization members. They concern taken-for-granted beliefs and values that can "determine behavior perception, thought and feeling" (Schein 2010, p. 24).

There is a vital interaction between these three levels of Schein's approach to organizational culture. The meaning and day-to-day influence of the surface level artifacts, including written rules, procedures, and evaluation standards, is embedded and constructed within the deeper organizational cultural fabric of the beliefs, values, and underlying assumptions (Schein 2010, p. 25).

2.2. Analyzing Toxicity in Corporate Culture

As Schein's influential model of organizational culture suggests, any assessment of organizational culture includes both tangible and intangible elements. Schein, and most management science organizational culture specialists, do not provide much information about a toxic organizational culture that induces legal rule breaking. To understand how organizational culture can induce and sustain offending and harmful behavior and to trace the toxic elements in the corporate culture that are responsible for the wrongdoing, we shall draw on insights from sociology, anthropology, psychology, and criminology.

A first insight from sociological and anthropological accounts of law is that organizations and communities may come to form their own norms and these norms can come to oppose and resist those of the law, thus sustaining rule breaking. Sally Falk Moore showed in her seminal 1973 paper that very different communities (e.g., the garment industry in New York City; Tanzanian coffee farmers) both formed what she called *semi-autonomous social fields*. These are social fields (communities) that are open to the influence of the law, yet also form their own norms and rules that can come to resist those of the law (Moore 1973). As she explained: "A court or legislature can make custom law. A semi-autonomous social field can make law its custom" (Moore 1973, p. 744).

Similarly, Carol Heimer has found that legal norms can come to compete with norms of different communities they have to interact with. She found this in her study of neonatal intensive care units, where legally mandated institutions in hospitals tasked to implement the law had to compete with medical norms of the hospital staff, and familial norms of the families of children treated (Heimer 1999). She found that hospital staff would adopt in earnest only legal norms that were directly useful to them, and would ignore or resist other legally mandated procedures and practices. Instead of the law shaping hospital practices, she found the hospital routine shaped the law, as legal procedures had to adapt to the practices, interests, and even time-table of the hospital staff (Heimer 1999).

Heimer's findings demonstrate how organizations can develop norms that can successfully resist and compete with the law (for this point see also (Clinard and Yeager 1980, p. 58)). However, that raises the question of how exactly this occurs. Vaughan's study of the fatal NASA decision to launch the Space Shuttle Challenger in 1986 can shed light on this question. Her study focused on why NASA had gone ahead with the launch of the Challenger shuttle, even though there had been repeated evidence going back to 1977 of a particular technical risk with the so-called "O-Rings" that were "designed to seal a tiny gap created by pressure at ignition in the joints of the Solid Rocket Booster" (Vaughan 1997, p. xi). Even on the eve of the launch, several concerned NASA engineers had argued against the launch as they feared that these O-Rings might threaten flight safety (Vaughan 1989, p. 331). Vaughan has argued that NASA's Solid Rocket Booster group had "normalized deviance" (Vaughan 1997, pp. 62–63). In other words, the Solid Rocket Booster Group had developed an organizational norm that could successfully oppose safety norms.

What is vital about her study is that it shows how such organizational normalization of deviance developed over a process. As Vaughan has shown, the normalization occurred in several stages. First, came the warning signals, starting all the way back in 1977, that there may be a technical deviation. These signals were then reinterpreted and finally labeled "an acceptable risk" (Vaughan 1997, p. 65). Thus, deviance became the standard. And this in turn became "a collectively constructed cultural reality, incorporated into the worldview of the group." (Vaughan 1997, pp. 65–66). The culturally embedded norm in the group became that "risk had to be renegotiated" (Vaughan 1997, p. 66). And this did not just play out on the eve of the launch, it was a repeated process that had before already become deeply engrained within the Solid Rocket Booster Group.

Vaughan's research illuminates processes within an organization that can help to develop norms that run against those of the law and can become embedded in the organization's values. Social psychology offers further insights about such social norms and how they can come to sustain illegal behavior. And although these psychological insights have been studied in the interactions and behaviors of individuals and in rather simple situations, they provide important insights relevant for understanding the interactive processes between social and legal-type norms. It should be noted that the insights discussed here come from field experiments in which real behavior outside of the lab was observed and analyzed.

The psychological study of social norms has demonstrated that social norms are very strong influences on individual behavior. Psychologists distinguish two kinds of social norms. First are injunctive social norms—these concern what people think others think they should do. Second are descriptive social norms, which consist of the behavior of others (Cialdini et al. 2006). A first insight from the psychological study of social norms is that human responses to others do not just flow through values, as Schein and the socio-legal approaches previously discussed focus on, but also through behavioral practices (Cialdini 2003, 2007; Cialdini and Goldstein 2004). A second insight is that social norms are not necessarily conscious: people respond to the behavior of others even when they are not aware that they are doing so (Cialdini 2003, 2007; Cialdini and Goldstein 2004). Social norms can become embedded in the social environment, creating automated situational norms where people subconsciously respond to cues in their environment that activate social norms (Aarts and Dijksterhuis 2003; Aarts et al. 2003).

Social psychologists have identified the processes through which social norms and legal norms interact, offering insights into how toxic norms may spread in organizational environments. First, when a negative social norm exists that is opposed to the legal norm—for instance, if most people steal valuable wood in a forest where this is not allowed—people will be more likely to break such legal rule (Cialdini and Goldstein 2004). In corporate settings, Baucus and Neal have found that firms with a longer history of violating the law (and thus firms who have developed social norms that violate legal norms) are more likely to violate again (Baucus and Near 1991). Simpson and Koper, similarly found that past illegal involvement predicted future offending (Simpson and Koper 1997). It is vital to prevent such negative social norms from being triggered or strengthened. Here, public messages—even messages by law enforcement—matter. Any message that stresses the scale of rule violation (even if it is to show how many people are punished) must be avoided lest more rule breaking will result (Cialdini 2007). And when there is a negative social norm with regard to one type of law (for instance when there is illegal graffiti) there is a danger of contagion to also create more rule violation for another legal norm (enhancing theft or littering) (Keizer et al. 2008).

A second situation occurs when a social norm supports compliance with the law (Cialdini 2007). When most people wear their seatbelt, others are more likely to comply with seatbelt laws, even when there is little enforcement. In this situation, it is vital to prevent legal interventions that erode these positive social norms. When punishment is introduced in an environment with strong positive social norms, this can send a signal that compliance is only necessary because of the punishment, not because of its intrinsic value. Consequently, in this way, punishment can erode positive social norms (Gneezy et al. 2011; Gneezy and Rustichini 2000).

A third situation occurs when a discrepancy exists between an injunctive social norm and a descriptive social norm. In other words, when what people perceive others to be telling them they should do is different from what others are actually doing. Keizer and colleagues have carried out a series of field experiments, where they looked at what would happen when they placed a sign clearly indicating what people should do (i.e., not litter, or not park their bike) in an environment where this behavior was common and where it was not common, also comparing this to when no sign had been there in both situations. Their findings indicate that compliance is best when there are no existing violations (when there is a positive descriptive social norm) and when there is a prohibition sign. They are second best when there is no sign and no existing violations. They are worse when there are existing violations, but compliance is the worst when there are existing violations and a sign forbidding such behavior. In other words, when there are actually negative descriptive social norms, the practice of emphasizing positive injunctive social norms can backfire (Keizer et al. 2011).

Organizational psychologists and management scientists have looked at what fosters an unethical climate that can stimulate rule breaking and immoral conduct. As Scholten and Ellemers (2016) have summarized the literature, three aspects are key here. First is the way organizations deal with errors and what sort of error management culture they have (cf. Van Dyck et al. 2005; Homsma et al. 2009). Organizations that promote ethical behavior recognize that errors are part of normal work and foster employees to acknowledge errors and learn from them. Organizations will foster unethical behavior if they respond in an ineffective way to errors. Such ineffective responses include denial that errors can and do occur, failing to act when they do occur and failing to assess what had caused the errors and make necessary changes to prevent future errors, or blame and punish employees, which may hamper successful learning and increase anxiety and stress and willingness to comply with organizational rules (Scholten and Ellemers 2016; Van Dyck et al. 2005; Homsma et al. 2009).

Second, organizational psychologists and management scientists also have shown that organizations where small differences in performance can cause high differences in how employees are treated and what opportunities they get can breed more unethical behavior as employees feel treated unfairly and develop envy of colleagues (Cohen-Charash and Mueller 2007; Cohen-Charash and Spector 2001; Zoghbi-Manrique-de-Lara and Suárez-Acosta 2014; Scholten and Ellemers 2016). And third, finally, these scholars point to particular organizational traits that create so-called *dysfunctional moral climates*. These include organizations that do not focus on the moral implications of organizational activities and decisions (moral neglect), organizations where there is awareness of moral problems but no ability and opportunity to act against them (moral inaction), and organizations that reframe immoral actions to distort a proper understanding of moral content (moral justification) (Moore and Gino 2013; Scholten and Ellemers 2016).

There are also important criminological insights that apply to how organizational culture can come to stimulate corporate rule breaking and wrongdoing. Corporate crime criminologists have for a long time recognized that corporate culture matters. As Clinard and Yeager state: "ethical behavior [...] is also the product of cultural norms operating within a given corporation or even industry that may be conducive to produce violations" (Clinard and Yeager 1980, p. 58). One strand of criminological theory finds that crime originates in distress, in so-called "strain." Breaking rules or committing crime is a way for some people to cope with such strain. Two of the three core sources—strain originally identified in Agnew (1992) General Strain Theory—are the presentation of negative stimuli (physical or verbal assaults) and the inability to reach a desired result (Agnew 1992).

While strain originally pointed to the response to the strain of low socio-economic conditions, it can be applied to an organizational environment. If the environment puts stress on employees, employees may respond to the strain by violating laws (Agnew et al. 2009). Clinard and Yeager (1980) analysis of corporate crime points to the importance of economic performance, showing that violating firms are on average "less financially successful, [and] experience poorer growth (Clinard and Yeager 1980, p. 132). Baucus and Near's model of illegal corporate behavior shows that corporations with a scarcity of resources are likely to break the law, but corporations with plentiful resources are even more likely to offend, while poor performance does not predict corporate offending (Baucus and Near 1991).

Criminologists have also shown how criminals are better able to break the law if they are able to "neutralize" the shame and guilt that comes with offending behavior. Sykes and Matza demonstrate several such neutralization techniques. These include: denying responsibility, denying injury, or reframing the victim into someone that deserves the harm (Sykes and Matza 1957). While these insights were originally developed for individual street crime, corporations can just as well develop organizational values, practices, and even structures that neutralize offending behavior (Stadler and Benson 2012; Gottschalk and Smith 2011; Benson 1985). Here, criminologists have recognized that other neutralization techniques like the defense of necessity (Minor 1981), the claim of normality (Benson 1985; Maruna and Copes 2005), and the metaphor of the ledger (where having done good acts balances out bad acts) (Klockars 1974; Piquero et al. 2005) play important roles in explaining corporate offending.

Criminologists have further focused on how the context in which a potential offender exists can create more or less opportunities for crime (Belknap 1987; Cohen and Felson 1979; Felson 1987; Osgood et al. 1996). These theories (including routine activity, situational crime prevention, and ecological criminology) all point to the fact that crime needs more than a motivated offender: it also requires such an offender to have access to an unguarded target, lacking a capable guardian. This is highly relevant for corporate offending and corporate culture. Some corporate cultures may produce organizational structures (rules and incentives), values, and practices that provide members with easier opportunities to break the law, for instance when external oversight is difficult (as the crimes are hidden inside the organization), when there is less internal auditing, when employees are left large discretion, or when rule breaking is normally condoned. An important context is the amount of dynamism and change that a corporation operates under, with the more changes in the market a corporation must adapt to the more likely the company will offend (Baucus and Near 1991). Here Baucus notes that a key issue is that corporations respond to dynamism by spreading out responsibility for decision making (Baucus and Near 1991). For similar points on the complexity of structures and corporate offending see (Clinard and Yeager 1980). Spreading decision making power reduces the ability of successful oversight while giving more people in the firm the power to make decisions that can result in offending and harmful behavior.

A vital insight from these three bodies of criminological literature is that organizational deviancy does not solely come from organizational structures, values, and practices that produce social norms that are opposed to the law, but can also originate from social norms that obstruct compliance (through strain), or that enable rule breaking (through neutralization and opportunity creation).

2.3. Levels, Aspects, Types of Toxicity and Processes

In sum, an assessment of toxic corporate cultures must take into account an organization's tangible and intangible manifestations (Schein 2010), and in particular, the organizational structures (rules, authority lines, and incentives) (Schein 2010), organizational values (injunctive social norms), and organizational practices (descriptive social norms) (Cialdini 2007; Cialdini et al. 2006; Cialdini and Goldstein 2004). These form the core three organizational levels at which organizational culture can be assessed. They are entry points to do a cultural assessment, but are not wholly distinct, as structures can derive from and shape values and practices, and values can originate in structures and practices, and, of course, practices can follow the structures and values of an organization. Table 1 outlines the three levels of organizational culture that a forensic ethnographer can assess to identify toxic elements.

Table 1. Levels of Organizational Cultural Analysis.

Level	Aspects		
1. **Structures**	Rules	Targets and Incentives	Hierarchy
2. **Values**	Explicit Shared Values	Injunctive Social Norms	Hidden Assumptions
3. **Practices**	Visible common behavior	Unaware Common Behavior	Situational Norms

To do a full forensic ethnography, one must then look at toxic elements at these three levels of an organizational culture. As the sociological, anthropological, psychological, management science, and criminological studies discussed above show, this process requires looking for norms at all three levels that are either directly opposed to the law, and thus have values or practices that undermine the law, or other law-type norms protecting against corporate harm (Moore 1973; Heimer 1999; Cialdini et al. 2006; Cialdini and Goldstein 2004). Thus, when common practices can come to normalize deviancy and damaging behavior (Vaughan 1989; Keizer et al. 2008; Scholten and Ellemers 2016), enable rule breaking through neutralization (Sykes and Matza 1957; Gottschalk and Smith 2011; Maruna and Copes 2005; Minor 1981; Siponen et al. 2012) or opportunity creation (Belknap 1987; Cohen and Felson 1979; Felson 1987; Osgood et al. 1996), obstruct rule following—through not providing sufficient informational or technical support to learn from errors (Scholten and Ellemers 2016; Homsma et al. 2009)—by creating strain and inducing negative rule breaking or harmful responses to such strain (Agnew 1992, 2001; Agnew et al. 2009; Simpson and Koper 1997; Scholten and Ellemers 2016; Homsma et al. 2009), toxic organizational norms and processes are achieved Finally, we must look at how the stated rules and values of the corporation are at odds with the practices and implied values, as this will stimulate extra rule offending as it delegitimizes compliance (when organizations stress values in line with the law that are commonly broken in practice) (Keizer et al. 2011). Table 2 below outlines these types of toxic norms and their processes.

Table 2. Toxic Organizational Norms and Processes.

Type of Toxic Norms	Processes	
Directly Opposed	Resist and Compete with Legal Norms	Normalize Deviancy
Enabling Rule Breaking	Create Opportunity to Violate	Neutralize Offending
Obstructing Compliance	Lack of Support to Follow the Law and Learn from Errors	Strain Employees away from Compliance
Practice runs against Values	Delegitimize Positive Social and Legal Norms	

3. Assessing Toxic Culture at BP, VW, and Wells Fargo

The goal of this paper is not to test the theories discussed above, nor to offer new empirical insights about which of these theories best predicts toxic corporate behavior. Rather, this paper illustrates how these ideas can be used to assess what aspects in organizations constitute a negative culture and how they sustain misbehavior. The remainder of this paper will analyze how the cultures in BP, VW, and Wells Fargo have come to support the deviant practices that culminated in the massive scandals introduced above. It will draw on extensive investigative journalism, court records, published internal reports, and academic literature available on all three cases to outline the core elements of deviancy in the organizational cultures that were at play. It will discuss key cultural elements these reports have found stimulate wrongdoing and offending behavior, and will analyze them in light of the social and behavioral science about toxic corporate culture. All three cases have been extensively reported, providing a wealth of information to draw from to analyze the toxic elements in their corporate cultures. For VW this paper relies heavily on the excellent reporting by *New York Times* journalist Jack Ewing published in his 2017 monograph, as it provides the most comprehensive discussion of all sources as well as balanced and critical reporting. Where necessary we have added other sources as updates or to provide a different perspective.[3]

The remainder of this section will assess the toxicity in the three corporate cultures. To structure the analysis of toxic elements in the cultures of these three organizations, the paper will focus on different relevant aspects of the business operations that are directly relevant for the illegal and harmful behavior these companies were engaging in. In each of these different aspects, it will offer a short sub-conclusion that highlights what toxic elements, referring back to Table 2, were at play at which levels of the culture (as outlined in Table 1 above).

First, this paper looks at how all three organizations developed their overall goals and strategies, and how this has been implemented in structures, values, and practices. Second, it explores how people in the corporations could respond to these goals and strategies and to what extent there was room for dissent and adaptation. Third, it analyses the extent to which there was illegal behavior and whether this behavior was condoned or disciplined internally. Fourth, it recounts what the companies did after the illegal behavior was discovered and made public, and to what extent they took responsibility or tried to deflect blame. And finally, it looks at how the companies' messages over the years have compared to their practices in order to find out whether there was cognitive dissonance. After discussing these aspects separately, the final section examines the broader patterns of toxic cultural elements and explores what these patterns mean for attempts at cultural change.

---

[3]   Although there is a wealth of available sources, these data do not inform us about the deepest levels of values and practices, since many of the social norms at play are unaware, unconscious, and automated. Such an analysis would require a true ethnography, combined with psychological experimentation, to understand exactly what descriptive, injunctive, and situational norms shaped offending behavior.

3.1. Goals and Strategies

BP, VW, and Wells Fargo all started as underdogs with high ambitions. In the early 1990s, BP was struggling as oil prices had declined, many oil reserves in the Middle East had been nationalized by local countries, and the production costs of onshore drilling had hampered profits (Lustgarten 2012; Steffy 2010). At that time, Volkswagen had major difficulties in the U.S. market, where it had been unable to find a successor to the counterculture successes of the Beetle and the Transporter Van in the 1960s. Further, it struggled with the image of being unreliable and requiring frequent repair, had high labor and production costs, and barely broke even financially in 1992 (Ewing 2017). Wells Fargo was a local bank operating largely in California (Colvin 2017).

Yet, all three developed grand ambitions as new CEOs came to power. When John Browne became CEO of BP in 1995, he saw that BP could close its gap with the largest petroleum giants by rigorously focusing on divesting on-shore operations with low profits, by cutting costs, and by doing new oil exploration for major off-shore fields (so-called "Elephants") in areas with higher risk but also higher profits (Lustgarten 2012). When Ferdinand Piëch, grandson of Ferdinand Porsche who had designed the original Beetle for Hitler, took over as CEO of VW, he soon declared that by 2018 the German carmaker should become the largest in the world (Ewing 2017). And when Richard Kovacevich became CEO of Wells Fargo, after it had been acquired by Minneapolis-based Norwest in 1998 that opted to drop its old name, he adopted the "Go for Gr-Eight" motto, seeking to guide the bank to the national and global top by outselling competitors and selling eight products per customer—four times the average rate for banks (Colvin 2017).

In each of these cases, high ambitions focused on growth and profit increase, and with risk-prone means to achieve the goals. Wells Fargo had to go where no bank had gone before—to achieve fast growth, and reach the highly ambitious sales target, it had to somehow convince its clients not to buy two of its products (e.g., credit cards, insurance, special accounts), but eight.

At BP, the risk came as the new strategy required two opposed interventions: cutting costs and laying off a large part of the engineering expertise on the one hand, and developing new oil exploration in high risk areas that required extra engineering resources (Steffy 2010). At VW, the mission to become number one could only be achieved by becoming competitive in the number one car market, the U.S. When Martin Winterkorn became CEO, he wanted to increase car production from six million to ten million in the next ten years, surpassing both GM and Toyota, which would mean that VW would finally have to succeed in the difficult U.S. car market.

To do so, Winterkorn bet on clean diesel and a new diesel engine: the EA 189. The problem was that the company had been unable to develop an engine that was actually economical, practical, and clean and could compete in the U.S. market. VW's option—to cut the toxic NOx emissions that the higher temperature burning diesel engines produce—came with its own problems of higher price, occupying precious storage space, and requiring more frequent maintenance, which would all prohibit a successful strategy (Ewing 2017). Thus, VW set itself a target that may well have been impossible to achieve.

It was not long before the new ambitions and values they represented turned into practices and structures that produced risks of wrongdoing and damages. At BP, this was most evident in cost-saving reforms. After John Browne took the helm, he started to cut costs aggressively, with across-the-board cuts of 25%, first in 1999 and then again in 2004. This affected not just material costs, but also personnel, resulting in forced lay-offs, thus shrinking BP's pool of engineering talent (Steffy 2010). It was not long until these general cuts started to affect the safety at BP operations. In the years prior to the 2005 Texas City explosion, BP had decided not to replace outdated equipment that later caused the massive accident. BP simply wanted to save on the $150,000 investment that was needed. One employee, as reported by PBS, wrote: "We need to decide if we want to invest $150,000 now to save money later on" (PBS 2010). And a senior manager wrote "that capital expenditure is 'very tight. Bank the $150,000 in savings right now'" (PBS 2010). It is no wonder that former Secretary of State James Baker, who headed one of the two investigations into the Texas City explosion, concluded that "BP has not adequately embraced safety as a core value" (Baker et al. 2007). In the 2006 Alaskan spill, the leak occurred in a corroded pipe, "which hadn't been cleaned in over a decade" (PBS 2010). In Alaska, BP had for years, as a subsequent investigation found, sacrificed proper maintenance for profit. Investigators found that "'unacceptable' maintenance backlogs ballooned as BP tried to sustain profits ... even though production was declining" (Lustgarten and Knutson 2010). The investigation clearly concluded that these issues are at the heart of BP's value system: "There is a disconnect between ... management's stated commitment to safety and the perception of that commitment" (Lustgarten and Knutson 2010). And preceding the Gulf spill in 2010, BP managers "were shaving maintenance costs with the practice of 'run to failure,' under which aging equipment was used as long as possible" (Lustgarten and Knutson 2010). In sum, BP in its day-to-day operations valued profits over anything else, even at the repeated sacrifice of safety and the environment.

The overall targets of cost reduction played a crucial role in BP safety issues, as the Chemical Safety and Hazard Investigation Board (CSB) concluded in its 341 page report after the 2005 report in response to the Texas explosion that had killed 15 (U.S. Chemical Safety and Hazard Investigation Board 2007). As a supervisor told lower-level managers who had questioned the 2004 budget cuts and their implications for ensuring operations: "Which bit of 25 percent do you not understand?" (Steffy 2010, p. 117). Another manager explained how this forced them towards risky and illegal practices: "The focus on controlling costs was acute at BP, to the point it became a distraction. They just go after it with a ferocity that's mind-numbing and terrifying. No one's ever asked to cut corners or take a risk, but often it ends up like that" (Steffy 2010, p. 58).

At VW, Winterkorn's ambitious target, to sell ten million cars and focus on clean diesel, put engineers in a bind. They could develop a clean diesel engine. To do so, they could use technology from Daimler, called BlueTec, that sprayed a chemical substance called urea into the exhaust to help breakdown NOx emissions (Ewing 2017). However, it came with an extra cost of about $350 dollars for each car, and also required installing an extra tank that would take up cargo space and require owners to do frequent refills.

The other option was a so-called "lean NOx trap" that separated nitrogen oxide molecules into harmless oxygen and diatomic nitrogen. This technique was cheaper and did not need an extra tank, but it required an exhaust gas recirculation system that produced more carcinogenic fine particle emissions, and also caused the soot filter to wear out faster (Ewing 2017). Considering U.S. law obliged car makers to have emissions control systems effective for the entire lifespan of the vehicle, the soot filter wear was a core problem.

Nonetheless, VW's highly ambitious targets played such a strong role that by late 2007, engine specialists had never seriously considered adjusting them to the engineering realties they faced. Rather than give up on the targets, VW engineers were forced to look for alternative solutions. They not only adopted the lean NOx trap, but also installed the software "defeat device" that would only switch on the emissions control system during emissions testing, so that during normal driving the soot filter would remain intact longer (Ewing 2017). Because of VW's cost reduction efforts to make as many models as possible share the same parts, the decision to install cheating devices on the EA 189 engine came to affect over ten million cars VW produced and sold.

At Wells Fargo, the push for growth through the extremely high sales targets was to be achieved through bank employee incentive systems. The bank's branches started to set product sales goals for employees to meet. This put tremendous pressure on Wells Fargo bankers to sell more products to their clients. Employees would be under constant scrutiny with daily and monthly "Motivator" reports tracking their sales volumes (Frost 2017). If they failed to meet targets, employees would undergo "coaching sessions." One employee explained later to National Public Radio (NPR) journalists that these sessions were not there to support the workers but just to pressure them to sell more (Arnold 2016). Another employee explained how, when she failed to meet her target, two managers would lecture her at her desk and then perp-walk her while colleagues were watching. As she explained: "It's like being called into the principal's office. Sit down at the large conference table, no windows in this room, they shut the door, lock the door" (Arnold 2016). After that she was forced to sign a "formal warning" and was warned: "If you don't meet your solutions you're not a team player. If you're bringing down the team then you will be fired and it will be on your permanent record" (Arnold 2016). She was simply afraid to lose her job and fearful not to get another one with the bad state of the economy. This employee said that things got so bad that she vomited under her desk.

Another employee compared his Wells Fargo job to "being in an abusive relationship" (Arnold 2016). Things were worst during special sales campaigns, such as the "Jump into January" campaign that sought to start the year with strong sales. During such campaigns, employees were to reach even higher targets than usual, sometimes even up to twenty per customer. In one local branch office, employees were forced to "run the gauntlet" by running past costumed district managers to write their sales numbers on a white board (Frost 2017). It became increasingly clear that employees had started to resort to creating unauthorized or fake accounts in response to these extreme pressures to boost their sales targets and achieve the overall goals set in the company. Yet, for a long time no change was made to the targets themselves or the pressures through which they were implemented. As one report found, Wells Fargo "was hesitant to end the program because (Carrie) Tolstedt (the head of community banking at the time) was 'scared to death' that it could hurt sales figures for the entire year" (Frost 2017).

And the strategy worked. In 1999, BP, after cutting costs and taking over several competitors, quadrupled in value, and finally caught up with the top oil companies. Its stocks soared, and its CEO, Browne, was dubbed "Sun King" in British newspapers. VW finally became successful in the U.S. market with its clean diesel, and eventually even after the emission scandal was discovered became the largest car company in the world in 2015, three years ahead of the planned schedule (Ewing 2017, p. 187). And Wells Fargo jumped from the ninth most valuable bank in America, to the most valuable one in the world in 2015. Wells Fargo achieved 18 consecutive quarters of over $5 billion in profits—a feat it shares only with Apple (Colvin 2017).

In sum, this analysis of how these companies set their targets and responded to challenges in the business environment demonstrates how toxic elements came to exist in these three cases. The most important type of toxic norm, from those discussed in Table 2 earlier, is strain (Agnew 1992, 2001; Agnew et al. 2009; Simpson and Koper 1997). What we see here is that the companies themselves were under strain of the shareholder's expectations of growth and revenue formation. New leaders responded to these pressures by setting highly ambitious goals that because of their high risk and low feasibility nature brought the external strain into the company's operations and ultimately to the employees, which in crucial instances forced them to make or go along with decisions that were damaging, and at worst illegal. These negative responses to strain and its resultant negative influences came at the cultural level of structures (see Table 1), as it was laid down in targets and incentives (cf. Schein 2010), but soon moved deeper into explicit shared values and visible common behavior (see Table 1).

3.2. Management and Employee Responses to Goals and Strategies

So why did BP employees, VW employees, and Wells Fargo employees go along with these goals? Why did they not successfully resist or change these goals or the practices they produced, even though they must have seen they were not realistic or risk free? To answer these questions, we must look at the corporate structures in the companies and how they shaped internal communication as well as the way responsibility for targets and work was shared.

BP and Wells Fargo have hierarchies that are strikingly different from Volkswagen. VW had a highly centralized structure with strong power vested in the CEO at the top. There was a centralized authority in decision-making that forced decisions to go up the chain of command. As one former manager trainee described it: "VW was like North Korea without the labor camps. You have to obey everyone" (Ewing 2017, p. 93). VW's CEO played a central and direct role in day-to-day decisions, with first Piëch, and later his successor Winterkorn, as engineers who micro-managed engineering decisions all the way to the interior color of cars promoted at auto shows.

By contrast, Wells Fargo and BP had highly decentralized structures. Under Browne's leadership, BP established business units that were to operate at autonomous companies within the overall BP structure. Each had its own targets, its own profit reporting, and its own leadership. At some point BP had over 300 such decentralized units. As Steffy argues, this created an unwieldy structure, with each unit leader caring for his own goals without focusing on how these affected the whole (Steffy 2010). BP also often used sub-contractors and outsourced key aspects of its work, further delegating responsibilities, but now outside of its own employees (Bozeman 2011). Wells Fargo was very similar to BP in that its operation was split amongst business units. Wells Fargo's CEO Kovacevich nicely illustrated the structure when he called himself a "CEO of CEOs" (Colvin 2017).

While the three companies had such different hierarchical structures, in all three there was limited possibility to resist top-down targets and have effective dissent. Comparing the cases reveals that the overall hierarchy itself was not the core issue here, but rather how information flowed across the structure from bottom to top and top to bottom. Clearly, VW's highly centralized hierarchy meant lower level employees had trouble getting their information heard at higher levels. Thus, at VW it was hard for lower level employees to correct faulty central level decision making and targets.

However, BP and Wells Fargo's decentralized structures did not allow for much better information flow that might have corrected unrealistic budget cuts and sales targets. At BP for instance, in 1999, a group of 77 workers at the Alaskan operations—where later a major spill would occur—wrote a desperate letter to CEO John Browne trying to sway him from the intended cuts as they feared it would further undermine the already appalling safety conditions (Lustgarten 2012). The letter points to the difficulty of communicating critical information upwards: "Anything we say either stays at this level or gets filtered on the way up to a version of 'can do sir' . . . Our feedback is ignored because it doesn't support the preordained agenda . . . Your frontline management and supervision will continue to cut as long as you direct and sanction it, right up to the precipice of disaster and over" (Lustgarten 2012). John Browne did not reply and instead, a month later, announced another $4 billion budget cut.

Five years later, in 2004, the new BP Texas City Refinery Plant manager also tried to get attention from higher executives at the London office. He presented a detailed report entitled "Texas City is Not a Safe Place to Work," about the horrible safety record at the plant, where over three decades 23 workers had died—one of the worst records in the industry. He also conducted a survey amongst workers that unearthed widespread safety concerns that had long gone unheard and unaddressed. The new manager used the report to ask for a budget increase to upgrade the safety at the plant. The main office denied his request and asked him to focus on the 25% budget cuts he had to meet for 2004, all the while the refinery was making $100 million a month for BP (Steffy 2010, p. 67).

Similarly, Wells Fargo senior executives refused to respond to challenges by regional leaders of the bank who had come forward to complain that the sales goals were too high and had become "increasingly untenable" (Frost 2017). What was at play here was not so much the structure itself, but the failure of higher level employees to adequately allow lower level employees to provide input and be heard. Targets were formulated in a top-down fashion and implemented while disregarding critique, regardless of the decentralized structure at Wells Fargo and VW.

In all three companies, the composition of the labor force and executive management practices made dissent difficult. At Wells Fargo the high strain of the job resulted in massive staff turnover, reaching up to 41% in one year (Colvin 2017). This left the bank with highly inexperienced employees, less likely to successfully raise concerns over the targets they had to meet. Through its mass lay-offs, BP similarly got rid of a large swatch of its senior engineers, who would have been in the best position to speak out against the safety hazards that were becoming increasingly apparent (Steffy 2010). BP CEO John Browne wanted a bench of followers, which he dubbed his "turtles," referring to the Ninja Turtle cartoon (Steffy 2010, p. 58). And at VW, CEOs Piëch and later Winterkorn often fired executives they did not like, keeping only those who would agree with them and support their positions (Ewing 2017).

At BP, meanwhile, frequent executive job rotations, which were a standard management practice, incentivized these lower level leaders to focus on short term targets while disregarding the longer term consequences, and thus made them more concerned with meeting the targets set by the company headquarters than enhancing long term safety (Lyall 2010).

Dissenting opinions were also suppressed through intimidating management practices. An investigative report following the 2010 Deep Water Horizon Spill found at BP "a pattern of intimidating workers who raised safety or environmental concerns" (Lustgarten and Knutson 2010). At Wells Fargo, as discussed above, daily intimidation practices were used to cajole and publicly shame employees to keep focused on their targets and the overall growth of the bank. Employees at all levels worked on the pressure of constant, sometimes hourly ranking of their sales rates in comparison with peers. When found to be lagging, they risked demotion or dismissal. As one employee recalled: "We were constantly told we would end up working for McDonald's if we did not make the sales quotas ... we had to stay for what felt like after-school detention, or report to a call session on Saturdays" (Reckard 2013). This clearly did not produce an atmosphere conducive to voicing critical opinions.

At VW, intimidation occurred at the highest levels. CEO Winterkorn was known for his Tuesday top executive meetings that included the highest-level officials in charge of major brands like Audi or Seat. At the meetings, with all present, Winterkorn would mercilessly criticize any executive that had failed to meet set targets. Ewing explains the humiliating tactics that Winterkorn used: "Managers who were favorites one week could suddenly fall from grace the next. Sometimes they learned they had been demoted or dismissed not from Winterkorn or a colleague but from reading about it in a German business publication, like *Manager Magazine*, that had somehow been tipped off" (Ewing 2017, p. 157). Similarly, at Wells Fargo the head of community banking, Tolstedt, an internal board review found, was "insular and defensive and did not like to be challenged or hear negative information. Even senior leaders within the Community Bank were frequently afraid of or discouraged from airing contrary views" (Colvin 2017).

Let us here also look at what we can draw out from these three cases about how toxic cultures form.

The most important insight here is that in all three cases a strong social norm (injunctive but also in the form of visible common (and probably unaware common) behavior) developed that dissent was not appreciated and that targets had to be met. A strong norm developed in all three companies not to resist or disagree with higher level targets and commands. This norm in and of itself is not directly opposed to the legal norms at play here. It does not support breaking safety standards, creating defeat devices, or fraudulently opening false or unauthorized bank accounts. This social norm here rather obstructs behavior that supports compliance. It makes it harder for employees or executives to come to speak out and resist practices that break the law. As such, it also undermines checks and balances within the company, especially over policies and practices of higher level leaders that come to break the law. In turn, this creates a larger opportunity to break the law (Belknap 1987; Cohen and Felson 1979; Felson 1987; Osgood et al. 1996), and when such rule breaking is allowed to occur without critique, it thus becomes condoned and even normalized (Vaughan 1989, 1997). As such employees here operated in an inactive moral climate, where there may have been recognition of unethical and immoral problems, but a very limited space to act on them (cf. Moore and Gino 2013; Scholten and Ellemers 2016).

In this context, the social norm against critique and dissent can work in tandem with generating further strain (Agnew 1992, 2001; Agnew et al. 2009; Simpson and Koper 1997). Specifically, employees and managers were under pressure due to the strong coercive processes as well as the fierce competition and job insecurity some had. As such, in light of Table 2's framework to understand toxic organizational norms and processes, our analysis of employee and management participation in goals and targets shows that four toxic processes were at play in the organizational culture: obstruct behavior that supports compliance, strain away from compliance, normalization of deviancy, and creating opportunity to violate the law. Here, in light of Table 1's outline of the levels and aspects of organizational cultural analysis, we see that these toxic processes developed first at the level of values, they became reinforced by the structures of hierarchy and incentives, and became deeply embedded as they developed into common practices (cf. Schein 2010).

3.3. Illegal Behavior and Internal Responses

By the time the scandals became public, all three companies had already engaged in the damaging and rule breaking behavior for years or even decades. BP had, from the 1990s onwards, developed an appalling safety record at its operations. Its operations were so bad that it had one of the worst safety records in the industry, paying one multimillion dollar fine and settlement after another to the EPA and OSHA, only to be found breaking the same safety standards again (Lustgarten 2012; Mattera 2016; Steffy 2010). Even after the major 2005 Texas Refinery explosion that had killed 15 workers and wounded 170, BP's major safety problems continued. In the three years following the explosion, and after paying $20 million in fines to OSHA, and after being forced to do a $1 billion upgrade to the facilities, another four people were killed at the refinery. And another two were killed in another BP refinery in Washington State. BP thus had five fatalities in two facilities, while there had been a total of nine fatalities in all other 146 non-BP refineries in the U.S. (Steffy 2010, p. 139).

For comparison purposes, consider how BP had had 700 OSHA safety violations in three years, whereas Exxon, which after the Valdez disaster completely improved its safety record, had only one (Steffy 2010, p. 150). BP never seriously responded to the concerns of its employees, its lower level managers, or even regulators. Each time, BP would negotiate a settlement or simply pay the fine, and do what was demanded in paying for upgrades or installing safety management. But it would not end its relentless pursuit for higher profits by cutting costs and pursuing high risk high reward exploration and refinery. The norm in BP thus became that safety hazards were part of the job, that deviating from safety norms was normal, and that redress rather than prevention was the way to address them (Lustgarten 2012; Steffy 2010).

Volkswagen and Wells Fargo had similarly normalized deviancy. As we saw already, Volkswagen had used defeat devices all the way back to 1973, when it was first caught and ordered to pay a $120,000 fine to the EPA. Then, in 2005, VW had to pay a $1.1 million fine to the EPA for emissions cheating in Mexico. And starting in 1999, the company had installed a device in the software controlling the highly polluting noise control system in its Audi engines that would switch off this system and reduce pollution when it recognized the car was being tested (Ewing 2017). So, when engineers frantically sought to find a solution to make the new VW diesel clean, but also economical and practical, they had models to turn to. In fact, the Audi device served as a direct example for the much more widespread cheating that VW would do with the EA 189 engine. During a meeting where 15 engineers, including the head of VW engine development, met to discuss how to create an economical engine that would pass stringent U.S. emissions tests, the idea of this defeat device was presented and debated. While some pointed out of the risks breaking the law by adopting this device, others stated that this was normal and that many carmakers did so and VW had to do so as well if it were to keep up with competition (Ewing 2017, p. 122). According to Ewing's analysis of the meeting, most engineers would not see this as "a grave violation of Volkswagen standards. There was plenty of precedent for using shortcuts to cope with inconvenient regulations" (Ewing 2017, p. 123). In all the earlier instances of cheating, VW as a company had turned a blind eye and condoned the behavior that had occurred, paying the fines should they come, without creating clear boundaries that this was unacceptable behavior. And once they had started using the cheat in their diesel engine there was no more stopping. As Ewing explains, "defeat devices which may have begun as a stopgap had become a habit" (Ewing 2017, p. 178).

Since adopting the ambitious Going for Gr-eight targets, Wells Fargo learned about more and more instances where its employees had opened fake and unauthorized accounts, from 63 in 2000, to 680 in 2004, to 288 in a single quarter in 2007, to 1469 in a single quarter in 2013 (Colvin 2017). In 2002, it was discovered that a whole Colorado branch had been opening unauthorized and fake accounts simply to reach their sales targets. The bank responded simply by firing individual employees involved, but not by addressing this as a systemic problem caused by their own targets. Bank leaders were actually positive about the numbers, as it showed them that only 1% of the work force had to be fired for cheating, while they assumed the other 99% were in compliance. As then CEO Stumpf said in an email to another bank leader: "Do you know only around 1% of our people lose their jobs [for] gaming the system, and about 2/3 of those are for gaming the monitoring of the system, i.e., changing phone numbers, etc. Nothing could be further from the truth on forcing products on customers. In any case, right will win and we are right. Did some do things wrong—you bet and that is called life. This is not systemic" (Colvin 2017).

While the company would fire employees caught red-handed in defrauding clients or the bank, it turned a blind eye to ongoing practices, never seeking to proactively find out how widespread they were and end them. Neither did Wells Fargo fully make clear that reaching sales targets was less important than compliance. As increasingly more employees started to cheat, a norm developed. As Colvin explains: "The message was clear to everyone in the retail bank: Everyone knew the goals were sheer fantasy for many branches and employees. At some branches not enough customers walked in the door, or area residents were too poor to need more than a few banking products. Bank leaders called overall quotas '50/50 plans' because they figured only half the regions could meet them. Yet no excuses were tolerated. You met the quotas or paid a price" (Colvin 2017).

In all three companies, norms thus developed that normalized risky, rule breaking, and damaging practices that would come to shape the values and assumptions of corporate employees and executives. This was not merely a passive process in which the corporations allowed the practices to develop in response to the structures of budget cuts and highly ambitious targets. At times corporations would directly condone these practices. Volkswagen never strongly responded to any of the earlier cases where its engineers had installed defeat devices. At BP for instance, an independent investigation found that the oil company allowed "pencil whipping" and the fabrication of inspection data. One employee said that "BP workers felt pressure to skip key diagnostics, including pressure testing, cleaning of pipelines, and checking for corrosion, in order to cut costs" (Lustgarten and Knutson 2010). A former Wells Fargo assistant vice president and regional private banker has sued the bank claiming that she was fired when she refused "to participate in a scheme to manipulate accounts and sell products that weren't in customers' best interest." She alleged that her superiors were running the scheme (Associated Press 2017). Other employees have come forth complaining that they were fired after trying to report the illegal practices to the ethic's hotline (Egan 2017). In another case, a former branch manager had found out that bankers had swayed a homeless person to open six bank accounts getting her to pay $39 per month. She explained: "It's all manipulation. We are taught exactly how to sell multiple accounts" (Reckard 2013). She reported the situation to higher executives but never received any answer (Reckard 2013). Or as another former employee explained: "Training in questionable sales practices was required or you were to be fired" (Colvin 2017). Clearly, at Wells Fargo this was not simply a matter of lower employees breaking Wells Fargo rules. And it was not simply a common practice: It had become something that was endorsed and for which no internal complaints were accepted, let alone seriously acted upon to change the root causes that sustained it.

The ongoing illegal behavior and internal responses to it in all three cases offer us further insight into toxic elements in their culture. Again, we will first discuss the types of toxic norms and their processes (drawing on Table 2 above) and then look at what level of culture we find these in (drawing on Table 1). A first clear toxic process was that in all three cases the existence of illegal practices formed visible common behavior (a descriptive social norm (cf. Cialdini et al. 2006)) that was directly against the law and thus came to compete and resist with the law (cf. Moore 1973; Heimer 1999). The lack of company responses to such illegal behavior spurred two further negative cultural processes. As illegal behavior could continue unaddressed, the companies normalized deviance (Vaughan 1989, 1997) and failed to foster learning processes that could prevent future misconduct (Homsma et al. 2009). As the companies turned a blind eye to the ongoing illegal practices, and never sought to proactively detect and stop them, they also created an opportunity for employees to cut corners at very little risk. As long as it did not create a major scandal with outside complaints or regulatory investigations, the companies were not proactively seeking to find violators or hold them accountable. And thus, the companies left the henhouse open to the foxes. Or in the terms of the Routine Activities Theory, "committed offenders" had access to "suitable targets" as there were no "capable guardians" (Cohen and Felson 1979). The negative cultural processes here started at the practice level, with visible common behavior, that probably became unaware common behavior, and then moved into the values, especially the injunctive social norms and hidden assumptions, as what people saw converged with what they came to think.

3.4. Responses to Exposure of Scandals

So, what happened when the three companies came to face strong public and legal scrutiny when each had its scandals exposed? Organizational responses to crisis offer a clear window into what values a company communicates both outwards and inwards to its own employees at the most critical moments. Crucially, responses to scandals are major organizational moments that can have a strong impact on the organizational culture and the extent to which it is toxic. In all three, the companies deflected blame, defended themselves from liability, and some, most notably VW, even tried to downplay the damages of their actions. By doing so, the companies neutralized their own culpability, thus enabling further rule breaking.

The Wells Fargo response to over a decade of fraudulent practices was to blame the individual employees, and not the unrealistic sales targets, lack of response to complaints, and threatening practices that had stimulated these lower level bankers to start cheating. As Frost explains: "It was convenient instead to blame the problem of low quality and unauthorized accounts and other employee misconduct on individual wrongdoers" (Frost 2017). At Wells Fargo, the fragmented corporate structure enabled blame shifting and obstructed taking responsibility for malpractice elsewhere in the company. As Colvin analyses: "For example, the corporate chief risk officer had no authority over the retail bank's risk officer, who reported only to Tolstedt (who headed community banking). The HR department regarded employee misbehavior as an issue of training, incentive compensation, and performance management. The law department's employment section focused mainly on litigation risks from firing employees. Each concerned itself with its assigned slice of the issue; no one looked for the root cause or envisioned big-picture consequences" (Colvin 2017).

Wells Fargo tried to persist in this strategy even in 2016, after the true scale of the fraudulent behavior became public and the company had to respond to news that it had defrauded millions of U.S. customers. Its first response was to blame individual employees and fire 5300 lower level bankers, without taking responsibility at the top. In a hearing before the Senate Banking Committee on 20 September 2016, CEO Stumpf apologized for not ending the illegal practices earlier and promised that the bank would undergo reform (Corkery 2016). Senators were angry that he did not offer any concrete steps against executives, including himself, and had just shifted blame and punishment to those at the bank's lower levels. As Senator Elizabeth Warren asked him: "Have you returned one nickel of the money that you earned while this scandal was going on? Have you fired any senior management, the people who actually oversaw this fraud?" After Mr. Stumpf, answered that he had not, Warren retorted: "Your definition of accountability is to push this on your low-level employees. This is gutless leadership." But Mr. Stumpf persisted stating: "The 5300 (fired employees) were dishonest, and that is not part of our culture. That is not scapegoating" (Corkery 2016). In a statement to National Public Radio inquiries following the hearings, Mr. Stumpf said: "Although the vast majority of our team members do the right thing, every day, on behalf of our customers, these allegations and accusations are very serious. And if any of these things transpired, it's distressing and it's not who Wells Fargo is" (Arnold 2016).

Senators also pushed the CEO about whether the bank would seek to claw back the millions of compensations of top executives who had failed to fulfil their duty to stop the scandal. Here they especially focused on Carrie Tolstedt, who had been in charge of community banking where all the issues had happened. She retired at age 56 with a package of tens of millions of dollars, just three months before the hearing. Mr. Stumpf explained that although Ms. Tolstedt had let the illegal practices go on for three years after they were first discovered in 2013, he did not want to fire her because she performed so well in her other duties (Corkery 2016).

BP's first response to major scandals was to deflect blame. One tactic was to try to place on blame on individual workers, at worst the ones who had been directly hurt in accidents. These were the same workers who had been concerned over the safety of the operations, as years and years of budget cuts had created a very hazardous working environment. And when things then did go wrong, as was likely to happen with the budget cuts, their company would blame them. Workers at the Texas Refinery, which was the site of the deadly 2005 explosion, had been interviewed previously about safety issues. One explained: "Yes I have been hurt and had management punish me and made a fool out of me. Need I say more?" (Steffy 2010, p. 66). Another, who had been hurt because of a mechanical failure: "I was blamed in the end. I was not the root cause" (Steffy 2010, p. 66).

And after the 2005 explosion at the Texas refinery facility BP followed a strategy of stonewalling and blame shifting (Smithson and Venette 2013). It first put the refinery on lockdown for eight days, not letting anybody in, claiming that it was too hazardous. Then two months later, it issued its internal investigation report and placed blame squarely on the low level employees who were alleged to have overfilled and overheated the raffinate splitter (Steffy 2010, p. 89). Steffy summarized BP's response: "Human error-or workers not following rules-meant that BP itself wasn't to blame" (Steffy 2010, pp. 89–90). Ironically enough, a BP executive had chaired the development of safety guidelines by the Center for Chemical Process Safety that concluded that "errant employees aren't the root cause of an accident but rather its symptom" (Steffy 2010, p. 90).

Five years later, following the Deepwater Horizon spill, BP also sought to deflect blame. Its first tactic was to try to steer out of the scandal, when media during the initial 12 days focused on Transocean, the owner of the rig. Transocean could act as a good shield (Steffy 2010, p. 182). In one of the early statements BP CEO Hayward stated: "We are responsible, not for the accident, but we are responsible for the oil" (Smithson and Venette 2013, p. 402). He said this in spite of Transocean's reliance for most of its business on BP for most of its business and the big oil company's major influence in day-to-day operational decisions—decisions that enhanced risks and neglected industry standards, all to expedite the drilling and save costs (Smithson and Venette 2013, p. 402). Therefore at first, BP tried to use its decentralized structure with sub-contractors to defect blame. It had done so earlier. In the 1990s for instance, BP had blamed a sub-contractor, Doyon, when it was found that BP Alaska had been illegally injecting its toxic waste into the ground, even though BP was again directly in charge and Doyon relied for 80% of its income on BP (Lustgarten 2012, p. 61).

BP leadership also tried to downplay the role they themselves played in all this. This was most apparent in CEO Hayward's testimony during the U.S. congressional hearings. He kept on deflecting critical questions about how BP had managed risk. Hayward instead focused on how much money the company had spent on safety (Smithson and Venette 2013, p. 402). Whenever he was pressed about problems, Hayward would insist that the investigation was ongoing and no firm conclusions about the role BP had played in all this could be made yet. When Representative Bart Stupak asked him, "Are you trying to tell me you have not reached a conclusion that BP really cut corners here?" Hayward answered simply: "I think it's too early to reach conclusions, with respect, Mister Chairman. The investigations are ongoing" (Smithson and Venette 2013, p. 403). When Hayward was asked about BP's decisions about particular aspects of the operation that had caused the risk, he would explain that he was not involved in the decision making. When pressed on details, he would claim ignorance. For instance, when Representative Michael Burges asked a question about why BP had installed fewer than the recommended number of centralizers that were to ensure the proper flow of cement, Hayward said: "I can't answer that question, I'm not a cement engineer I'm afraid" (Smithson and Venette 2013, p. 404). But Hayward does have a PhD in geology, 28 years of experience in oil and gas exploration, and had been CEO of BP America for the three years prior. As Smithson and Venette conclude: "The suggestion that someone with Hayward's experience and knowledge had insufficient information to determine whether BP made risky decisions was ridiculous" (Smithson and Venette 2013, p. 404).

BP did not stop there. It even tried to downplay the damage of the spill. At first, BP had stated that that oil was leaking at 1000 barrels a day, a relatively modest spill. That would indicate that the spill would only reach Exxon Valdez levels after one year. A little later, BP raised that figure from 1000 to 5000 barrels a day (Steffy 2010, p. 184). In fact, oceanographers from Florida had used satellite imaging data and found that the size of the leak was much larger at 30,000 barrels a day, meaning the leak could surpass the Valdez spill in only two weeks. CEO Hayward dismissed these findings saying that their own information was the most accurate: "A guestimate is a guestimate and the guestimate remains at 5000 barrels a day" (Steffy 2010, p. 184). When BP was forced to release its live video feed from the wellhead or face a congressional subpoena, experts found that the leak was even larger—about 60,000–70,000 barrels per day (Steffy 2010, p. 185). Hayward later even went as far as to deny that such a massive spill caused much damage. In an interview with the Guardian he stated: "The Gulf of Mexico is a very big ocean . . . the amount of oil and dispersant we are putting into [it] is tiny in relation to the total water volume" (Kollewe 2010).

But no one tried to deflect blame like Volkswagen. Soon after Volkswagen learned about the West Virginia University study that had demonstrated that the on-road emissions were many times higher than lab tested emissions, the head of product safety, Bern Gottweis, sent a memo to CEO Winterkorn. The memo concluded that "A thorough explanation for the dramatic increase in NOx emissions cannot be given to the authorities" (Ewing 2017, p. 177). He concluded that in further testing, the authorities would find out that there was a cheat device. And VW could revise the software to decrease emissions during road testing, but not to a compliant level (Ewing 2017). So very early on in the development of the scandal, the highest level executives at VW knew that regulators would find the defeat device and there was no way to salvage the situation. But rather than coming clean with the Californian and federal environmental regulators, VW opted to stall, to cheat even more, to deflect blame, and even to try to argue that the harm was limited. Soon after VW learned of the tests, there was a presentation that discussed the costs and benefits of different response options: refuse to acknowledge the problem and continue to stonewall and lie, offer an update to the engine software that would decrease emissions but not to the compliant level, or admit to the problem and buy back diesel cars in the US. The last option, Ewing concludes, "does not appear to have been seriously discussed at the time" (Ewing 2017, p. 179).

By this time, in May 2014, Volkswagen came to adopt a new NOx control system by installing urea tanks that catalyzed NOx into harmless oxygen and nitrogen. However, Volkswagen never installed a tank big enough to truly control the emissions at a sufficient level. So, the cars continued to have cheat devices that would only allow a sufficient level of urea to be used during lab testing, and not during road driving so that owners would not have to fill up their tanks with an extra chemical (Ewing 2017). In light of the investigation, Volkswagen tweaked its EPA application, indicating that owners would have to fill their tank "approximately" every ten thousand miles. This was a major change, as Ewing explains Volkswagen thus no longer promised that the system could work long enough through the full circle between regular oil changes. Volkswagen also updated the software so that the cars would use more urea to better catalyze NOx, and reduce the difference between road emissions and laboratory emissions, which would still not bring the true road emissions within the standards. In this way, Volkswagen tinkered and improved its cheating device, even when they already knew that in time it would be discovered. It continued to sell large volumes of cars that were not as clean as they claimed (Ewing 2017, p. 181).

Meanwhile, Volkswagen stalled and obstructed the CARB investigation into why there was a difference between the lab and road emissions. CARB at that time did not expect deliberate wrongdoing; they simply just tried to understand the cause and fix it. Volkswagen, however, was not really cooperative. As Ewing details: "The Volkswagen executives responsible for dealing with regulators gave answers that the regulators regarded as evasive, non-sensical, or dismissive. CARB's testing was wrong, Volkswagen complained. The outside air temperature threw off the results.

The routes followed [during the road tests] were inconsistent" (Ewing 2017, p. 182). As this process went on and started to consume more and more CARB time, Volkswagen informed the regulators that they would do a recall to update the software and "optimize" the emission control equipment in all clean diesels it had sold (Ewing 2017, p. 182). This was no admission of what actually had been happening, and instead gave the false promise that this would bring emissions within standards. Volkswagen also lied about the recall to customers and dealers, claiming that the recall was necessary to deal with a malfunction light defect (Ewing 2017, p. 183).

Most shocking, Volkswagen in fact used the recall to improve the effectiveness of the cheating software. It improved the car's ability to detect when it was being tested in the lab, switching on its fully effective emissions controls only when the steering wheel was stationary for a longer time while driving, as it would only be at the lab (Ewing 2017, p. 183). The regulators responded with further and more stringent tests, and asked questions about other models with larger engines, which by then had also had defeat devices. And Volkswagen, even though by then it knew for sure that the game would soon be up, just continued its stonewalling and deceit.

Volkswagen executives became especially worried when they learned CARB was going to test an older clean diesel model. One internal email stated: "If the Gen I goes on to the roller at CARB then we'll have nothing to laugh about" (Ewing 2017, p. 193). CARB also demanded that Volkswagen show them the software that controlled the urea injections in the new 2016 cars.

Volkswagen continued its cover-up all the way until it could no longer do so. It was forced to come clean and admit the existence of the defeat device only after CARB threatened that if Volkswagen failed to show them the software, it would refuse to approve the 2016 models onto the Californian market, which would keep them from the whole U.S. market (Ewing 2017, pp. 192–93). At first Volkswagen still would not admit to using the cheating software. A legal memo had estimated that the risk Volkswagen was running was still manageable. By now, Volkswagen had stalled and obstructed the CARB investigation for over a year. The company provided CARB a thick binder with the latest technical information, which seemed to indicate that VW had finally solved the problem. When CARB looked deeper into the information provided it found it was "all nonsense" (Ewing 2017, p. 197). The only explanation, CARB also now saw was that VW had been using a defeat device all along. It was August 2015, and CARB had still not approved the 2016 VW models, which were waiting in port to enter the market. And CARB was still waiting for the software information it had requested, and further it asked VW for a 2016 model car for new testing. This proved to be the final straw, as Volkswagen eager to get its cars on the US market ready for 2016, finally confessed that its cars had had defeat devices (Ewing 2017, pp. 197–98).

Volkswagen later claimed that it had failed to disclose the issue earlier because executives had not known about this. According to VW, it was only a small group of technicians who knew about the device. Top executives, Volkswagen claimed, had only learned about "conclusive proof" for the defeat device just before its confession to CARB (Ewing 2017, p. 200). And thus, Volkswagen moved from stonewalling, deceit and denial, to shifting blame downwards in the company. VW's new CEO, Müller, has maintained this discourse since then. Stating, in an interview with a German newspaper: "Based on what I know today only a few employees were involved." Defending his former CEO Winterkorn, he said: "Do you really think that a chief executive had time for the inner functioning of engine software?" (Ewing 2017, p. 216). Volkswagen leadership maintained this line, even when former CEO and grand architect of the Volkswagen growth strategy in the 1990s and early 2000s, Piëch came forward to claim that he had learned of the emissions problems in February 2015 while still chairing the board and that at the time Winterkorn had told them that there was nothing to worry about (Ewing 2017, p. 271).

Volkswagen ended up suspending several dozens of its midlevel engineers and executives, including the head of quality control and a member of the Audi management board (Ewing 2017, pp. 223, 256). Yet VW never addressed the more than a year period VW had tried to stall, obstruct, and deceive the ongoing investigations. Nor did VW seriously explore that the scandal involved a larger plot involving the highest level executives (Ewing 2017, p. 223). The company's supervisory board never took any disciplinary action against the company's top level executives who served on the management board (Ewing 2017, p. 256). And the car maker still paid out $33.9 million dollar in top executive bonuses, even when it reported a record $1.6 billion loss. This meant that even Winterkorn, who had been CEO during most of the saga, received a total compensation package of $8 million in 2015, and that was for ten months only, as he had retired in October (Ewing 2017, pp. 242–43). Volkswagen employees ended up paying the brunt of the costs, as in November 2016 the company announced it would cut 14,000 jobs (Ewing 2017, p. 258).

Volkswagen also tried to downplay that it had broken the law. VW CEO Müller tried to paint what had happened in a much more positive light. In an interview, he stated: "It was a technical problem ... An ethical problem? I cannot understand why you [the reporter] say that." As he explained, they did not have: "the right interpretation of the American law ... We didn't lie. We didn't understand the question first. And then we worked since 2014 to solve the problem" (Glinton 2016). Meanwhile in Europe, Volkswagen took a directly confrontational legal approach, claiming that what had happened was not against the law there. A Volkswagen representative called to share the company's response to the scandal to the UK House of Commons Transport Select Committee, called the software a "drive trace" and said that it "was not defined as a defeat device in Europe." When members pressed that this was incorrect, the company's representative simply stated that "in the understanding of the Volkswagen Group it is not a defeat device" (Ewing 2017, pp. 232–33).

The crassest deflection attempt of all was when Volkswagen tried to deny that it had damaged public health. It simply tried to refute that NOx was harmful. In a statement issued in late 2016 VW said: "A reliable determination of morbidity or even fatalities for certain demographic groups based on our level of knowledge is not possible from a scientific point of view" (Reuters 2016). In 2018, a German newspaper reported that Volkswagen had tried to back up its claims by exposing monkeys for hours to exhausts from the "clean diesel" engine of a 2016 Beetle, and compare them with monkeys exposed to the fumes from a 1997 heavy duty gasoline Ford F250 pick-up truck. Volkswagen had kept the study quiet, not in the least because the results had shown that the old Ford was less damaging to the monkeys than the state of the art Beetle. Several studies have now proven that the health effects are real. One of the most recent studies by MIT scientists, published in Environmental Research Letters, estimates that the extra NOx emissions emitted because of VW's cheating will cost 1200 premature deaths in Europe, each dying a decade early (Chossière et al. 2017).

In conclusion, all three companies clearly tried to deflect blame, doing so each time they had a scandal and when the most major scandals erupted over the last years. Blame deflection had become a regular practice in all three companies, and with it came values that were harmful for compliance. The blame deflection resulted in several toxic cultural norms and processes. Again, we shall discuss these here referring back to Table 2 for the norms and processes and Table 1 for the levels these played out in within the cultures.

The first toxic process we see here is neutralization. By shifting away blame from the company and its executives to sub-contractors and lower level workers, the company neutralized the culpability of the corporation and its leaders, and it failed to take responsibility itself that could foster organizational learning from the wrongdoing that would help to prevent it (Homsma et al. 2009). This "denial of responsibility" can enable further rule breaking, as corporate executives rationalize and legitimize illegal practices in their firm as they reiterate time and again that it was not the corporation, that this is not who we are, or that it was just a few bad apples (cf. Maruna and Copes 2005; Minor 1981; Sykes and Matza 1957). This mentality prevents the corporation from developing normative values, from taking responsibility for mistakes, and from acknowledging that what happened was unacceptable and must be prevented at all cost. BP and Volkswagen also denied the damaging impact of the rule violations, claiming that the oil spill was but a drop in the ocean and that the NOx emissions were not damaging to health. This "denial of injury" is another classic neutralization technique that directly enables continued offending behavior, as it allows future rule breakers to tell themselves that this is not as bad as what people make it out to be

(Maruna and Copes 2005; Minor 1981; Sykes and Matza 1957). In VW's case, a different neutralization technique not discussed in the original criminological literature can be identified—a legal neutralization that occurred when the company claimed that its actions were not against the law. Again, this claim enabled offending and damaging behavior by appealing to the letter of the law to justify behavior was so clearly against its spirit.

The deflection of blame further strengthened the normalization of deviancy (cf. Vaughan 1989, 1997). As blame is pushed downward and outward, discipline for higher level leaders remains lagging. In all three cases, stronger internal action, to the extent that it did happen, only came after outside pressure. Wells Fargo, for instance, sought to claw back bonuses after relentless critique that it had not done so. And through this, the deflection of blame practices further enabled rule breaking and normalized deviancy, as it failed to establish a clear norm that offending behavior is not tolerated.

The deflection of blame does not play out in a vacuum, but exists as a response to the broader economic and legal forces companies operate in and thus interacts with the responses to strain these companies are under (Agnew 1992, 2001; Agnew et al. 2009; Simpson and Koper 1997). Blame deflection is not just part of the toxic culture at these three companies, but a much more common practice for firms that are trying to repair their image in the aftermath of scandals (Benoit 2014). Blame deflection is also a direct response against legal forms of strain that come with criminal and civil liability. With the push for punishment and compensation—that is highly justified and also necessary to end impunity—also comes the risk of steering companies towards blame deflection. Blame deflection undermines the value of taking true responsibility and setting true internal norms and, as is evident in all three cases, acknowledging that such behavior is not acceptable. And, in turn, the push to punish the highest levels of corporate leadership may instead lead to a shifting of blame onto those individual leaders, without truly addressing the toxic corporate culture.

Here we see that these toxic processes started most clearly at the level of values in the form of explicit shared values that came with statements from the companies. But when companies respond to a longer series of scandals, as BP so clearly did, employees will begin to expect that their company deflects blame and does not take responsibility, and at some point this is can become a hidden assumption, and thus become more deeply embedded in the corporate culture, reaching the levels of hidden assumptions.

3.5. Mixed Messages and Corporate Dissonance

None of the companies openly claimed that their actions of defrauding customers, cheating on emissions, or chafing of safety standards were good or intentional. All three companies ostensibly had ethical standards, positive corporate messages, and even branding and commercials that were highly aligned with compliance and the goals of the law. The expressed values all three companies promoted formally, however, were in stark contrast with their actual practices and the values the public observed through these practices. As New York Federal Reserve President William Dudley said about Wells Fargo: "There was a serious mismatch between the values Wells Fargo espoused and the incentives that Wells Fargo employed" (Puzzanghera 2017).

BP and Volkswagen provide the most detailed information about such "corporate dissonance" between preached values and practiced norms (Ewing 2017). During the 1990s, both companies had made environmental protection part of their core image. Volkswagen started with the development of the turbo charged direct injection diesel engine. The new technology that VW brought to market in 1989 made the fuel-efficient diesel cleaner and less noisy, thus making diesel a palatable option for small and midsized cars. The company dubbed this technology—associated with power and fuel efficiency—"TDI", and made it a core part of its brand (Ewing 2017). In the 2000s, VW went a step further and developed "clean diesel," which was promoted as an equally clean, fuel efficient, but more powerful and economical alternative to the hybrid models Toyota and other companies started to advertise. To promote the new technology, VW commissioned several new commercials. One series of commercial featured three old ladies driving in a VW clean diesel car and discussing "old wives tales" about diesel. Each commercial ended by suggesting that Volkswagen's new clean diesel led to less noise, more power, and, most importantly, clean exhaust emissions . In one commercial, one of the elderly women placed her white handkerchief behind the exhaust just to show how clean the diesel was (Ewing 2017, p. 147). Another commercial, played during the break of the American Super Bowl, depicted environmental police busting people for minor issues, from not separating their trash to using the wrong lightbulbs. In the final scene, a police checkpoint verified if cars were environmentally friendly enough. A man driving a Volkswagen is waved through by a friendly cop who says: "Volkswagen Clean Diesel. Sir, you are good to go."[4]

Volkswagen's green branding and advertising stood in stark contrast to its actual practices, which were anything but clean. For those who had been in some way involved in the defeat device, the contrast between the public image of Volkswagen as environmentally friendly and the practice they knew was absolute.

This corporate dissonance between what was stated and what was practiced became even larger the moment the California regulators began to look into the discrepancy in VW lab and road test results. For over a year, VW's official stance was that the testing had problems and that it was not accurate, but not that the company had been cheating. As the pressure escalated, VW executives must have come to know of the defeat device, and the more they strategized how to continue to deflect blame, the more the discrepancy grew between what VW said and what happened in the company. This is especially clear with the recall VW organized, formally letting regulators know it was to fix the emissions problem, and telling dealers that it was to fix a safety light, while in fact it was a deliberate attempt to make the cheating even better (Ewing 2017, pp. 182–83). What employees and executives learned at VW was that what the company said, whether in advertisements, against regulators, and against the public, had little to no relation to what it practiced. This continued after even VW admitted it had a defeat device, as it tried to argue that it had not broken EU law, that the emissions were not toxic, that leadership had not been involved, and that this was not a problem in the culture, but just the work of a small group of bad apples. All public statements, and all statements VW executives knew or came to know, were not true.

BP had a similar disconnect between its corporate communication and its actual practices. While BP cut costs and focused on risky exploration—resulting in a long stream of spills, hazards, and accidents—it sought to be seen as an environmentally responsible company. In 1997, BP CEO Browne announced that the link between greenhouse gases and global climate change was real and could no longer be ignored. He announced that BP would invest in alternative energy operations and research. A few years after, the company dropped its longer name, "British Petroleum", and simply became BP, but with a new slogan "Beyond Petrol." Also it launched a new shield logo of an upbeat yellow sun, signifying solar energy, surrounded by "what looked like leaves" (Steffy 2010). In the following years, and even after the Gulf disaster, the company repeatedly issued statements proclaiming that it was strongly committed to the environment. Yet this was in stark contrast not only to the company's continued exploration operations, which were trying to get as much fossil fuels as possible out of the ground and sold to consumers to burn into the air (Frey 2002), but also to its appalling disregard for safety and the oil spills it could, and indeed would, cause. BP's new imagine was not welcomed everywhere. Greenpeace said that a more fitting logo for the company would be "a miserable polar bear on an icecap shrinking because of global warming" (Frey 2002). And the environmental NGO honored CEO John Browne for the "Best Impression of an Environmentalist" (Frey 2002).

BP also claimed that it cared about safety—especially at times following major incidents. In 2000, for instance, BP's Grangemouth refinery in Scotland had three separate accidents, all in one week. As a result, BP received a criminal fine of £750,000. The investigation found that BP's quest for

---

4   https://www.youtube.com/watch?v=Ky8x0ykF_tQ.

cost reductions had created the safety hazards, and that its fractured management structure had undermined a safety prevention strategy (Steffy 2010, p. 62). BP's response was to state that it had gotten the message and that it had "shared the lessons it learned with its 11 other refineries in the world" (Steffy 2010, p. 62). While in fact, BP did not change its practices of cost cutting, ignoring safety concerns, and deflecting blame, even on those who had been hurt themselves in accidents BP had caused. With each new incident, BP claimed improvement and change, yet real change did not happen. Instead, BP's internal communication on safety focused on minor, low-cost matters. As one former exploration engineer recalls, the company and its executives "focused so heavily on the easy part of safety, holding the hand rails, spending hours discussing the merits of reverse parking and the dangers of not having a lid on a coffee cup, but were less enthusiastic about the hard stuff, investing in and maintaining their complex facilities" (Steffy 2010, p. 57).

Real change did not even come when BP's new CEO, Hayward, took over from Browne. Hayward promised to make safety a priority; he promised a "new BP." Hayward promised a less complex organization with more transparency and accountability. He promised to hire 1000 engineers and improve safety in all of BP's global operations (Steffy 2010, p. 151). However, Hayward never took full accountability for how BP's cost cutting had led to the major accidents that had occurred before his tenure. He even resumed cost reductions, cutting $4 billion in 2009 in response to the 2008 crisis (Steffy 2010, p. 162). He was also unable to convince his executives that safety should become the priority, in part because English executives saw this as an American problem, and in part because he was not as popular as his predecessor Browne (Steffy 2010, p. 152).

Under Hayward's tenure, BP would not change its core safety problems. As Steffy summarizes: "Its management structure was still convoluted, accountability was hard to find, decisions were made by committee, and cost cutting and financial performance continued to overshadow operations" (Steffy 2010, p. 160). A good illustration of this is a 2009 OSHA inspection at the Texas City refinery. The inspection resulted in one of the highest fines in OSHA history—$87 million. OSHA fined BP especially for hazards that had been identified before, but that BP had failed to fix. During another inspection in the BP refinery in Toledo, Ohio, OSHA found that BP had only done the repairs it had specifically mentioned, while leaving similar problems in other part of its operation unaddressed. As Steffy summarizes: "Hayward's 'laser' was so precise that it was able to separate the letter of the rules from the intent" (Steffy 2010, p. 162). The more Hayward promised, as new CEO in the aftermath of the Texas refinery, to change BP, the more he undermined his own credibility and thus his ability to institute reform when practices on the ground did not actually change.

Here, again, we can analyze what this means for the corporate culture. Drawing on Table 2, we see that the most important type of toxic norm at play here is the disconnect between what the companies express as their values and what their actual day to day practice has been. A disconnect between the expressed values in support of compliance (safety, environmental protection, consumer protection) and practices that run directly counter to it will damage corporate compliance. When employees and executives hear one thing in corporate messaging, but see the complete opposite in everyday practices, they will not be convinced that their company and leaders are truly committed. This will either undermine the authority and credibility of corporate leadership within the company, or it will mean that lower level executives and employees learn that these messages are just for show, just to demonstrate commitment, but that what is truly expected is the opposite. This is very similar to findings in psychology that placing prohibition signs in environments where they are clearly being violated will create more offending (Keizer et al. 2011).

The damage in this case, however, can get worse. Once corporate employees and executives begin to doubt their leaders, achieving reform in corporate values and practices becomes very difficult. When CEOs preach improvement and preach that what has happened is not in line with the corporate culture year after year (or incident after incident), how will employees know when they truly mean it and when they should truly change what they do and think is right? Consequently, the corporate cognitive dissonance derived from conflicting corporate messages and practices can be viewed as the ultimate toxic element in a corporate culture—one that can obstruct any attempt to detoxify the culture.

4. Toxic Culture, Some Lessons

We have now discussed toxic norms and processes (drawing on Tables 1 and 2) in these three cases by looking separately at five relevant business aspects: how goals and targets were established, how employees and managers could participate and dissent from these, what illegal behavior existed and how it was responded to, how the corporations responded to scandals, and what disconnect there was between public messaging and day to day practices. In this section, we analyze what we can learn when we combine these five aspects.

A first insight is that much of the toxic culture at BP, VW, and Wells Fargo did not come in the form of norms that were directly opposed to the law. We see that norms that enable rule breaking (by creating opportunity or neutralizing offending), norms that obstruct compliance (through strain and obstructing support), and norms that undermine the authority of either positive social norms or legal norms are highly important. This provides a very different view of what toxic culture is (cf. Moore 1973; Heimer 1999; Cialdini et al. 2006; Cialdini and Goldstein 2004; Vaughan 1989, 1997; Scholten and Ellemers 2016). It means that assessing toxicity requires identifying the norms that enable rule breaking, obstruct compliance, and delegitimize both the law and the social norms that support it.

A second insight is that toxic culture in these three cases was a matter of converging toxic processes. Strain in the market resulted in highly ambitious and risky targets that resulted in strain in the company (cf. Agnew 1992, 2001; Agnew et al. 2009; Simpson and Koper 1997). The same strain restricted management and employee input and dissent, which obstructed successful critique of high risk targets and reporting on illegal practices and resulted in both normalizing illegal behavior (cf. Vaughan 1989, 1997) and creating more opportunity for rule breaking (cf. Belknap 1987; Cohen and Felson 1979; Felson 1987; Osgood et al. 1996). Considering companies did not respond strongly to rule breaking when it did occur, such rule breaking itself became normalized, and organizations never fostered the learning from error that could help to prevent it (Homsma et al. 2009; Scholten and Ellemers 2016).

When the corporate wrongdoing ultimately ended in public scandals, political hearings, and legal investigations, the companies deflected blame towards lower employees, sub-contractors, and some executives. However, they rarely took full responsibility by admitting that this was a pervasive corporate issue. With the deflection, the corporations neutralized the company's culpability (cf. Sykes and Matza 1957; Gottschalk and Smith 2011; Maruna and Copes 2005; Minor 1981; Siponen et al. 2012). It was not their fault, they could not help it, they did not know, it was not illegal, and there were no damages. All of these techniques of neutralization: (1) reinforced that norm violation was not an endemic problem that needed to be addressed, and (2) furthered the normalization of deviancy.

Ultimately, when companies were forced to state their guilt, address their culture, and change the tone at the top, it was too late. After years of dissonance between the ethical values the corporation had preached and the rule violating practices in their everyday operations, the company had undermined its own norms towards compliance (cf. Keizer et al. 2011). Consequently, employees and executives became less inclined to believe the leadership's lofty promises to change the culture at the company and to reduce risk and rule breaking. Importantly, this is the ultimate ingredient in a toxic corporate culture, as the cognitive dissonance between values and practices undermines the authority of new leadership and values that support compliance. Figure 1 below outlines the convergence of these elements, and where they have occurred in the business processes: in normal business strategy and operations, in responses to rule breaking, and in corporate communications and advertising.

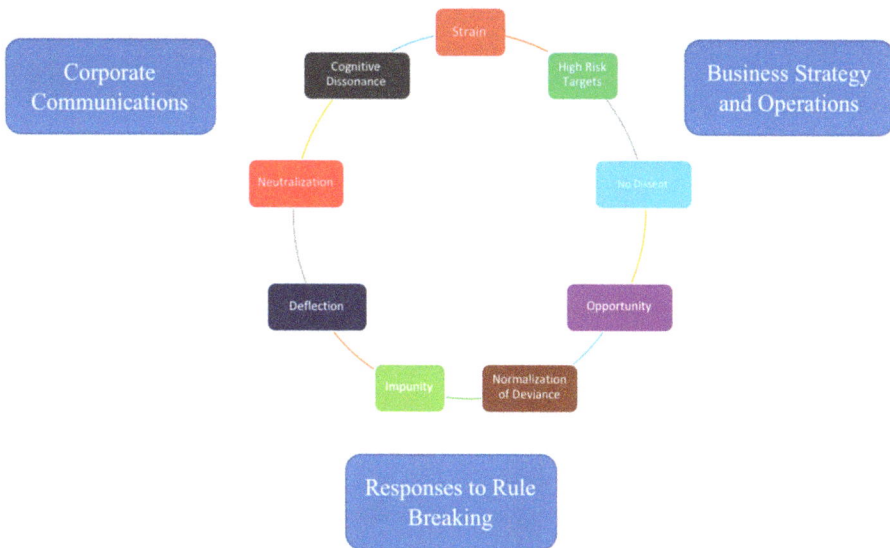

Figure 1. Converging elements of a toxic culture at VW, BP, and Wells Fargo.

A third insight, closely related to the first two, is that the toxic cultural processes occurred at all three levels of the corporate culture: structures, values, and practices. Moreover, just as Schein (2010) argued, the three levels of corporate culture interact. For instance, explicit values (e.g., the public deflection of blame) become embedded in practices and structures, that structures (e.g., the high risk and high growth targets) shape values and practices, and that practices (e.g., the condoning of ongoing violations) become embedded in values and hidden assumptions. Although beyond the scope of this paper, it is very likely that what started as conscious and deliberative values and practices became more deeply embedded in hidden assumptions, unaware common practices, and situational norms, and thus more deeply engrained in the culture.

A fourth insight is that the culture in these three cases did not become toxic by design or by any singular influence. Toxic culture was not just a matter of one bad CEO, one bad set of incentives, or the tone at the top. Certainly, the fish can rot from the head, but that certainly is not the only way it rots. Indeed, most toxic processes within these companies were not directly against the law. Moreover, the processes interacted, and no one had full knowledge and control over this interaction and what it would cause. And finally, the toxic processes did not just exist in designed structures and formal policies, but also in values and practices that were shared throughout the company. Consequently, while individual blame and responsibility for elements and aspects of the toxic cultural processes can be found and should be assigned (such as the high-risk targets, or the organization of coercive personnel practices that stymied dissent), these are not responsible for the whole culture.

Of course, not all toxic cultures are the same. But these three specific cases illustrate how we can assess toxic culture at the level of structures, values, and practices, by identifying norms that run against the law, norms that enable rule-breaking, norms that obstruct compliance, and conflicting messages that undermine the authority of positive and legal norms.

5. Detoxing Corporate Culture

Once we learn what toxic corporate cultures are, the next question is what to do about them. In the case of VW, BP, and Wells Fargo, investigators and reporters have concluded that toxic culture was to blame and must be addressed. Naturally, changing a toxic corporate culture is remarkably difficult. Nonetheless, deriving from the analysis of the three cases, this paper offers some observations about detoxing corporate culture and suggests several possible steps.

For any toxic corporate culture, the first step begins with the *proper assessment* of the toxicity. Such assessment requires a deep analysis of structures, values, and practices that run against the law, that enable rule breaking, that obstruct compliance, and that delegitimize the law and norms supporting it. Unfortunately, common responses to assess corporate culture tend to latch on to singular elements that are thought to signify the culture. Most discussion of cultural change at Wells Fargo focuses on the incentive structures, while forgetting the strained environment and lack of proper venues for dissent they operate in, let alone the condoning, blame shifting, and neutralization of guilt that has taken place in response to public scandal.

To assess the toxicity, one's initial reaction may be to turn to a survey. Certainly, there are several survey tools in academia designed to measure organizational and corporate culture. A widely-cited example of an academic survey measuring corporate culture is the one by Denisen that analyzes four cultural traits: mission, consistency, adaptability, and involvement (Denison 1990). Further, we can turn to Hofstede's influential work that used surveys worldwide to identify organizational cultures along four dimensions: power distance, uncertainty avoidance, individualism vs collectivism, and masculinity vs femininity (Hofstede 1980, 1998; Hofstede et al. 1991, 1990). These surveys allow us to understand general traits of organizations that have often been linked to economic performance.

However, existing academic surveys or organizational culture have not focused on studying *toxic* elements in particular. The problem with surveys is that they can only measure what people know and what they are willing to share. As such, surveys only provide access to the conscious values and practices, and not to the hidden assumptions and automatic, unconscious habits. Moreover, once surveys focus on toxic cultural traits, they would necessarily touch on aspects of illegal or wrongful behavior. It is extremely difficult to get people to admit to rule-breaking or immoral values and practices without protection from prosecution. In addition, surveys that ask closed questions do not allow for learning about elements in a culture that the survey designers had not thought of, and thus may overlook vitally important toxic elements in corporate cultures. That is, our insights are limited to what we thought to measure.

To assess a company's toxic culture, then, assessment cannot come solely through a survey. What is needed is a forensic ethnography, as outlined previously in this paper. Here, we have just done a first-level, desk-analysis using available resources from investigative reporting, company reports, and legal investigations. A true forensic ethnography would ask the same questions, but would do so through in-depth, open-response communication with current and former employees and executives involved in both operations and strategy of the company. Ideally, this should be done by investigators with training in qualitative social science research methods and ethnography, such as anthropologists and sociologists.

Step 2 is to *change toxic structures* of the corporation. This is the most straightforward way to start the corporate detox. Structures are the tangible, man-made, and changeable aspects of corporations. Should toxicity be found in such structures, as for instance the Wells Fargo incentives or the BP budget cut targets, then all that needs to be done is change such incentives and targets. This is simpler than it may look. First of all, the targets and incentives exist for a reason. Wells Fargo developed its targets under the strain of its overall performance in the market, and once it achieved growth with the incentives, it became very hard for leadership to let them go. Reformers may need to overcome resistance to change toxic structures, but that may well mean that first, they must address the strain that has caused them.

The second issue is that changing the structures will not eradicate negative behavior in and of itself, if such structures have become embedded in the deeper values and practices of the corporation. For instance, in the aftermath of the crisis, Wells Fargo ended its sales targets. Nonetheless, bank employees continued to feel the pressure to grow their sales and employees were still asked how many products they sold to each client and informally pushed to hit a certain target, even though such targets were no longer part of the official policy (Roberts 2017). Once toxic elements have moved from the structures into the values and practices, eradicating them through policy reform will not be enough. This has vital ramifications for how assessing toxic culture may undermine successful interventions. Most assessments focus on the structures because they are most visible, stimulating responses that sound good, but do not get to the root of the problem.

Step 3 is to *address top executives*. We see that CEOs played an important role in all three cases. They were the ones that had developed the risky targets. They had put strain on their executives to avoid critiquing these targets and to follow them compliantly, which the executives translated downwards. They turned a blind eye to the rule-breaking effects the targets were having. They failed to take disciplinary action against rule breakers. And they failed to take responsibility when the rule breaking became public. By deflecting blame, they neutralized culpability, and when they issued statements of support for the law that were in reality disconnected from the corporate practices and its actual values, they undermined the legitimacy of the law as well as their own legitimacy as the highest, internal leaders for compliance. Consequently, even when the CEOs and top executives were not directly involved in the rule breaking or had adopted policies that directly promoted rule breaking, they played a vital role in the toxic cultural elements that enabled rule breaking and obstructed compliance.

It seems natural to call for the replacement and punishment of these highest leaders—this may well be what is needed immediately. Replacement can start, or at least signal, the beginning of a shift in the culture of the firm. Punishment can show that what had happened in the past is wrong and should not happen again. However, while these may be necessary steps, they are not sufficient to change toxic culture and may even backfire. Discharging one CEO and hiring the next one, who enters an organization operating in a strained environment with toxic elements embedded in the values and practices, may inadvertently force the next CEO to adapt to the culture and continue the same problems. A good example is BP. Hayward vowed a turnaround when he succeeded Browne, promising an end to budget cuts and a true pledge to safety. Within a couple of years, however, it became clear that economic concerns forced him back to cost cutting, just like his predecessor.

Another challenge is knowing if the potential new CEO has the right values and is truly committed to compliance before taking the position. In this realm, management science may offer some insight on the characteristics of ethical leadership, which provides surveys to help discern the ethical style of the CEO candidates (Brown and Treviño 2006; Brown et al. 2005; Treviño et al. 2003). In practice, however, it is difficult to predict which leaders will be truly committed to compliance and will help solidify a compliance culture in a turnaround process.

Of course, addressing CEOs also means assigning accountability and punishment. Doing so could theoretically deter CEOs from allowing their companies to violate the law and cause harm. As we outlined at the outset of this paper, achieving deterrence in practice has proven difficult. But our analysis here shows that one of the unintended consequences of trying to prosecute executives is that it may harm a cultural detox. Trying to make CEOs liable for corporate misconduct, as seems to be so very justified with the impunity following the financial crisis, may result in more blame shifting, legal deflection, and a neutralization of guilt and culpability that only further strengthens the toxic culture. Also, it forces CEOs to continually come forth with public messages that run counter to the values and practices, and thus undermine credibility. Ideally, CEOs that come to clean up toxic cultures would be able to speak honestly and take responsibility. Unfortunately, this works best if they are under less pressure of potential liability and punishment.

This has insights for changing the *tone at the top* (Baggett 2003; Hansen et al. 2009; Schwartz et al. 2005). Analyses of toxic corporate cultures often point to the importance of a good, ethical, and compliant tone at the top. Indeed, such tone is vital, but it also needs to match the values and practices within the organization. When they are opposed, such as when leadership supports compliance while the organization does not actually practice it, the net result will be even more negative because it undermines the authority of the law and the CEO. Change in tone, therefore, must coincide with a true change in values and practices.

Further, the tone is not just about supporting ethics and compliance, but also, and maybe more importantly, about changing the norms that enable rule breaking and obstruct compliance. Here we can think of CEOs that express and initiate real support for worker empowerment and voice, for realistic targets, for honesty and transparency, for long-term over short-term goals. Detoxing the tone at the top must be honest and realistic for it to stimulate any meaningful change. This is especially important for a CEO unfortunate enough to face a long history of cognitive dissonance. Their first order of business is to convince the corporation that they stand by their word and that their expressed values will be matched by action.

Step 4 is to *address managers and employees*. Even when the structures are successfully altered, and there is new leadership with the right matching values and practices, corporations still face lower-level managers and employees whose values and habits may stimulate, enable, or sustain wrongdoing, or even simply obstruct compliance. One way to address this problem is to replace employees with toxic values and practices. However, how does the corporation exactly know who to fire, and who to hire? Of course, those caught breaking the law are clearly candidates for termination. But what about people who have simply not voiced dissent towards unrealistic targets, managers who have pressed their employees to meet these targets, or workers who have grown used to seeing violations around them? None of them may have broken the law, but their values and habits may well continue a toxic culture, and new hires may adopt similar practices and values. In some sectors, for instance in the automobile industry and its diesel emissions violations, rule breaking is more pervasive, as are norms and practices that sustain it (Ogbonna and Harris 2002). In some cases, everyone is involved in rule breaking to some degree. In 2002, Wells Fargo found that in one of its Colorado branches, all employees had been involved in defrauding clients. At first, Wells Fargo decided to fire all employees, but later had to rehire a number of them as it could no longer run its branch (Colvin 2017). A further problem with firing employees and managers is that it creates blame-shifting downwards, deflects responsibility from the company, and neutralizes its overall culpability—precisely the issues that need to be addressed within the toxic culture.

Consequently, replacing staff, while clearly necessary for the worst offenders, is not a silver bullet to achieve a cultural turnaround. The key challenge is to change the values and practices of existing employees. This is by far the most challenging step. Management science offers some ideas on how to do so, although it does not specifically focus on toxic cultures that promote rule breaking (Alvesson and Sveningsson 2015; Bass and Avolio 1993; Cameron and Quinn 2006; Harrison and Stokes 1992; Hatch 1993; Hofstede et al. 1990; Jones et al. 2005; Scalzi et al. 2006; Scott et al. 2003; Warren et al. 2014; Schein 2010).

One idea is to "unfreeze" organizations first (Schein 2010). This process prepares organizational staff and management to unlearn deeply-engrained practices, values, beliefs, and assumptions. The goal of unfreezing is to help employees overcome their natural resistance to letting go. Unfreezing starts by embedding so-called *survival anxiety* in the staff by shocking them into realizing that the organization, as well as their own position, are threatened unless there is a fundamental change.

Next, Schein (2010) stresses that to change an organizational culture requires creating so-called "psychological safety." By this, he means that organizations must show their staff that changes are feasible and learnable. Once these first two steps have been successfully deployed, staff are ready to relearn new values and practices. These are major learning processes, as they run counter to what employees have experienced, both consciously and subconsciously. Schein explains that such learning involves a cognitive restructuring of the basic values and assumptions that underlie their behavior. Companies can initiate this cognitive restructuring when they relabel all core organizational concepts, tasks, and job descriptions. To do so, they have to redevelop core evaluation processes and standards, to stress the values of an open culture for worker complaints, and to formulate a long-term vision on sustainable development. This vision should include the long-term costs of unsafe and risky operations, and strive to eliminate any internal inconsistency between the tone at the top and the operations on the ground.

A core aspect of this relearning process is to "de-neutralize" the values that have come to legitimize rule breaking. After years of blame deflection, employees may have learned to see regulations as unfair, or the issues at their company as originating from a few bad apples. They may even deny that the rule breaking resulted in real injury. One option to de-neutralize the company's employees and managers is through sessions where they meet with victims of the company's actions. These sessions can be an opportunity for employees to come face-to-face with the injury caused, see the role the company played in the injury, and consider whose interests the law is actually protecting. Wells Fargo bankers, for example, would meet defrauded clients and mistreated former employees; VW engineers and executives would meet affected car owners and people suffering from pollution-related illnesses; and BP staff would meet the victims of its spills and accidents (Braithwaite 2010).

In these sessions, honesty, combined with realistic goals, is essential. Anyone who tries to initiate these change-processes may face a lack of credibility and inertia from staff who have heard it all before and who do not believe their leaders after years of corporate cognitive dissonance. Consequently, the final key element in addressing staff is empowerment.

Empowerment has two functions. First of all, staff need to be allowed to participate actively in the detoxing process. Only when they have a stake in the cultural overhaul will they come to support and stimulate a successful cultural change (Parker and Gilad 2011; Treviño et al. 2008; Weaver et al. 1999; Parker 2002; Hutter 2001). Second, worker empowerment is vital to creating a critical mass in the company that can resist unfeasible targets and overcome intimidation, in order to freely report wrongdoing and offending behavior. Empowerment entails much more than giving workers rights to speak out. As Garry Gray has shown, giving workers rights without giving them the ability to actually speak out may shift more blame on such employees when accidents and rule breaking happen (Gray 2009; Gray and Silbey 2014). Actual empowerment, therefore, must allow for workers to organize independently, to participate in decision making on issues that directly concern their work, and to have strong protections in disputes against superiors.

6. Conclusions

Toxic culture is the ultimate challenge when trying to prevent corporate crime and wrongdoing. Talking about toxic culture is easy, but actually analyzing its processes in order to change them is much harder. This paper has shown how toxic culture exists at the levels of structures, values, and practices in corporate organizations. Most crucially, it has shown that toxicity does not exist only when organizations develop norms that go against the law and promote rule breaking. As the cases at BP, Wells Fargo, and Volkswagen demonstrate, toxicity also exists when organizations have norms that enable rule breaking, obstruct compliance, and delegitimize the authority of the law or norms that support it.

Toxic cultures at BP, Wells Fargo, and Volkswagen resulted from a convergence of several core processes. Among these processes, this paper identified: the strain on the company and employees; unfeasible and risky targets; obstruction of dissent; the opportunity for rule breaking based on condoning ongoing violations; the normalization of deviance as increasingly more people break rules; deflecting blame away from the company; neutralizing company culpability and legitimizing offending behavior; and delegitimizing the law because of a dissonance between preached values and illegal practices. Many of these processes in of themselves are not illegal, nor do they directly promoting rule breaking, but rather they enable violations and make compliance harder.

In these cases, the toxic culture did not develop by some grand design or because of a singular act or actor. While CEOs and high-level executives played a major role in these processes, they did not plan them or fully control them. They instigated some (e.g., targets, blame deflection), while simply letting others develop unaddressed.

All this has important implications for how we address deeply embedded corporate wrongdoing. The normal impulse is to seek blame and punishment as high up as possible. The idea is that ending impunity will cure further wrongdoing. Of course, ending impunity is a necessary condition for successful behavioral change. However, when wrongdoing is endemic in the culture, it indicates that it is not the fault of a singular leader, but part and parcel of the broader organization.

The core task becomes to challenge the culture. To detox corporate culture means addressing all of the converging elements. This does include ending impunity of leaders. In fact, simply placing more pressure on top leaders may result in more blame shifting, neutralization, and corporate dissonance. Rather than solely focusing on holding the highest executives liable, detoxing corporate culture must also come with a full overhaul.

Detoxing culture begins with a full assessment of toxicity in the structures, values, and practices, as developed in this paper. Subsequently, detoxing must take into account both changes made in the structures along with addressing the values and practices of executives and employees. As a first step to creating meaningful change in the culture, it is important to create a balance between ensuring accountability for those found to have done wrong and creating an open and safe space for all organizational members to truly discuss what happened, why it happened, and what harm it caused. The legal responses to mass corporate wrongdoing have much to learn from the field of transitional justice, particularly its analysis of legal responses to war and mass atrocity and its ideas on how to balance justice (holding perpetrators accountable) and peace (ensuring that warring parties refrain from future conflict) (Bell 2009; Lambourne 2009; Laplante 2008). Detoxing corporate culture, then, may well require the creation of Truth and Reconciliation Commissions. These commissions would allow corporate wrongdoers to confront victims in a safe and open exchange and would focus on unearthing truth and giving insights rather than on punishment and retribution, paralleling post-apartheid South Africa (Wilson 2001).

This paper hopes to aid practitioners tasked with detoxing corporate cultures. A better understanding of toxic corporate processes may lead to the development of better ways to reform them; however, it is important to caution against promises of an easy fix. Cultures are notoriously difficult to change, and lofty promises of changed cultural values and practices can generate more corporate dissonance when real change does not occur (Ogbonna and Wilkinson 2003). Therefore, any successful corporate detox must begin with resisting the pressure for a quick fix or a quick turn-around. Successful cultural overhaul starts and ends with honesty and patience.

Author Contributions: B.v.R. conceived of the paper idea, conducted the majority of the initial theoretical analysis, and wrote the first draft of the manuscript. A.F. provided critical revisions to the framework, analysis, and manuscript.

Conflicts of Interest: The authors declare no conflicts of interest.

References

Aarts, Henk, and Ap Dijksterhuis. 2003. The silence of the library: Environment, situational norm, and social behavior. *Journal of Personality and Social Psychology* 84: 18–28. [CrossRef] [PubMed]

Aarts, Henk, Ap Dijksterhuis, and Ruud Custers. 2003. Automatic normative behavior in environments: The moderating role of conformity in activating situational norms. *Social Cognition* 21: 447–64. [CrossRef]

Agnew, Robert. 1992. Foundation for a general strain theory of crime and delinquency. *Criminology* 30: 47–88. [CrossRef]

Agnew, Robert. 2001. Building on the foundation of general strain theory: Specifying the types of strain most likely to lead to crime and delinquency. *Journal of Research in Crime and Delinquency* 38: 319–61. [CrossRef]

Agnew, Robert, Nicole Leeper Piquero, and Francis T. Cullen. 2009. General strain theory and white-collar crime. In *The Criminology of White-Collar Crime*. Berlin: Springer, pp. 35–60.

Alvesson, Mats, and Stefan Sveningsson. 2015. *Changing Organizational Culture: Cultural Change Work in Progress.* Abingdon: Routledge.

Apel, Robert. 2013. Sanctions, perceptions, and crime: Implications for criminal deterrence. *Journal of Quantitative Criminology* 29: 67–101. [CrossRef]

Apel, Robert, and Raymond Paternoster. 2009. Understanding "criminogenic" corporate culture: What white-collar crime researchers can learn from studies of the adolescent employment–crime relationship. In *The Criminology of White-Collar Crime*. Berlin: Springer, pp. 15–33.

Arnold, Chris. 2016. Former Wells Fargo Employees Describe Toxic Sales Culture, Even At HQ. *NPR*. October 4. Available online: https://www.npr.org/2016/10/04/496508361/former-wells-fargo-employees-describe-toxic-sales-culture-even-at-hq (accessed on 16 March 2018).

Associated Press. 2017. Wells Fargo Fired a Worker for Refusing to Scam Customers, Lawsuit Says. *LA Times*. April 17. Available online: http://www.latimes.com/business/la-fi-wells-fargo-lawsuit-20170417-story.html (accessed on 16 March 2018).

Baggett, Walter O. 2003. Creating a culture of security: The OECD standards for systems security provide internal auditors with a tool for operationalizing tone at the top. *Internal Auditor* 60: 37–41.

Baker, James, Nancy Leveson, Frank L. "Skip" Bowman, Sharon Priest, Glenn Erwin, Isadore "Irv" Rosenthal, Slade Gorton, Paul V. Tebo, Dennis Hendershot, Douglas A. Wiegmann, and et al. 2007. *The Report of the BP U.S. Refineries Independent Safety Review Panel*. Washington, DC: U.S. Chemical Safety and Hazard Investigation Board.

Barringer, Felicity. 2006. Large Oil Spill in Alaska went Undetected for Days. *New York Times*. March 15. Available online: https://www.nytimes.com/2006/03/15/us/large-oil-spill-in-alaska-went-undetected-for-days.html?_r=0 (accessed on 16 March 2018).

Bass, Bernard M., and Bruce J. Avolio. 1993. Transformational leadership and organizational culture. *Public Administration Quarterly* 17: 112–21. [CrossRef]

Baucus, Melissa S., and Janet P. Near. 1991. Can illegal corporate behavior be predicted? An event history analysis. *Academy of Management Journal* 34: 9–36.

Belknap, Joanne. 1987. Routine activity theory and the risk of rape: Analyzing ten years of national crime survey data. *Criminal Justice Policy Review* 2: 337–56. [CrossRef]

Bell, Christine. 2009. Transitional Justice, Interdisciplinarity and the State of the 'Field' or 'Non-field'. *International Journal of Transitional Justice* 3: 5–27. [CrossRef]

Benoit, William L. 2014. *Accounts, Excuses, and Apologies: Image Repair Theory and Research*. Albany: SUNY Press.

Benson, Michael L. 1985. Denying the guilty mind: Accounting for involvement in a white-collar crime. *Criminology* 23: 583–607. [CrossRef]

Bozeman, Barry. 2011. The 2010 BP Gulf of Mexico oil spill: Implications for theory of organizational disaster. *Technology in Society* 33: 244–52. [CrossRef]

Braithwaite, John. 2010. Diagnostics of white-collar crime prevention. *Criminology & Public Policy* 9: 621–26.

Brown, Don W. 1978. Arrest rates and crime rates: When does a tipping effect occur? *Social Forces* 57: 671–82. [CrossRef]

Brown, Michael E., and Linda K. Treviño. 2006. Ethical leadership: A review and future directions. *The Leadership Quarterly* 17: 595–616. [CrossRef]

Brown, Michael E., Linda K. Trevino, and David A. Harrison. 2005. Ethical leadership: A social learning perspective for construct development and testing. *Organizational Behavior and Human Decision Processes* 97: 117–34. [CrossRef]

Cameron, Kim S., and Robert E. Quinn. 2006. *Diagnosing and Changing Organizational Culture: Based on the Competing Values Framework*. San Francisco: Jossey-Bass Inc. Pub.

Carrington, Damian, Gwyn Topham, and Peter Walker. 2016. Revealed: Nearly All New Diesel Cars Exceed Official Pollution Limits. *The Guardian*. April 23. Available online: https://www.theguardian.com/business/2016/apr/23/diesel-cars-pollution-limits-nox-emissions?CMP=Share_iOSApp_Other (accessed on 16 March 2018).

Chamlin, Mitchell B. 1991. A longitudinal analysis of the arrest-crime relationship: A further examination of the tipping effect. *Justice Quarterly* 8: 187–99. [CrossRef]

Chossière, Guillaume P., Robert Malina, Akshay Ashok, Irene C. Dedoussi, Sebastian D. Eastham, Raymond L. Speth, and Steven R. H. Barrett. 2017. Public health impacts of excess NOx emissions from Volkswagen diesel passenger vehicles in Germany. *Environmental Research Letters* 12: 034014. [CrossRef]

Cialdini, Robert B. 2003. Crafting normative messages to protect the environment. *Current Directions in Psychological Science* 12: 105–9. [CrossRef]

Cialdini, Robert B. 2007. Descriptive social norms as underappreciated sources of social control. *Psychometrika* 72: 263–68. [CrossRef]

Cialdini, Robert B., Linda J. Demaine, Brad J. Sagarin, Daniel W. Barrett, Kelton Rhoads, and Patricia L. Winter. 2006. Managing social norms for persuasive impact. *Social Influence* 1: 3–15. [CrossRef]

Cialdini, Robert B., and Noah J. Goldstein. 2004. Social influence: Compliance and conformity. *Annual Review of Psychology* 55: 591–621. [CrossRef] [PubMed]

Clinard, Marshall Barron. 1983. *Corporate Ethics and Crime; The Role of Middle Management*. Beverly Hills: Sage Publications.

Clinard, Marshall Barron, and Peter C. Yeager. 1980. *Corporate Crime*. New York: Free Press.

Coglianese, Cary, and David Lazer. 2003. Management-based regulation: Prescribing private management to achieve public goals. *Law & Society Review* 37: 691–730.

Cohen, Lawrence E., and Marcus Felson. 1979. Social change and crime rate trends: A routine activity approach. *American Sociological Review* 44: 588–608. [CrossRef]

Cohen-Charash, Yochi, and Jennifer S. Mueller. 2007. Does perceived unfairness exacerbate or mitigate interpersonal counterproductive work behaviors related to envy? *Journal of Applied Psychology* 92: 666–80. [CrossRef] [PubMed]

Cohen-Charash, Yochi, and Paul E. Spector. 2001. The role of justice in organizations: A meta-analysis. *Organizational Behavior and Human Decision Processes* 86: 278–321. [CrossRef]

Colvin, Geoff. 2017. Inside Wells Fargo's Plan to Fix Its Culture Post-Scandal. *Fortune*. June 11. Available online: http://fortune.com/2017/06/11/wells-fargo-scandal-culture/ (accessed on 16 March 2018).

Corkery, Michael. 2016. *Elizabeth Warren Accuses Wells Fargo Chief of 'Gutless Leadership'*. New York: The New York Times Company, Video.

Cowley, Stan. 2017. Wells Fargo Review Finds 1.4 Million More Suspect Accounts. August 31. Available online: https://www.nytimes.com/2017/08/31/business/dealbook/wells-fargo-accounts.html (accessed on 16 March 2018).

Denison, Daniel R. 1990. *Corporate Culture and Organizational Effectiveness*. Hoboken: John Wiley & Sons.

Department of Justice. 1998. DOJ, EPA Announce One Billion Dollar Settlement with Diesel Engine Industry for Clean Air Violations. October 22. Available online: https://www.justice.gov/archive/opa/pr/1998/October/499_enr.htm (accessed on 16 March 2018).

Edelman, Lauren B., Stephen Petterson, Elizabeth Chambliss, and Howard S. Erlanger. 1991. Legal ambiguity and the politics of compliance: Affirmative action officers' dilemma. *Law & Policy* 13: 73–97.

Edelman, Lauren B., and Shauhin A. Talesh. 2011. To Comply or Not to Comply—That Isn't the Question: How Organizations Construct the Meaning of Compliance. In *Explaining Compliance: Business Responses to Regulation*. Cheltenham: Edward Elgar Publishing, pp. 103–22.

Egan, Matt. 2017. More Wells Fargo Workers Allege Retaliation for Whistleblowing. *CNN*. November 7. Available online: http://money.cnn.com/2017/11/06/investing/wells-fargo-retaliation-whistleblower/index.html (accessed on 16 March 2018).

Eriksen, Thomas Hylland. 2001. *Small Places, Large Issues, an Introduction to Social and Cultural Anthropology*. London and Sterling: Pluto Press.

Ewing, Jack. 2017. *Faster, Higher, Farther: The Volkswagen Scandal*. New York: Norton.

Felson, Marcus. 1987. Routine Activities and Crime Prevention in the Developing Metropolis. *Criminology* 25: 911–32. [CrossRef]

Frey, Darcy. 2002. How Green is BP? *New York Times*. December 8. Available online: https://www.nytimes.com/2002/12/08/magazine/how-green-is-bp.html (accessed on 16 March 2018).

Frost, William. 2017. Wells Fargo Report Gives Inside Look at the Culture that Crushed the Bank's Reputation. *CNBC*. April 10. Available online: https://www.cnbc.com/2017/04/10/wells-fargo-report-shows-culture-that-crushed-banks-reputation.html (accessed on 16 March 2018).

Geertz, Clifford. 1973. Thick Description: Toward and Interpretive Theory of Culture. In *The Interpretation of Cultures, Selected Essays by Clifford Geertz*. Edited by Clifford Geertz. New York: Basic Books, pp. 3–30.

Gilad, Sharon. 2010. It runs in the family: Meta-regulation and its siblings. *Regulation & Governance* 4: 485–506.

Glazer, Emily, and Christina Rexrode. 2017. As Regulators Focus on Culture, Wall Street Struggles to Define It. *Wall Street Journal*. February 1. Available online: https://www.wsj.com/articles/as-regulators-focus-on-culture-wall-street-struggles-to-define-it-1422838659 (accessed on 22 June 2018).

Glinton, Sonari. 2016. *We Didn't Lie,' Volkswagen CEO Says Of Emissions Scandal*. Washington, DC: National Public Radio.

Gneezy, Uri, Stephan Meier, and Pedro Rey-Biel. 2011. When and why incentives (don't) work to modify behavior. *The Journal of Economic Perspectives* 25: 191–209. [CrossRef]

Gneezy, Uri, and Aldo Rustichini. 2000. A Fine Is a Price. *Journal of Legal Studies* 29: 1–17. [CrossRef]

Goldenberg, Suzanne. 2010. US Oil Spill Inquiry Chief Slams BP's 'Culture of Complacency'. *The Guardian*. November 9. Available online: https://www.theguardian.com/environment/2010/nov/09/oil-spill-inquiry-culture-complacency-bp (accessed on 16 March 2018).

Gottschalk, Petter, and Robert Smith. 2011. Criminal entrepreneurship, white-collar criminality, and neutralization theory. *Journal of Enterprising Communities: People and Places in the Global Economy* 5: 300–8. [CrossRef]

Gray, Garry C. 2009. The responsibilization strategy of health and safety neo-liberalism and the reconfiguration of individual responsibility for risk. *British Journal of Criminology* 49: 326–42. [CrossRef]

Gray, Garry C., and Susan S. Silbey. 2014. Governing Inside the Organization: Interpreting Regulation and Compliance. *American Journal of Sociology* 120: 96–145. [CrossRef]

Gray, Wayne B., and John T. Scholz. 1991. Analyzing the Equity and Efficiency of OSHA enforcement. *Law & Policy* 13: 185–214.

Gray, Wayne B., and John M. Mendeloff. 2005. The declining effects of OSHA inspections on manufacturing injuries, 1979–1998. *Industrial & Labor Relations Review* 58: 571–87.

Hansen, James, Nathaniel M. Stephens, and David A. Wood. 2009. Entity-level controls: The internal auditor's assessment of management tone at the top. *Current Issues in Auditing* 3: A1–A13. [CrossRef]

Harrison, Roger, and Herb Stokes. 1992. *Diagnosing Organizational Culture*. Zürich: Pfeiffer.

Hatch, Mary Jo. 1993. The dynamics of organizational culture. *Academy of Management Review* 18: 657–93. [CrossRef]

Heimer, Carol A. 1999. Competing Institutions: Law, Medicine, and Family in Neonatal Intensive Care. *Law & Society Review* 33: 17–66.

Henriques, Diana B. 2011. *The Wizard of Lies: Bernie Madoff and the Death of Trust*. Basingstoke: Macmillan.

Hofstede, Geert, Bram Neuijen, Denise Daval Ohayv, and Geert Sanders. 1990. Measuring organizational cultures: A qualitative and quantitative study across twenty cases. *Administrative Science Quarterly* 25: 286–316. [CrossRef]

Hofstede, Geert. 1980. Culture and organizations. *International Studies of Management & Organization* 10: 15–41.

Hofstede, Geert. 1998. Attitudes, values and organizational culture: Disentangling the concepts. *Organization Studies* 19: 477–93. [CrossRef]

Hofstede, Geert, Gert Jan Hofstede, and Michael Minkov. 1991. *Cultures and Organizations: Software of the Mind*. London: McGraw-Hill, vol. 2.

Homsma, Gert J., Cathy Van Dyck, Dick De Gilder, Paul L. Koopman, and Tom Elfring. 2009. Learning from error: The influence of error incident characteristics. *Journal of Business Research* 62: 115–22. [CrossRef]

Hutter, Bridget M. 2001. *Regulation and Risk: Occupational Health and Safety on the Railways*. Oxford: Oxford University Press.

Independent Directors of the Board of Wells Fargo. 2017. Sales Practice Investigation Report. April 10. Available online: https://www08.wellsfargomedia.com/assets/pdf/about/investor-relations/presentations/2017/board-report.pdf (accessed on 16 March 2018).

Interligi, Lisa. 2010. Compliance culture: A conceptual framework. *Journal of Management & Organization* 16: 235–49.

Jones, Renae A., Nerina L. Jimmieson, and Andrew Griffiths. 2005. The impact of organizational culture and reshaping capabilities on change implementation success: The mediating role of readiness for change. *Journal of Management Studies* 42: 361–86. [CrossRef]

Keizer, Kees, Siegwart Lindenberg, and Linda Steg. 2008. The spreading of disorder. *Science* 322: 1681–85. [CrossRef] [PubMed]

Keizer, Kees, Siegwart Lindenberg, and Linda Steg. 2011. The reversal effect of prohibition signs. *Group Processes & Intergroup Relations* 14: 681–88.

Kellaway, Lucy. 2015. Wells Fargo's Happy: Grumpy Ratio Is No Way to Audit Staff. *Financial Times*. February 8. Available online: https://www.ft.com/content/31967ba6-aacb-11e4-81bc-00144feab7de (accessed on 16 March 2018).

Klockars, Carl B. 1974. *The Professional Fence*. New York: Free Press.

Kollewe, Julia. 2010. BP chief executive Tony Hayward in his own words. *The Guardian*, May 14.

Lambourne, Wendy. 2009. Transitional justice and peacebuilding after mass violence. *International Journal of Transitional Justice* 3: 28–48. [CrossRef]

Lange, Bettina. 1999. Compliance Construction in the Context of Environmental Regulation. *Social & Legal Studies* 8: 549–67.

Laplante, Lisa J. 2008. Transitional Justice and Peace Building: Diagnosing and Addressing the Socioeconomic Roots of Violence through a Human Rights Framework. *International Journal of Transitional Justice* 2: 331–55. [CrossRef]

Lubin, Joann S. 2017. After Uber and Wells Fargo, Boards Wake up to Culture. *Wall Street Journal*. October 5. Available online: https://www.wsj.com/articles/after-uber-boards-wake-up-to-company-culture-1507046401 (accessed on 16 March 2018).

Lustgarten, Abrahm. 2012. *Run to Failure: BP and the Making of the Deepwater Horizon Disaster*. New York: WW Norton & Company.

Lustgarten, Abrahm, and Ryan Knutson. 2010. Years of Internal BP Probes Warned That Neglect Could Lead to Accidents. *ProPublica*. June 7. Available online: https://www.propublica.org/article/years-of-internal-bp-probes-warned-that-neglect-could-lead-to-accidents (accessed on 16 March 2018).

Lyall, Sarah. 2010. In BP's Record, a History of Boldness and Costly Blunders. *New York Times*. July 12. Available online: https://www.nytimes.com/2010/07/13/business/energy-environment/13bprisk.html (accessed on 16 March 2018).

Maruna, Shadd, and Heith Copes. 2005. What have we learned from five decades of neutralization research? *Crime and Justice* 32: 221–320. [CrossRef]

Mattera, Philip. 2016. BP: Corporate Rap Sheet. *Corporate Research Project*. August 1. Available online: https://www.corp-research.org/BP (accessed on 16 March 2018).

Mills, Russell W., and Christopher J. Koliba. 2015. The challenge of accountability in complex regulatory networks: The case of the Deepwater Horizon oil spill. *Regulation & Governance* 9: 77–91.

Minor, W. William. 1981. Techniques of neutralization: A reconceptualization and empirical examination. *Journal of Research in Crime and Delinquency* 18: 295–318. [CrossRef]

Moore, Celia, and Francesca Gino. 2013. Ethically adrift: How others pull our moral compass from true North, and how we can fix it. *Research in Organizational Behavior* 33: 53–77. [CrossRef]

Moore, Sally Falk. 1973. Law and social change: The semi-autonomous social field as an appropriate subject of study. *Law & Society Review* 7: 719–46.

Nagin, Daniel S. 2013. Deterrence in the Twenty-first Century. *Crime and Justice* 42: 199–263. [CrossRef]

National Association of Corporate Directors. 2017. Report of the NACD Blue Ribbon Commision on Culture as a Corporate Asset. Available online: https://www.nacdonline.org/files/NACD%20BRC%20Culture%20as%20Corporate%20Asset.pdf (accessed on 16 March 2018).

Needleman, Martin L., and Carolyn Needleman. 1979. Organizational crime: Two models of criminogenesis. *The Sociological Quarterly* 20: 517–28. [CrossRef]

Ogbonna, Emmanuel, and Lloyd C. Harris. 2002. Organizational culture: A ten year, two-phase study of change in the UK food retailing sector. *Journal of Management Studies* 39: 673–706. [CrossRef]

Ogbonna, Emmanuel, and Barry Wilkinson. 2003. The false promise of organizational culture change: A case study of middle managers in grocery retailing. *Journal of Management Studies* 40: 1151–78. [CrossRef]

Osgood, D. Wayne, Janet K. Wilson, Patrick M. O'malley, Jerald G. Bachman, and Lloyd D. Johnston. 1996. Routine activities and individual deviant behavior. *American Sociological Review* 61: 635–55. [CrossRef]

Parker, Christine. 2002. *The Open Corporation: Effective Self-Regulation and Democracy*. Cambridge: Cambridge University Press.

Parker, Christine, and Sharon Gilad. 2011. Internal Corporate Compliance Management Systems: Structure, Culture and Agency. In *Explaining Compliance: Business Responses to Regulation*. Edited by Christine Parker and Vibeke Nielsen. Cheltenham: Edward Elgar Publishing.

PBS. 2010. BP's Troubled Past. *Frontline*. October 26. Available online: http://www.pbs.org/wgbh/pages/frontline/the-spill/bp-troubled-past/ (accessed on 16 March 2018).

Pertiwi, Kanti. 2018. Contextualizing Corruption: A Cross-Disciplinary Approach to Studying Corruption in Organizations. *Administrative Sciences* 8: 12. [CrossRef]

Piquero, Nicole Leeper, Stephen G. Tibbetts, and Michael B. Blankenship. 2005. Examining the role of differential association and techniques of neutralization in explaining corporate crime. *Deviant Behavior* 26: 159–88. [CrossRef]

Plambeck, Erica L., and Terry A. Taylor. 2015. Supplier Evasion of a Buyer's Audit: Implications for Motivating Supplier Social and Environmental Responsibility. *Manufacturing and Service Operations Management (Articles in Advance)* 18: 184–97. [CrossRef]

Pontell, Henry N., Kitty Calavita, and Robert Tillman. 1994. Corporate crime and criminal justice system capacity: Government response to financial institution fraud. *Justice Quarterly* 11: 383–410. [CrossRef]

Puzzanghera, Jim. 2017. What's Wrong with Bank Culture? A Top Fed Official Points to Wells Fargo Scandal. *LA Times*. March 21. Available online: http://www.latimes.com/business/la-fi-wells-fargo-fed-20170321-story.html (accessed on 16 March 2018).

Reckard, E. Scott. 2013. Wells Fago's pressure-cooker sales culture comes at a cost. *LA Times*, December 21.

Reuters. 2016. VW Says Defeat Device in Conformity with European Law. *Reuters*. November 3. Available online: https://www.reuters.com/article/us-volkswagen-emissions-lawsuit/vw-says-defeat-device-in-conformity-with-european-law-idUSKBN12Y2VJ (accessed on 22 June 2018).

Roberts, Dean. 2017. A Year after Scandal, Claims of Sales Pressure Linger at Wells Fargo. *Charlotte Observer*. September 2. Available online: http://www.charlotteobserver.com/news/business/banking/article170791647.html (accessed on 16 March 2018).

Ross, Ezra, and Martin Pritikin. 2010. The Collection Gap: Underenforcement of Corporate and White-Collar Fines and Penalties. *Yale Law & Policy Review* 29: 453.

Scalzi, Cynthia C., Lois K. Evans, Alan Barstow, and Kathryn Hostvedt. 2006. Barriers and enablers to changing organizational culture in nursing homes. *Nursing Administration Quarterly* 30: 368–72. [CrossRef] [PubMed]

Schein, Edgar H. 2010. Organizational Culture and Leadership, 4th ed.San Francisco: Jossey-Bass.

Scholten, Wieke, and Naomi Ellemers. 2016. Bad apples or corrupting barrels? Preventing traders' misconduct. *Journal of Financial Regulation and Compliance* 24: 366–82. [CrossRef]

Schwartz, Mark S., Thomas W. Dunfee, and Michael J. Kline. 2005. Tone at the top: An ethics code for directors? *Journal of Business Ethics* 58: 79. [CrossRef]

Scott, Tim, Russell Mannion, Huw Davies, and Martin Marshall. 2003. The quantitative measurement of organizational culture in health care: A review of the available instruments. *Health Services Research* 38: 923–45. [CrossRef] [PubMed]

Silbey, Susan S. 2009. Taming Prometheus: Talk about safety and culture. *Annual Review of Sociology* 35: 341–69. [CrossRef]

Simpson, Sally, Melissa Rorie, Mariel Elise Alper, Natalie Schell-Busey, William Laufer, and N. Craig Smith. 2014. Corporate Crime Deterrence: A Systematic Review. *Campbell Systematic Reviews* 10. [CrossRef]

Simpson, Sally S., and Christopher S. Koper. 1997. The changing of the guard: Top management characteristics, organizational strain, and antitrust offending. *Journal of Quantitative Criminology* 13: 373–404. [CrossRef]

Siponen, Mikko, Anthony Vance, and Robert Willison. 2012. New insights into the problem of software piracy: The effects of neutralization, shame, and moral beliefs. *Information & Management* 49: 334–41.

Smithson, Joy, and Steven Venette. 2013. Stonewalling as an image-defense strategy: A critical examination of BP's response to the Deepwater Horizon explosion. *Communication Studies* 64: 395–410. [CrossRef]

Stadler, William A., and Michael L. Benson. 2012. Revisiting the guilty mind: The neutralization of white-collar crime. *Criminal Justice Review* 37: 494–511. [CrossRef]

Steffy, Loren C. 2010. *Drowning in Oil: BP & the Reckless Pursuit of Profit*. New York: McGraw Hill Professional.

Sutherland, Edwin H. 1940. White-collar criminality. *American Sociological Review* 5: 1–12. [CrossRef]

Sykes, Gresham M., and David Matza. 1957. Techniques of neutralization: A theory of delinquency. *American Sociological Review* 22: 664–70. [CrossRef]

Talesh, Shauhin. 2015. Rule-Intermediaries in Action: How State and Business Stakeholders Influence the Meaning of Consumer Rights in Regulatory Governance Arrangements. *Law & Policy* 37: 1–31.

Talesh, Shauhin A. 2009. The privatization of public legal rights: How manufacturers construct the meaning of consumer law. *Law & Society Review* 43: 527–62.

Thornton, Dorothy, Neil Gunningham, and Robert A. Kagan. 2005. General Deterrence and Corporate Environmental Behavior. *Law & Policy* 27: 262–88.

Treviño, Linda Klebe, Michael Brown, and Laura Pincus Hartman. 2003. A qualitative investigation of perceived executive ethical leadership: Perceptions from inside and outside the executive suite. *Human Relations* 56: 5–37. [CrossRef]

Treviño, Linda Klebe, Gary R. Weaver, and Michael E. Brown. 2008. It's lovely at the top: Hierarchical levels, identities, and perceptions of organizational ethics. *Business Ethics Quarterly* 18: 233–52. [CrossRef]

U.S. Chemical Safety and Hazard Investigation Board. 2007. *Investigation Report: Refinary Explosion and Fire BP Texas City, March 23, 2005*. Washington, DC: U.S. Chemical Safety and Hazard Investigation Board.

Van Dyck, Cathy, Michael Frese, Markus Baer, and Sabine Sonnentag. 2005. Organizational error management culture and its impact on performance: A two-study replication. *Journal of Applied Psychology* 90: 1228–40. [CrossRef] [PubMed]

Vaughan, Diane. 1989. Regulating Risk: Implications of the Challenger Accident. *Law & Policy* 11: 330–49.

Vaughan, Diane. 1997. *The Challenger Launch Decision: Risky Technology, Culture, and Deviance at NASA*. Chicago: University of Chicago Press.

Warren, Danielle E., Joseph P. Gaspar, and William S. Laufer. 2014. Is formal ethics training merely cosmetic? A study of ethics training and ethical organizational culture. *Business Ethics Quarterly* 24: 85–117. [CrossRef]

Weaver, Gary R., Linda Klebe Trevino, and Philip L. Cochran. 1999. Integrated and decoupled corporate social performance: Management commitments, external pressures, and corporate ethics practices. *Academy of Management Journal* 42: 539–52.

Wilson, Richard. 2001. *The Politics of Truth and Reconciliation in South Africa: Legitimizing the Post-Apartheid State*. Cambridge: Cambridge University Press.

Zoghbi-Manrique-de-Lara, Pablo, and Miguel A. Suárez-Acosta. 2014. Employees' reactions to peers' unfair treatment by supervisors: The role of ethical leadership. *Journal of Business Ethics* 122: 537–49. [CrossRef]

*administrative
sciences*

MDPI

Article

Corruption in Organizations: Ethical Climate and Individual Motives

Madelijne Gorsira [1],*, Linda Steg [2], Adriaan Denkers [1] and Wim Huisman [1]

[1]   Department of Criminal Law and Criminology, VU University Amsterdam, 1081 HV Amsterdam,
     The Netherlands; adriaandenkers@icloud.com (A.D.); w.huisman@vu.nl (W.H.)
[2]   Department of Psychology, University of Groningen, 9712 TS Groningen, The Netherlands; e.m.steg@rug.nl
*   Correspondence: m.gorsira@vu.nl

Received: 22 December 2017; Accepted: 14 February 2018; Published: 19 February 2018

Abstract: The aim of this research was to examine how organizational and individual factors, in concert, shape corruption. We examined whether the ethical climate of organizations is related to corruption, and if so, whether it affects corruption *through* individual motives for corruption. A large-scale questionnaire study was conducted among public officials (n = 234) and business employees (n = 289) who were in a position to make corrupt decisions. The findings suggest that public and private sector employees who perceive their organizational climate as more egoistic and less ethical are more prone to corruption. This relationship was fully mediated by individual motives, specifically by personal and social norms on corruption. These results indicate that employees who perceive their organization's ethical climate as more egoistic and less ethical experience weaker personal and social norms to refrain from corruption, making them more corruption-prone. Hence, strategies addressing the interplay between organizational factors and individual motives seem promising in curbing corruption. To effectively withhold employees from engaging in corruption, organizations could deploy measures that strengthen an organizations' ethical climate and encourage ethical decision-making based on concern for the wellbeing of others, as well as measures increasing the strength of personal and social norms to refrain from corruption.

Keywords: bribery; corruption; ethical climate; organizations; personal and social norms

---

1. Introduction

Increasingly, organizations are being held responsible for their employees' unethical and illegal behavior (Victor and Cullen 1988; Wells 2014). This is especially true for corruption. For example, under the United Kingdom Bribery Act 2010, UK-connected companies can be held criminally liable for employees' acts of bribery unless the company can prove it had in place 'adequate procedures'[1] designed to prevent bribery (Lord and Levi 2016). In February 2016, the company Sweett Group PLC was the first to be convicted[2] of having failed to take such adequate steps, and was ordered to pay £2.25 million.[3] As a result, organizations are becoming progressively concerned about[4] and are taking steps[5] to prevent bribery in their organization. Yet, which measures are actually effective in preventing

---

[1]   www.legislation.gov.uk/ukpga/2010/23/section/7.
[2]   This was the first conviction, but not the first case to be dealt with using the s.7 corporate offence. In November 2015,
     the Serious Fraud Office (SFO) and Standard Bank reached a deferred prosecution agreement (DPA) for a failure to prevent
     bribery, contrary to section 7 of the Bribery Act 2010 (www.sfo.gov.uk/2015/11/30/sfo-agrees-first-uk-dpa-with-standard-
     bank/).
[3]   www.sfo.gov.uk/2016/02/19/sweett-group-plc-sentenced-and-ordered-to-pay-2-3-million-after-bribery-act-conviction/.
[4]   www.willis.com/documents/publications/Industries/Financial_Institutions/Directors_Liability.pdf.
[5]   www.ey.com/Publication/vwLUAssets/EY-managing-fraud-bribery-and-corruption-risks-in-the-mining-and-metals-
     industry/$FILE/EY-managing-fraud-bribery-and-corruption-risks-in-the-mining-and-metals-industry.pdf.

corruption is largely unknown. Hence, a key question is which factors cause corruption, and which strategies may be effective in preventing it.

The vast majority of empirical corruption studies focus on differences between countries (Dong et al. 2012; Svensson 2003), and look at macro-level determinants of corruption, such as political institutions (Lederman et al. 2005), and the culture in a country (Jha and Panda 2017). Such research may offer explanations for why corruption is more common in some countries than in others. It does not, however, reveal why within countries corruption seems to flourish more in some sectors and organizations than in others, nor why within organizations some people engage in corruption while their colleagues do not. Furthermore, country-level factors are generally very stable and difficult to alter. As a result, explanations on the macro level may not be very helpful in designing practical anti-corruption measures (Rose-Ackerman 2010). Hence, a better understanding of why certain individuals within certain organizations commit corruption seems vital. For this reason, we examine which organizational and individual factors may explain employees' engagement in corruption. Hence, we aim to identify the 'bad barrels' and the 'bad apples' (Kish-Gephart et al. 2010). More specifically, we conduct a questionnaire study among a large sample of employees who are likely to face corruption-prone situations, as questionnaires can provide insight into multiple key correlates of corruption (Andvig et al. 2001). Corruption is most often defined as the abuse of public power for private benefit (Aguilera and Vadera 2008; Tanzi 1998). This definition includes many unethical behaviors, such as embezzlement, conflicts of interests, and forgery. In this paper, we focus on a specific form of corrupt behavior: bribery. Bribery is not only unethical but also illegal; it is criminalized in both national and international legislation (e.g., The United Kingdom Bribery Act 2010 and the United Nations Convention Against Corruption). The present study takes both sides of bribery, the giver and the taker, into account. Bribery most commonly occurs in interactions between public and private sectors (Rose-Ackerman 1997; Rose-Ackerman 2007). When bribery involves a public official and a business employee, it is likely that the latter bribes the former. If so, the business employee engages in *active* bribery and the public official in *passive* bribery (Beets 2005; Huberts and Nelen 2005). In this paper, we therefore focus on the bribery of public officials by business employees. Below, we first review the empirical literature concerning individual factors influencing corruption. Next, we discuss a prominent organizational factor that may affect corruption. Subsequently, we discuss how these individual and organizational factors might be related, and how they, in concert, may shape corruption.

1.1. Individual Factors Explaining Corruption

Corruption ultimately results from decisions made by individuals. Various disciplines have postulated explanations for why some individuals are more prone to corruption than others, specifically economics, criminology, and social psychology (Gorsira et al. 2016). The most prominently explanations include incentives (Dong et al. 2012; Prabowo 2014; Shover and Bryant 1993; Andvig et al. 2001; Dimant 2013), opportunities (see, for instance, Aguilera and Vadera 2008; Pinto et al. 2008; Graycar and Sidebottom 2012), and norms (see, for instance, Powpaka 2002; Köbis et al. 2015; Rabl and Kühlmann 2008; Tavits 2010). A recent study demonstrated that all of these factors were, indeed, related to proneness to corruption (Gorsira et al. 2016). The study showed that public officials and business employees who perceived higher benefits of corruption, e.g., financial gains, excitement, and pleasure, and perceived lower costs of corruption, i.e., a lower chance of detection, and a less severe punishment, were more prone to engage in corruption (Gorsira et al. 2016). Similarly, employees who perceived more opportunities to engage in, and less opportunities to refrain from, corruption reported to be more prone to it. Employees who reported weaker personal norms, i.e., who felt less morally obliged to refrain from corruption, and who reported weaker social norms, i.e., those who thought their close colleagues approved of and engaged in corruption, also reported to be more prone to corruption. The outcomes of this study further suggest that the motives that contribute uniquely to employees' proneness to corruption, when other motives were controlled for, were the perceived opportunity to refrain from corruption and personal and social norms on corruption. Importantly, the pattern of results was identical for public and private sector respondents when business employees were asked about their proneness to active bribery, and public officials about their proneness to passive bribery. This indicates that the same motives underlie both sides of bribery (Gorsira et al. 2016). In the present study, we expect these individual motives to be related to public officials' and business employees' proneness to corruption.

1.2. Organizational Factors Explaining Corruption

Individuals do not operate in a vacuum; corruption occurs within an organizational context. Hence, it seems important to not only look at the 'bad apples', but also at possible 'bad barrels'. A relevant organizational-level predictor of (un)ethical behavior in organizations is the culture (Jha and Panda 2017; Kaptein 2011)[6] or climate of an organization (Victor and Cullen 1988). One meta-analysis revealed an organizations' ethical climate as a particularly relevant organizational factor explaining a wide range of unethical decisions of employees (Kish-Gephart et al. 2010; Peterson 2002).[7] We, therefore, focus on the ethical climate, rather than on ethical culture. An organization's ethical climate affects which issues organization members consider ethically relevant, whose interests they consider when deciding on moral issues, and which ethical criteria they use to determine what constitutes the 'right behavior' (Victor and Cullen 1988; Martin and Cullen 2006). As such, ethical climate refers to the most commonly used *types* of moral reasoning, rather than to the content of decisions (Victor and Cullen 1988). The assumption underlying the concept of ethical climate is that members of an organization share, at least to some extent, a form of moral reasoning.

In deciding whether it is acceptable to pay or to accept bribes, organizational members can consider different ethical criteria. The dominant considerations are maximizing self-interest (egoistic reasoning), maximizing joint interests (benevolent reasoning), or adherence to principles (principled reasoning; Victor and Cullen 1988). In an egoistic climate, people base their decisions, first and foremost, on what will best promote their self-interest (Martin and Cullen 2006). In such a climate, organizational members perceive that self-interest commonly guides behavior, even if it is at the expense of others (Wimbush and Shepard 1994). In a benevolent climate, ethical decision-making is seen to be predominantly based on concern for the wellbeing of others, which may be others within the organization itself, or society at large (Martin and Cullen 2006). In a principled climate, ethical decision-making is primarily presumed to be based on external codes, such as the law or professional codes of conduct (Martin and Cullen 2006).

More recently, a simplified model and measure of ethical climate has been postulated (Arnaud 2010; Arnaud and Schminke 2006, 2012; Abernethy et al. 2012). This model proposes that organizational members typically base ethical decisions either on what best promotes their self-interest, or the interests of others. If the former form of moral reasoning is seen to predominate within an organization or department, the ethical climate can be characterized as primarily self-focused, which is likely to inhibit ethical behavior. If the latter is perceived to prevail, the ethical climate within the organization or department is predominantly other-focused, stimulating ethical behavior (Arnaud 2010; Arnaud and Schminke 2006). In the current paper, we use the terms 'egoistic climate' to refer to the former and 'ethical climate' to refer to the latter. Notably, we regard the two organizational-climate types as two ends of a single dimension, as it seems unlikely that an organizational climate is predominantly focused on maximizing self-interest and, at the same time, on maximizing the interests of others.

Empirical studies have generally found that employees who perceive their organizational climate as more egoistic report more unethical behavior, while employees who perceive their organizational

---

[6] Ethical culture is defined as "the perception about the conditions that are in place in the organization to comply or not comply with what constitutes unethical and ethical behavior", e.g., role-modeling of managers, and rewards and punishment (Kaptein 2011, p. 846).

[7] When ethical climate and ethical culture are considered as predictors simultaneously, ethical culture does not contribute uniquely to (un)ethical behavior (Kish-Gephart et al. 2010).

climate as more ethical report less unethical behavior (Kish-Gephart et al. 2010; Peterson 2002; Wimbush and Shepard 1994; Treviño et al. 1998; Mayer 2014).

Many scholars have also proposed a link between an organization's ethical climate and, specifically, corruption (Pinto et al. 2008; Grieger 2006; Motwani et al. 1998; Simha and Cullen 2012; Hess 2015; Martin et al. 2009). Few, however, have actually demonstrated one. One study found support for a relationship between an egoistic climate and corruption in organizations (Stachowicz-Stanusch and Simha 2013). Another study found that employees who perceived their organizational climate as more ethical were less likely to give gifts or favors in exchange for preferential treatment, whereas the opposite was true for a more egoistic climate (Peterson 2002). We examine whether perceived ethical climate is related to engagement in corruption, in particular bribery, among both public officials and business employees, thereby focusing on both sides of bribery. We propose the following hypothesis:

Hypothesis 1 (H1). *The more ethical and the less egoistic public and private sector employees perceive their organizational climate to be, the less likely they are to engage in corruption.*

1.3. Interplay

An important question is whether and how ethical climate is related to individual corruption motives. We propose that corruption is the result of an *interplay* between individual and organizational factors. Notably, individual motives for corruption and ethical climate are likely to be related, and may, in concert, shape corruption. To date, studies on individual and organizational explanations for corruption have almost exclusively focused on either individual or organizational factors, and have examined the relationship of each factor to corruption independently (Den Nieuwenboer and Kaptein 2008). Studies that simultaneously include organizational and individual factors will enhance our understanding of why employees engage in corruption. For the first time, we aim to systematically investigate how individual and organizational factors are related not only to corruption, but also to each other. In particular, we examine how perceived ethical climate, which is typically considered to be an *organizational* characteristic (Arnaud 2010; Arnaud and Schminke 2006, 2012), is related to *individual* motives for *corruption* as a specific type of unethical behavior. We define ethical climate as one's perceptions of how people within an organization typically make ethical decisions in general. As such, ethical climate is likely to affect many ethical and unethical behaviors, including corruption, which is why we propose that the perceived organizational ethical climate may affect individual motives for corruption as a specific form of unethical behavior. Therefore, the perceived general ethical climate of organizations is likely to affect motives for various types of unethical behavior, including corruption of employees, rather than the other way around. More specifically, we hypothesize that perceived ethical climate is related to corruption *via* individual motives for corruption. In particular, ethical climate may weaken or strengthen the motives for corruption, thereby, increasing or decreasing the likelihood of corruption.

We propose that ethical climate particularly influences personal and social norms on corruption. Notably, ethical climate refers to the *most commonly* used types of *moral* reasoning within organizations (Victor and Cullen 1988; Arnaud 2010). As such, ethical climate may shape employees' personal and social norms on corruption. Some scholars indeed have speculated that ethical climate affects (un)ethical behavior through individual factors, particularly ethics-related ones (Kish-Gephart et al. 2010; Treviño et al. 1998; Webb 2012). Specifically, it has been proposed that awareness of moral obligation functions as a mediator and, notably, that an organization's ethical climate may strengthen or weaken employees' personal norms, which in turn affect the likelihood of unethical behavior (Wang and Hsieh 2013; Guthrie et al. 2006). Furthermore, there is initial empirical evidence to suggest that ethical climate affects unethical behavior (i.e., employees' illegal copying of software) through social norms on the behavior (Lin et al. 1999). To date, however, little is known about the mechanisms through which ethical climate exerts influence on the unethical and, more specifically, corrupt behavior of employees. In short, although it is unclear how ethical climate affects employees' unethical behavior and corrupt behavior specifically, ethical climate perceptions might especially influence normative motives, such as personal and social norms, which in turn, affect the likelihood of corruption. Hence, we aim to examine whether a more ethical and less egoistic climate elicits stronger personal and social norms to refrain from corruption, which, in turn, decreases the likelihood of corruption.

Additionally, we explore whether perceived ethical climate is related to other motives for corruption, in particular, the perceived costs and benefits of corruption and perceived opportunities to engage in and to refrain from corruption, and whether these motives also mediate the relationship between ethical climate and corruption.

On the basis of our reasoning above, we hypothesize that:

Hypothesis 2 (H2). *The more ethical and the less egoistic public and private sector employees perceive their organizational climate to be, in general, the stronger their personal and social norms to refrain from corruption, specifically, in turn resulting in less corruption.*

2. Materials and Methods

To gain a better insight into the key correlates of corruption, we conducted a large-scale study among a large sample of people who, in all likelihood, were in a position to bribe or to be bribed. That is, public officials and company employees who regularly interacted professionally with employees of the other sector, and who performed corruption-sensitive tasks. Our study was conducted in the Netherlands, which, according to the Corruption Perceptions Index of Transparency International, belongs to the least corrupt nations worldwide (Transprancy International 2016). In line with this, the number of Dutch people who report having had to pay a bribe is low compared to other European countries.[8] Nonetheless, the same survey indicates that more than half of the Dutch respondents think corruption is a widespread phenomenon in their country. Another study revealed that approximately 20%[9] of Dutch public officials reported having engaged in bribery-related behaviour in the past and/or to have an intention to do so in the near future (Gorsira et al. 2016).

2.1. Procedure and Respondents

A questionnaire study, preceded by a selection study, was conducted among members of a panel managed by an agency specializing in online research (www.flycatcher.eu[10]). Prospective participants had to meet the following criteria: they were employed either in the public or private sector; regularly interacted professionally with employees of the other sector (public officials with business employees and vice versa); and performed tasks over which they had discretionary powers.[11] In the selection study, 4318 panel members participated (a 70% response rate). On the basis of the selection criteria,

---

8   http://ec.europa.eu/commfrontoffice/publicopinion/archives/ebs/ebs_397_en.pdf.
9   Note that the respondents were selected, among others, on the basis of their discretionary powers.
10   The Flycatcher panel consists of approximately 16,000 members who have agreed to participate regularly in online surveys. On average, panel members receive eight surveys a year and, in exchange for completing the questionnaires, receive a small reward in the form of points, which can be converted into gift vouchers. The Flycatcher panel meets the ISO quality standards for social science research and is used exclusively for research, and not for any other purposes such as sales or direct marketing. Panel members may terminate their membership at any time and cannot select the type of surveys for which they wish to be invited.
11   A similar study was performed in 2013 by Gorsira et al. (2016). Panel members who participated in 2013 and who were still members of the Flycatcher-panel received an invitation to participate again. Of the 202 public officials who took part in 2013, 144 participated in the selection study (3.3%), of whom 73 participated in the main study (13.7%). Of the 200 business employees who took part in 2013, 140 participated in the selection study (3.2%), of whom 78 participated in the main study (14.9%). Hence, in total, 28.9% of the participants in the current study had participated in the 2013 study as well.

842 people received an invitation to participate in the questionnaire study.[12] Participation in the study was voluntary and anonymous. Given the sensitivity of the subject, the introduction stated that a study was being conducted by the Faculty of Law on integrity at work, rather than specifying that it was conducted by the Department of Penal Law and Criminology on corruption. The questions were presented in a randomized order, to counter order effects. To avert missing data, all questions had to be answered. A data quality check was performed on completion time, consistency of answers, and straight lining and, on the basis of this, 26 respondents were excluded due to poor response quality. The final sample, after the data quality check, consisted of 234 public officials and 289 business employees (a 62% response rate). Of the respondents to the questionnaire study, 53% were male. The participants' age ranged from 21 to 77 years, with a mean age of 44.8 (SD = 11.86). Compared to the general Dutch population, people with a higher level of education and income were overrepresented, which was expected, as the participants were selected on the basis of their discretionary powers, among other criteria.

Forty percent of respondents from the public sector interacted professionally with the private sector on a daily basis, 36% at least weekly, and 24% at least monthly. Of the respondents from the private sector, this was 37%, 54%, and 8%, respectively. These contacts were related to matters such as awarding contracts, purchasing goods and services, and enforcement and inspection, among others. On average, the public-sector respondents had been working at their organization for 4.3 years, at their current department for 3.5 years, and in their current function for 3.5 years. Of the private-sector respondents, this was 3.9 years, 3.6 years, and 3.5 years, respectively. Of the public-sector respondents, 22% held a management position and, of the private sector respondents, this was 31%.

2.2. Measures[13]

All measures were directed at the work context. The items measuring perceived ethical climate were derived from an instrument developed by Arnaud (2010). These items were the same for the public and private sectors. The items measuring motives for corruption and proneness to corruption were measured using a slightly modified version of a questionnaire developed by Gorsira et al. (2016).[14] This questionnaire consisted of two versions, one for the private sector and one for the public sector, the active and passive side of bribery respectively. Below, for each scale, we first provide an exemplary item for the private sector and then for the public sector. Unless otherwise noted, all items were scored on a 7-point scale ranging from strongly disagree (1) to strongly agree (7). Cronbach's alpha for all measures, as well as the means and standard deviations, are reported separately for the public and private sectors in Table 1.

Table 1. Summary statistics, disaggregated for the public sector (*n* = 234) and the private sector (*n* = 289).

Variables	Public Sector			Private Sector		
	α	M	SD	α	M	SD
Corruption-proneness	0.90	0.19	0.392	0.93	0.21	0.409
Perceived ethical climate	0.89	5.05	1.071	0.88	4.92	1.062
Personal norms on corruption	0.78	5.64	0.969	0.85	5.56	1.126
Social norms on corruption	0.76	4.87	1.111	0.83	5.70	1.133
Possibility to engage in corruption	0.61	3.22	1.370	0.65	2.66	1.342
Possibility to refrain from corruption	0.69	5.86	0.973	0.63	5.54	1.081

---

[12] The Ethics committee granted permission to conduct the study and, since fully disclosing the purpose of the study upfront could alter responses, waived the need to obtain participants' written consent.
[13] We only elaborate on the measures that are relevant for the current study.
[14] The full questionnaire is available from the first author upon request.

Table 1. *Cont.*

Variables	Public Sector			Private Sector		
	α	M	SD	α	M	SD
Costs of corruption	0.90	4.70	1.118	0.90	4.72	1.233
Benefits of corruption	0.84	2.36	1.070	0.92	2.53	1.304
Social desirability	0.83	5.66	0.937	0.86	5.55	1.016

2.3. Dependent Variable

Corruption was operationalized by probing bribery-related intention and behavior, without using the words 'corruption' or 'bribery'. Three items measured bribery-related intentions ("In the foreseeable future, I can imagine that at my work a situation could arise in which I offer/give/promise money, goods or services to a public official in exchange for preferential treatment" (for the private sector); and "In the foreseeable future, I can imagine that at my work a situation could arise in which I ask/accept/expect money, goods or services in exchange for preferential treatment" (for the public sector)) on a scale ranging from 1 'not at all' to 7 'to a great extent'. Three similar items measured past bribery-related behavior ("At my work, I have offered/gave/promised money, goods or services to a public official in exchange for preferential treatment" (for the private sector); and "At my work, I have asked/accepted/expected money, goods or services in exchange for preferential treatment" (for the public sector)) on a scale ranging from 1 'never' to 7 'often'. The two scales were strongly correlated ($r = 0.71$, $p < 0.001$). Therefore, they were combined into one scale measuring corruption-proneness. As the six items formed a reliable scale, mean scores were computed. The average scores across the six items indicated that the respondents from both sectors reported themselves not to be very corruption-prone. As the data were not normally distributed, the scale was dichotomized to a corruption-prone category (consisting of respondents with a score of four or higher on the intention scale, and a score of two or higher on the past behavior scale[15]) and a non-corruption-prone category. Of the respondents, 19% of public and 21% of private sector respondents were categorized as corruption-prone, while the others were classified as non-corruption-prone.

2.4. Independent Variables

Ethical climate of respondents' own department was measured using a 10-item instrument (Arnaud 2010; Arnaud and Schminke 2006; Arnaud and Schminke 2012), with five items reflecting an egoistic climate (e.g., "In our department, people are mostly out for themselves" and "People around here protect their own interest above other considerations") and five items reflecting an ethical climate (e.g., "The most important concern is the good of all the people in the department" and "In our department, it is expected that you will always do what is right for society"). After recoding the items relating to egoistic climate, mean scores for the 10 items were computed, which formed an internally reliable scale, where the higher the score, the more the organizational climate was perceived as ethical rather than egoistic. As Table 1 indicates, according to both public and private sector respondents, the ethical climate of their respective organizations could be characterized as more ethical than egoistic.

Personal norms on corruption were measured by ten items (e.g., "I would feel guilty if I gave a public official money, goods or services in exchange for preferential treatment" (for the private sector); "I would feel guilty if I gave somebody from outside of my organization preferential treatment in exchange for money, goods or services" (for the public sector); and "I think it is over the top to have rules about accepting or offering gifts to public officials" (for both sectors). The 10 items formed

---

[15] We decided that respondents with a score of less than four on the intention scale could not conclusively be regarded as corruption-prone. With regard to self-reported corrupt behavior in the past, however, we reasoned that someone either had or had not engaged in bribery-related behavior; consequently, respondents with a score of two or higher on the behavior scale were classified as corruption-prone.

a reliable scale. Hence, mean scores were computed. The mean scores indicated that respondents from both sectors felt morally obliged to refrain from corruption; hence, on average, respondents experienced strong personal norms on corruption.

Social norms on corruption were measured by six items (e.g., "I am convinced that my close colleagues sometimes give money, goods or services to public officials in exchange for preferential treatment",[16] and "I am convinced that my close colleagues would feel guilty if they gave a public official money, goods or services in exchange for preferential treatment" (for the private sector); and "I am convinced that my close colleagues sometimes give somebody from outside our organization preferential treatment in exchange for money, goods or services",[17] and "I am convinced that my close colleagues would feel guilty if they gave somebody from outside our organization preferential treatment in exchange for money, goods or services" (for the public sector)). The six items formed a reliable scale. Therefore, mean scores were computed. The mean scores indicated that respondents of both sectors expected their close colleagues to disapprove of and refrain from corruption.

Perceived opportunities to engage in corruption were measured by three items (e.g., "There are many occasions during my work where I could bribe public officials" (for the private sector); "There are many occasions during my work where I could be bribed" (for the public sector); and "The rules on bribery at my work are easy to avoid" (for both sectors)). The three-item scale had a satisfactory reliability. Therefore, average scores were calculated, which indicated that, in both sectors, respondents did not perceive many opportunities to engage in corruption.

Perceived opportunities to refrain from corruption were measured by five items (e.g., "I am well aware of the rules about giving money, goods or services to public officials (for the private sector); "I am well aware of the rules about accepting money, goods or services of business contacts" (for the public sector); and "It is difficult to comply with bribery rules at my work"[18] (for both sectors)). The five-item scale had a satisfactory reliability. Therefore, mean scores were computed, which indicated that respondents perceived it as easy to refrain from corruption.

Costs of corruption were measured by 12 items, measuring the perceived chance of detection (six items; "Imagine that it is discovered that you engaged in bribery. In your opinion, how likely is it that the following persons or agencies would discover this . . . e.g., a direct colleague of yours; a supervisor from your organization; an enforcement agency (for both sectors)), and the severity of punishment (six items; "Imagine that it is discovered that you engaged in bribery. In your opinion, how serious would the negative consequences be, if the discovery was made by . . . e.g., a direct colleague of yours; a supervisor from your organization; an enforcement agency (for both sectors)). Responses were given on a 7-point scales ranging from 1 'not likely at all/not serious at all' to 7 'very likely/very serious'. The twelve items formed a reliable scale and the mean scores were computed, which indicated that respondents from both sectors assessed the costs of engaging in corruption as relatively high.

Benefits of corruption were measured by eleven items measuring how likely it is, in the respondents' perception, that someone would initiate, or go along with, a corrupt exchange (three items; e.g., "How likely do you think it is that you might get preferential treatment from a public official if you would offer him or her money, goods or services" (for the private sector); and "How likely do you think it is that someone from outside your organization would offer you money, goods or services to receive preferential treatment" (for the public sector)), and the benefits this would render (eight items; e.g., "Engaging in bribery would . . . lead to financial gain."; . . . make my job more exciting."; . . . lead to fun and pleasure." (for both sectors)). Responses were given on a 7-point scale ranging from 1 'very unlikely/strongly disagree' to 7 'very likely/ strongly agree'. The eleven items formed a reliable scale. Therefore, mean scores were computed. The mean scores indicated that respondents from both sectors perceived the benefits of engaging in corruption as not very high.

---

[16] This item was reversed scored during scale construction.
[17] This item was reversed scored during scale construction.
[18] This item was reversed scored during scale construction.

2.5. Control Variable

Social desirability was measured to control for respondents' tendencies to deny undesirable beliefs or behavior; a risk of special concern in ethics research (Fukukawa 2002). The Marlowe-Crowne Social Desirability Scale (Crowne and Marlowe 1960) has been widely used to test for the presence of this type of response; however, the items of this scale are rather general (e.g., "I sometimes think when people have a misfortune they only got what they deserved"). Since all items in the current study are directed at people's working situation, a social desirability scale was used that was specifically directed at a work context (Gorsira et al. 2016). Social desirability was measured by seven items (e.g., "At my work it has happened to me that I ... benefitted from someone else"; " ... took something (even a pen or a pin) that wasn't mine"; " ... did not keep a promise" (for both sectors)). Responses were given on a 7-point scale ranging from 1 'never' to 7 'often'.[19] Mean scores were computed, which formed an internally reliable scale, and indicated that the respondents from both sectors responded in a rather socially desirable manner.

Independent-samples-*t*-tests were performed to investigate whether the two sectors differed regarding the average scores on the measures included in this study. The results suggested that public and private sector respondents did not significantly differ with regard to mean scores on: corruption-proneness; perceived ethical climate; personal norms; perceived costs of corruption; perceived benefits of corruption; and social desirability. However, compared to private sector respondents, public sector respondents perceived weaker social norms, which suggests that the public officials in the sample perceived corrupt behavior to be relatively more approved of and more common among their close colleagues compared to private sector respondents ($t(521) = 8.42$, $p < 0.001$). In addition, public sector respondents perceived more opportunities to engage in corruption ($t(521) = 4.66$, $p < 0.001$). Private sector respondents, on the other hand, perceived less opportunities to refrain from corruption than public sector respondents ($t(521) = 3.54$, $p < 0.001$).

2.6. Statistical Analyses

First, simple correlation coefficients were calculated for the public and private sectors, separately, to explore relationships between the variables included in the study. Next, a series of binary regression analyses were conducted over both sectors to test (a) whether perceived ethical climate explained corruption-proneness; (b) which motives for corruption uniquely explained corruption-proneness; and (c) whether the relationship between perceived ethical climate and corruption-proneness weakened or became statistically non-significant when the motives for corruption were included, the latter testing whether individual motives mediated the relationship between perceived ethical climate and corruption-proneness. Subsequently, for each motive, separately, we tested via bootstrapping (Zhao et al. 2010) which motives functioned as mediators in the relationship between perceived ethical climate and corruption-proneness. Additional analyses were performed to examine whether the same motives functioned as mediators in both the public and private sectors.

3. Results

The simple correlation coefficients between perceived ethical climate, individual motives for corruption, and corruption-proneness are displayed separately for the public and private sectors in Table 2. In both sectors, perceived ethical climate was negatively related to corruption. Hence, public and private sector respondents who perceived their organizational climate as more ethical and less egoistic reported to be less prone to corruption. This confirms the first hypothesis. In line with the results from another previous study (Gorsira et al. 2016), motives for corruption were significantly related to public and private sector respondents' corruption-proneness in the expected direction, except

---

[19]   All items were reversed scored during scale construction.

for perceived opportunities to engage in corruption in the public sector, which was not related to self-reported corruption-proneness. Furthermore, the results showed that perceived ethical climate was significantly related to personal and social norms on corruption; the more ethical and less egoistic public and private sector employees perceived their organizational climate to be, the more they felt morally obliged to refrain from corruption and the more they perceived their close colleagues to disapprove of and refrain from corruption. Furthermore, the results indicated that the more ethical and less egoistic public officials and business employees perceived their organizational climate to be, the less opportunities they perceived to engage in corruption; the more opportunities they perceived to refrain from corruption; the higher they assessed the costs of engaging in corruption; and the lower they assessed the benefits of corruption (but this relationship was only statistically significant for private sector respondents).[20] However, Table 2 shows that social desirability was significantly related to self-reported proneness to corruption in both sectors, as well as to perceived ethical climate in the private sector.[21] In the subsequent analyses, the influence of social desirability tendencies was, therefore, controlled for. Since the pattern of results appeared to be rather similar in both sectors, in order to enhance statistical power and to provide an overall view, the following analyses were performed over both groups and, thus, sectors, as the sector the respondents were employed in was included as a covariate.

Table 2. Simple correlations between corruption-proneness, ethical climate, and the motives for corruption, disaggregated for the public sector ($n = 234$) and the private sector ($n = 289$).

	Corruption-Proneness		Ethical Climate	
	Public Sector	Private Sector	Public Sector	Private Sector
Ethical climate	−0.18 **	−0.26 ***		
Personal norms on corruption	−0.30 ***	−0.41 ***	0.34 ***	0.46 ***
Social norms on corruption	−0.18 **	−0.49 ***	0.57 ***	0.52 ***
Possibilities to engage in corruption	0.06	−0.39 ***	−0.14 *	−0.20 *
Possibilities to refrain from corruption	−0.23 ***	−0.39 ***	0.39 ***	0.34 ***
Costs of corruption	−0.24 ***	−0.22 ***	0.26 ***	0.26 **
Benefits of corruption	0.19 **	−0.34 ***	−0.10	−0.22 *
Social desirability	−0.26 ***	−0.35 ***	0.10	0.29 ***

Notes: * $p < 0.05$, ** $p < 0.01$, *** $p < 0.001$.

The three models that were tested are displayed in Table 3. The first model confirmed the negative relationship between perceived ethical climate and corruption-proneness, when social desirability was controlled for. The second model indicated that, when all the motives for corruption were included into a single model, personal and social norms on corruption and perceived opportunities to refrain from corruption were the only significant predictors of corruption-proneness. This suggests that perceived opportunities to engage in corruption and the perceived costs and benefits of corruption did not significantly explain corruption-proneness when other motives were controlled for. The full model, including both perceived ethical climate and motives for corruption, revealed that the direct effect of perceived ethical climate on corruption-proneness, indeed, weakened and became statistically non-significant when motives for corruption were included in the model as well. Hence, motives for corruption may, indeed, function as mediators in the relationship between perceived ethical climate and

---

[20] We also performed a partial correlation analysis, which showed that, in the private sector, perceived ethical climate, motives for corruption, and corruption-proneness were all still significantly correlated when social desirability was included as a covariate. In the public sector, however, perceived ethical climate was no longer significantly related to perceived opportunities to engage in corruption, while social norms on corruption and the perceived benefits of corruption were no longer significantly related to corruption-proneness when social desirability was controlled for.

[21] Correlation analysis showed that social desirability was also related to all motives for corruption (in both sectors).

corruption-proneness (see Figure 1).[22] To test this further and for each motive separately, mediation analyses were performed via bootstrapping (Zhao et al. 2010; with 1000 resamples derived from the full sample).

Table 3. Binary logistic regression model of corruption-proneness (corruption-prone = 1, not corruption-prone = 0; $n = 523$).

Factor	Model 1		Model 2		Model 3	
	B	Wald	B	Wald	B	Wald
Sector	−0.028	0.014	−0.148	0.238	0.203	0.432
Social desirability	−0.710	36.133 ***	−0.442	11.039 **	−0.448	11.242 ***
Perceived ethical climate	−0.438	14.864 ***			0.152	0.888
Personal norms on corruption			−0.429	9.862 **	−0.456	10.556 **
Social norms on corruption			−0.385	8.644 **	−0.448	9.294 **
Possibility to engage in corruption			0.114	0.952	0.105	0.791
Possibility to refrain from corruption			−0.320	5.374 *	−0.337	5.841 *
Costs of corruption			−0.097	0.595	−0.111	0.759
Benefits of corruption			.238	3.351	0.238	3.317
Overall fit model 1: −2 Log likelihood = 458.715; Cox and Snel R² = 0.118; Nagelkerke R² = 0.187.						
Overall fit model 2: −2 Log likelihood = 393.136; Cox and Snel R² = 0.222; Nagelkerke R² = 0.351.						
Overall fit model 3: −2 Log likelihood = 392.233; Cox and Snel R² = 0.223; Nagelkerke R² = 0.353.						

Notes: * $p < 0.05$, ** $p < 0.01$, *** $p < 0.001$.

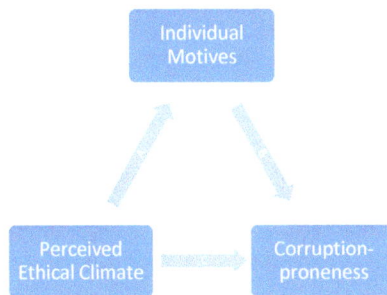

Figure 1. Model of individual motives as mediators of the ethical climate–corruption relationship.

Table 4 displays the mean indirect effect of motives for corruption ($a \times b$) and the 95% confidence intervals (see Figure 1). Table 4 also depicts the a and b coefficients, as well as the direct effects of perceived ethical climate on corruption-proneness (c) and the 95% confidence intervals, to determine whether full or partial mediation was found. The results suggest that personal norms on corruption mediated the relationship between perceived ethical climate and corruption-proneness, as the 95% confidence interval of the indirect effect excluded zero. Table 4 further shows that the 95% confidence interval of the direct effect did include zero, which means that the direct effect of perceived ethical climate on corruption-proneness was no longer statistically significant when personal norms were controlled for. This suggests full cf. indirect-only mediation, referred to by Zhao et al. (2010) as the "gold standard" (p. 198). The same results were found with regard to social norms on corruption: the indirect effect was significant but the direct effect was not. With regard to the other motives for corruption, Table 4 shows that all motives mediated the effect of perceived ethical climate on

---

[22] The pattern of results was similar for both men and women.

corruption-proneness, as the 95% confidence intervals of all indirect effects excluded zero. However, the 95% confidence intervals of the direct effects of perceived opportunities to engage in and to refrain from corruption and the costs and benefits of corruption excluded zero as well, which suggests partial mediation. To establish the type of mediation, Zhao et al. (2010) proposed calculating the product of $a \times b \times c$, where if the outcome is positive, this points to complementary mediation, indicating partial mediation. Since all products were positive, the results suggest that perceived opportunities for engaging and refraining from corruption and the perceived costs and benefits of corruption only partially mediated the relationship between perceived ethical climate and corruption-proneness.

Table 4. Results of the mediation analyses ($n = 523$).

	$a \times b$	95% CI of $a \times b$	a	b	c	95% CI of c
Personal norms on corruption	−0.226	[−0.341, −0.141]	0.351	−0.644	−0.207	[−0.462, 0.047]
Social norms on corruption	−0.374	[−0.534, −0.219]	0.538	−0.694	−0.064	[−0.335, 0.207]
Possibilities to engage in corruption	−0.051	[−0.111, −0.010]	−0.151	0.334	−0.402	[−0.627, −0.176]
Possibilities to refrain from corruption	−0.190	[−0.300, −0.104]	0.315	−0.601	−0.264	[−0.508, −0.019]
Costs of corruption	−0.079	[−0.152, −0.030]	0.241	−0.330	−0.369	[−0.600, −0.138]
Benefits of corruption	−0.051	[−0.110, −0.014]	−0.122	0.413	−0.408	[−0.635, −0.181]

The previous analyses were performed over both groups (while controlling for sector) to enhance statistical power, as well as to provide an overall view on whether, and if so which, individual motives mediated the relationship between perceived ethical climate and employees' corruption-proneness. To examine whether motives functioned as mediators in both the public and private sectors, the same analyses were conducted for the two sectors, separately. The results showed that personal norms on corruption fully mediated the relationship between perceived ethical climate and corruption-proneness, in both the public and private sectors; the mean indirect effects of personal norms were negative and significant, while the direct effects were not (see Table 5). With regard to social norms on corruption, however, the results indicated that social norms functioned as a mediator in the private but not in the public sector. In the private sector, the indirect effect was significant, whilst the direct effect was not, which indicates that social norms fully mediated the effect of perceived ethical climate on corruption in the private sector. Yet, in the public sector, neither the indirect nor the direct effect was statistically significant. Regarding other motives for corruption, the analyses reveal full (cf. indirect only) mediation effects of perceived opportunities to comply, in both sectors, and of perceived costs of corruption, in the public sector. Further, the results confirmed the partial (cf. complementary) mediation effect of perceived opportunities to engage in corruption and the perceived costs and benefits of corruption in the private sector, but not in the public sector.

Table 5. Results of the mediation analyses for the public sector ($n = 234$) and private sector ($n = 289$).

	Public Sector					Private Sector				
	$a \times b$	95% CI	a	b	c	$a \times b$	95% CI	a	b	c
Personal norms	−0.173	−0.317, −0.061	0.287	−0.601	−0.221	−0.268	−0.431, −0.135	0.397	−0.675	−0.191
Social norms	−0.085	−0.306, 0.145	0.575	−0.147	−0.310	−0.573	−0.862, −0.358	0.513	−1.118	0.150
Possibilities to violate	0.006	−0.037, 0.071	−0.148	−0.042	−0.398 *	−0.105	−0.235, −0.007	−0.160	0.654	−0.455 **

Table 5. *Cont.*

	Public Sector					Private Sector				
	$a \times b$	95% CI	a	b	c	$a \times b$	95% CI	a	b	c
Possibilities to comply	−0.152	−0.352, −0.019	0.347	−0.438	−0.254	−0.201	−0.358, −0.087	0.280	−0.720	−0.285
Costs of corruption	−0.118	−0.262, −0.020	0.254	−0.462	−0.275	−0.055	−0.142, −0.008	0.221	−0.250	−0.429 **
Benefits of corruption	−0.019	−0.085, 0.010	−0.068	0.286	−0.373 *	−0.081	−0.183, −0.014	−0.168	0.481	−0.437 **

Notes: * $p < 0.05$, ** $p < 0.01$.

4. Discussion

The purpose of this study was to examine how the ethical climate of organizations, in concert with individual motives for corruption, affects corruption, and bribery, in particular. The findings revealed a relationship between the perceived ethical climate of both public and private organizations and corruption. The more ethical and less egoistic the organizational climate was perceived to be, the less prone employees were to engage in corruption. Our study, therefore, provides the first empirical evidence for a relationship between ethical climate, a general organizational factor, and a specific type of unethical behavior, that is, corruption. Furthermore, in line with another previous study (Gorsira et al. 2016), the results suggest that personal and social norms on corruption were the most important individual-level predictors of employees' proneness to corruption. Extending previous research, we examined whether ethical climate appealed to or affected individual motives for corruption, and whether individual motives, in turn, affected whether or not employees engaged in corruption. As expected, the ethical climate–corruption relationship was fully mediated by personal norms on corruption (in both public and private sector organizations) and social norms on corruption (in private sector organizations). Moreover, the relationship between ethical climate and corruption was partially mediated by the other motives for corruption, the perceived costs and benefits, and perceived opportunities to engage in, and to refrain from, corruption. Hence, the perceived ethical climate seemed to be particularly linked to corruption *through* personal and social norms on corruption. This suggests that public officials and business employees who perceive their organizational climate as more egoistic (i.e., who perceive that self-interest is the dominant consideration within their organization in deciding what constitutes right behavior) feel less morally obliged to refrain from corruption, which in turn increases their proneness to corruption. In addition, private sector employees who perceived their organizational climate as more egoistic believed that corruption was more approved of and more common among their immediate co-workers, which, in turn, appeared to make them more corruption-prone. These results suggest that individual motives for engaging in corruption are the mechanisms through which a general organizational factor, ethical climate, impacts corrupt conduct. Interestingly, normative motives seemed to mediate the relationship between ethical climate and corruption in both the public and private sectors, which implies that normative motives account for the relationship between ethical climate and engagement in both active and passive bribery. This study followed a correlational design, which means that causal inferences are difficult to draw (Andvig et al. 2001; Tavits 2010). Notably, although it is, theoretically, more plausible that general ethical climate affects individual motives for corruption as a specific type of unethical behavior, which in turn influence proneness to corruption, our study does not allow for firm conclusions about causality. Therefore, we cannot rule out that personal and social norms on corruption affect perceptions of an organization's ethical climate, or that a third variable, for instance past corrupt behavior, affects both ethical climate perceptions and individual corruption motives. Longitudinal and experimental studies are necessary to test the causal ordering more thoroughly. Yet, a recent experimental study provides the first evidence that business culture causally affects employees' unethical behavior (Cohn et al. 2014). Another experimental study found that perceived ethical climate causally affected the corrupt decisions of employees (Gorsira 2018, doctoral dissertation). These experimental studies provide initial experimental evidence that ethical climate precedes corruption, providing further support for our theoretical model. However, more research is required to test whether ethical climate affects the likelihood of corruption via motives for corruption, and whether these, in turn, affect corrupt decisions. Yet, while more experimental research is needed, experiments can only test a limited number of variables at a time, and can create artificial situations that do not represent real-life situations (Sequeira 2012). In contrast, questionnaires enable us to gain insight into multiple key correlates of corruption by surveying large relevant samples, thereby providing insights into respondents' proneness to corruption in the real world. Therefore, it is important to study corruption and its explanatory factors using multiple methods, as different methods have their own strengths and weaknesses and can, thus, provide convergent evidence for the issue at stake (Abbink 2006). Another limitation of the present study was that all data originated from the same method and the same respondents at one point in time. Therefore, testing of the hypotheses may have suffered from common method bias, which usually results in an inflation of observed relationships (Peterson 2002; Podsakoff and Todor 1985). This may have affected our results. We considered the risk of common method bias, and, therefore, guaranteed anonymity and counterbalanced the question ordering, which are design techniques to counteract the influence of common method bias (Podsakoff and Todor 1985; Conway and Lance 2010). Moreover, as social desirability tendencies are another potential source of common method bias, we included a social desirability scale in the questionnaire (Podsakoff and Todor 1985). We have attempted to control for such biases by including a social desirability scale in the relevant regression models. The results indicated that both public and private sector respondents exhibited high social-desirability scores. Moreover, the results showed that social desirability was strongly related to the key factors of interest. Yet, even when we controlled for people's social desirable response tendencies, we found consistent support for our hypotheses. This suggests that the current study may have adequately tapped into the relationships between ethical climate, individual motives for corruption, and proneness to corruption.

We relied on respondents' perceptions to assess their organization's ethical climate. Perceptions may not always reflect the reality that would be observed by outsiders or captured through more objective measures (Martin et al. 2014). Hence, it is unclear how perceptions corresponded to *actual* ethical climates. Although research suggests that employees tend to share their perceptions of the organization's ethical climate, to some extent (Schneider 1975; Wang and Hsieh 2012), it is unclear whether respondents' perceptions of ethical climate were actually shared by others within their organization or department. In the end, however, the individuals' perception is what matters most, as people act upon their perception of a setting more so than upon the actual setting (Wikström 2004).

Our study was conducted in the Netherlands. Future research is needed to examine the extent to which similar results would be found when conducting this study in other cultures and societies. In doing so, researchers could, additionally, examine to what extent and how macro factors affect the individual and organizational factors we studied, and how the three types of factors affect corruption together. Moreover, we focused on only one organizational characteristic, perceived ethical organizational climate, which appeared to be a relevant factor. Future studies could explore the role of other characteristics, both *within* organizations, such as organizational strategy and organizational structure (Huisman 2016), and *outside* the organizations, such as market conditions, like fierce competition, and legal regulations and provisions (Bennet et al. 2013; Luo 2005). Notably, the latter factors may affect both the organization's ethical climate, and the individual motives for corruption of individual employees.

The current study has important practical implications. It suggests a considerable shift in thinking about the causes of corruption and corruption-control initiatives is needed. In their review on corruption research, Andvig et al. (2001, p. 39) concluded that "in recent years, economic explanations of corruption have been the most cited and probably also the most influential for policy formulations" (see also (Prabowo 2014; Shover and Bryant 1993; Dimant 2013; Svensson 2005)). Present organizational anti-corruption approaches appear to rest heavily on deterrence—detecting and punishing transgressions—and on diminishing opportunities for engaging in corruption—e.g., the 'four-eyes-policy'. The results of the present study do not provide strong support for the assumptions underlying this approach. Economic motives, the perceived costs and benefits of corruption, and perceived opportunities for engaging in corruption did not significantly contribute to explaining proneness to corruption; their influence was outweighed by other individual motives, notably personal and social norms and perceived possibilities for refraining from corruption (see also Gorsira et al. 2016). Hence, in spite of the anti-corruption approach that is now in vogue, our results suggest that combating corruption should not solely be focused on raising costs, diminishing benefits, and reducing opportunities (see also (Hess 2015; Treviño et al. 1999)).

A potentially effective way to motivate people to refrain from corruption is to bolster personal and social norms towards it, since personal and social norms seem to be important predictors of corruption, as well as important routes through which ethical climate affects corruption. Measures focused on norms may be more effective than traditional approaches that focus on threat of detection and severe fines. Organizations can activate personal and social norms through the use of normative messages, for example: "In this organization, people refrain from corruption", addressing the social norm on corruption (De Groot et al. 2013). However, such a message is only likely to lead to stronger social norms to refrain from corruption when people in that organization generally, indeed, refrain from corruption; when they do not refrain from it, such obviously incorrect information might very well backfire and lead to mistrust of the messenger and reinforcing the corrupt norm. In that case, increasing the saliency and strength of personal norms, instead of social norms, might work better, for example: "Do *you* care about honest decision-making? Do not act corruptly" (De Groot et al. 2013; Schultz et al. 2007). Interestingly, one study suggests that implicating the *self* in normative messages is more effective than focusing on the *action* (Bryan et al. 2013). Hence, a normative message might achieve its maximum effect when it is rephrased as follows: "Do *you* care about honest decision-making? Do not be corrupt". Another potentially effective way to encourage employees to hold and to act upon strong personal norms is the use of commitment strategies. Organizations can, for instance, request their employees sign an honor code before, instead of after, they engage in corruption-sensitive tasks, so that normative demands can be made salient at the right place and time (Mazar et al. 2008). Similarly, organizational members can be requested to take a professional oath, preferably in the presence of others (Cohn et al. 2014). An example of such an oath is the bankers oath that was introduced in the Netherlands after the recent financial crises. In this oath, bankers make a promise to execute their function in an ethical manner (Boatright 2013). Commitment strategies are built on the assumption that once people commit themselves to behave ethically, they are motivated to act in line with the promise they made, as they want to (appear to) be consistent (Abrahamse and Steg 2013; Steg 2016). Interventions like these can easily be implemented in both the public and private sectors. Moreover, since people's engagement in both active and passive bribery seems to be affected by normative motives, normative messages and commitment strategies might effectively target both sides of this illegal and unethical act.

Importantly, the present study suggests that corruption should not be seen as an isolated or purely personal issue. When looking at why employees engage in corruption and how to prevent it, organizations should, as well, pay attention to their ethical climate (see also (Hess 2015; Treviño et al. 1999)). The outcomes of the current study indicate that employees' personal and social norms on corruption depend on their organizations' ethical climate. Hence, without policies directed at the organizational level, the aforementioned strategies might be less effective, since an organizational climate that is perceived as egoistic may undermine the strength of employees' personal and social norms on corruption and, thus, encourage corruption.

Organizations can influence their ethical climate, for instance, by paying attention to the ethical issues employees may face in the workplace, by stimulating open discussion about these issues (e.g., by organizing interactive discussions) and by emphasizing which criteria, in the organization's view, should prevail in deciding on these issues. More specifically, organizations may reduce corruption risks by encouraging decision-making based on concern for the wellbeing of others and based on ethical principles, and by simultaneously discouraging an "everyone for him-/herself" atmosphere (Kish-Gephart et al. 2010). Leadership may matter here, as leaders may shape and reinforce employees' perceptions of the organization's ethical climate (Peterson 2002; Hess 2015; Dickson et al. 2001; Mayer et al. 2010; Schminke et al. 2007). To monitor if strategies targeted at the organization's ethical context have the desired effect on employees' perception, organizations can gauge their ethical climate using ethical climate questionnaires (e.g., Victor and Cullen 1988; Arnaud 2010).

The present study suggests that corrupt behavior, similar to other unethical behavior (Wikström 2004; Treviño 1986), is ultimately the result of the interplay between factors at different levels of analysis. However, it is at the organizational and the individual level, and not the country level, that organizations can take the necessary steps to reduce corruption. Particularly, interventions that cultivate an ethical organizational climate, in combination with practical tools that further strengthen personal and social norms on corruption, may contribute to the dwindling of this unethical and illegal behavior. For organizations that have, unfortunately, been confronted with corrupt employees, it seems unwise to exclusively concentrate on the 'bad apples' involved. It is key to not forget the barrel itself, or the public or private organization harboring a corrupt employee.

Acknowledgments: The study was funded by PricewaterhouseCoopers Advisory N.V. (PwC The Netherlands).

Author Contributions: M.G. and A.D. conceived and designed the experiments; M.G. performed the experiments; M.G. and L.S. analyzed the data; M.G., L.S., A.D. and W.H. wrote the paper.

Conflicts of Interest: The authors declare no conflict of interest.

References

Abbink, Klaus. 2006. Laboratory Experiments on Corruption. In *International Handbook on the Economics of Corruption*. Edited by Susan Rose-Ackerman. Cheltenham: Edward Elgar Publishing, pp. 418–35.

Abernethy, Margaret A., Jan Bouwens, and Laurence Van Lent. 2012. Ethics, Performance Measure Choice, and Accounting Manipulation. Available online: http://feweb.uvt.nl/pdf/2012/ethics.pdf (accessed on 20 September 2017).

Abrahamse, Wokje, and Linda Steg. 2013. Social Influence Approaches to Encourage Resource Conservation: A Meta-Analysis. *Global Environmental Change* 23: 1773–85. [CrossRef]

Aguilera, Ruth V., and Abhijeet K. Vadera. 2008. The Dark Side of Authority: Antecedents, Mechanisms, and Outcomes of Organizational Corruption. *Journal of Business Ethics* 77: 431–49. [CrossRef]

Andvig, Jens Chr, Odd Helge Fjeldstad, Inge Amundsen, Tone Sissener, and Tina Søreide. 2001. *Corruption. A Review of Contemporary Research*. Bergen: Chr. Michelsen Institute.

Arnaud, Anke. 2010. Conceptualizing and Measuring Ethical Work Climate Development and Validation of the Ethical Climate Index. *Business & Society* 49: 345–58.

Arnaud, Anke U., and Marshall Schminke. 2006. Beyond the Organizational Bases of Ethical Work Climates: A New Theory and Measure. *Administrative Science Quarterly* 33: 101–25.

Arnaud, Anke U., and Marshall Schminke. 2012. The Ethical Climate and Context of Organizations: A Comprehensive Model. *Organization Science* 23: 1767–80. [CrossRef]

Beets, S. Douglas. 2005. Understanding the Demand-Side Issues of International Corruption. *Journal of Business Ethics* 57: 65–81. [CrossRef]

Bennet, Victor Manuel, Lamar Pierce, Jason A. Snyder, and Michael W. Toffel. 2013. Customer-Driven Misconduct: How Competition Corrupts Business Practices. *Management Science* 59: 1725–42. [CrossRef]

Boatright, John R. 2013. Swearing to Be Virtuous: The Prospects of a Banker's Oath. *Review of Social Economy* 71: 140–65. [CrossRef]

Bryan, Christopher J., Gabrielle S. Adams, and Benoît Monin. 2013. When Cheating Would Make You a Cheater: Implicating the Self Prevents Unethical Behavior. *Journal of Experimental Psychology: General* 142: 1001–5. [CrossRef] [PubMed]

Cohn, Alain, Ernst Fehr, and Michel André Maréchal. 2014. Business Culture and Dishonesty in the Banking Industry. *Nature* 516: 86–89. [CrossRef] [PubMed]

Conway, James M., and Charles E. Lance. 2010. What Reviewers Should Expect from Authors Regarding Common Method Bias in Organizational Research. *Journal of Business and Psychology* 25: 325–34. [CrossRef]

Crowne, Douglas P., and David Marlowe. 1960. A New Scale of Social Desirability Independent of Psychopathology. *Journal of Consulting Psychology* 24: 349–54. [CrossRef] [PubMed]

De Groot, Judith I. M., Wokje Abrahamse, and Kayleigh Jones. 2013. Persuasive Normative Messages: The Influence of Injunctive and Personal Norms on Using Free Plastic Bags. *Sustainability* 5: 1829–44. [CrossRef]

Den Nieuwenboer, Niki A., and Muel Kaptein. 2008. Spiraling Down into Corruption: A Dynamic Analysis of the Social Identity Processes That Cause Corruption in Organizations to Grow. *Journal of Business Ethics* 83: 133–46. [CrossRef]

Dickson, Marcus W., D. Brent Smith, Michael W. Grojean, and Mark Ehrhart. 2001. An Organizational Climate Regarding Ethics: The Outcome of Leader Values and the Practices That Reflect Them. *The Leadership Quarterly* 12: 197–217. [CrossRef]

Dimant, Eugen. 2013. The Nature of Corruption: An Interdisciplinary Perspective. *Economics Discussion Papers*.

Dong, Bin, Dulleck Uwe, and Torgler Benno. 2012. Conditional Corruption. *Journal of Economic Psychology* 33: 609–27. [CrossRef]

Fukukawa, Kyoko. 2002. Developing a Framework for Ethically Questionable Behavior in Consumption. *Journal of Business Ethics* 41: 99–119. [CrossRef]

Gorsira, Madelijne. 2018. Corruption: Why Two Tango out of Step. Ph.D Dissertation, VU University, Amsterdam, The Netherlands, February 1.

Gorsira, Madelijne, Adriaan Denkers, and Wim Huisman. 2016. Both Sides of the Coin: Motives for Corruption among Public Officials and Business Employees. *Journal of Business Ethics*, 1–16. [CrossRef]

Graycar, Adam, and Aiden Sidebottom. 2012. Corruption and Control: A Corruption Reduction Approach. *Journal of Financial Crime* 19: 384–99. [CrossRef]

Grieger, Jürgen. 2006. *Corruption in Organizations-Some Outlines for Research.* Working Paper Number 203. Wuppertal: Department of Economics and Social Sciences, University of Wuppertal.

Guthrie, John, Sarah Todd, and Ainsworth A. Bailey. 2006. Retail Employee Theft: A Theory of Planned Behavior Perspective. *International Journal of Retail & Distribution Management* 34: 802–16.

Hess, David. 2015. Combating Corruption in International Business: The Big Questions. *Ohio Northern Law Review* 41: 679–96. [CrossRef]

Huberts, Leo, and Hans Nelen. 2005. *Corruptie in Het Nederlandse Bestuur: Omvang, Aard En Afdoening [Corruption in Dutch Government: Extent, Nature, and Settlement].* Utrecht: Uitgeverij Lemma BV.

Huisman, Wim. 2016. Criminogenic Organizational Properties and Dynamics. In *The Oxford Handbook of White-Collar Crime.* Edited by Shanna R. Van Slyke, Michael L. Benson and Francis T. Cullen. New York: Oxford University Press, pp. 435–62.

Jha, Chandan, and Bibhudutta Panda. 2017. Individualism and Corruption: A Cross-Country Analysis. *Economic Papers: A Journal of Applied Economics and Policy* 36: 60–74. [CrossRef]

Kaptein, Muel. 2011. Understanding Unethical Behavior by Unraveling Ethical Culture. *Human Relations* 64: 843–69. [CrossRef]

Kish-Gephart, Jennifer J., David A. Harrison, and Linda Klebe Treviño. 2010. Bad Apples, Bad Cases, and Bad Barrels: Meta-Analytic Evidence About Sources of Unethical Decisions at Work. *Journal of Applied Psychology* 95: 1–31. [CrossRef] [PubMed]

Köbis, Nils C., Jan-Willem Van Prooijen, Francesca Righetti, and P. A. M. Van Lange. 2015. "Who Doesn't?"—The Impact of Descriptive Norms on Corruption. *PLoS ONE* 10. [CrossRef] [PubMed]

Lederman, D., N. V. Loayza, and R. R. Soares. 2005. Accountability and corruption: Political institutions matter. *Economics & Politics* 17: 1–35.

Lin, Tung-Ching, Meng Hsiang Hsu, Feng-Yang Kuo, and Pei-Cheng Sun. 1999. An Intention Model-Based Study of Software Piracy. Paper presented at the Proceedings of the 32nd Annual Hawaii International Conference on Systems Sciences, Maui, Hawaii, January 5–8.

Lord, Nicholas, and Michael Levi. 2016. Organizing the Finances for and the Finances from Transnational Corporate Bribery. *European Journal of Criminology* 14: 365–89. [CrossRef]

Luo, Yadong. 2005. An organizational perspective of corruption. *Management and Organization Review* 1: 119–54. [CrossRef]

Martin, Kelly D., and John B. Cullen. 2006. Continuities and Extensions of Ethical Climate Theory: A Meta-Analytic Review. *Journal of Business Ethics* 69: 175–94. [CrossRef]

Martin, Kelly D., Jean L. Johnson, and John B. Cullen. 2009. Organizational Change, Normative Control Deinstitutionalization, and Corruption. *Business Ethics Quarterly* 19: 105–30. [CrossRef]

Martin, Kelly D., Jennifer J. Kish-Gephart, and James R. Detert. 2014. Blind Forces: Ethical Infrastructures and Moral Disengagement in Organizations. *Organizational Psychology Review* 4: 295–325. [CrossRef]

Mayer, David M. 2014. A Review of the Literature on Ethical Climate and Culture. In *The Oxford Handbook of Organizational Climate and Culture*. Edited by Benjamin Schneider and Karen M. Barbera. Oxford: University Press, pp. 415–40.

Mayer, David M., Maribeth Kuenzi, and Rebecca L. Greenbaum. 2010. Examining the Link between Ethical Leadership and Employee Misconduct: The Mediating Role of Ethical Climate. *Journal of Business Ethics* 95: 7–16. [CrossRef]

Mazar, Nina, On Amir, and Dan Ariely. 2008. The Dishonesty of Honest People: A Theory of Self-Concept Maintenance. *Journal of Marketing Research* 45: 633–44. [CrossRef]

Motwani, Jaideep, Ashok Kumar, and Zubair Mohamed. 1998. Ethical Behavior of Indian Purchasing Managers. *Transportation Research Part E: Logistics and Transportation Review* 34: 161–68. [CrossRef]

Peterson, Dane K. 2002. Deviant Workplace Behavior and the Organization's Ethical Climate. *Journal of Business and Psychology* 17: 47–61. [CrossRef]

Pinto, Jonathan, Carrie R. Leana, and Frits K. Pil. 2008. Corrupt Organizations or Organizations of Corrupt Individuals? Two Types of Organization-Level Corruption. *Academy of Management Review* 33: 685–709. [CrossRef]

Podsakoff, Philip M., and William D. Todor. 1985. Relationships between Leader Reward and Punishment Behavior and Group Processes and Productivity. *Journal of Management* 11: 55–73. [CrossRef]

Powpaka, Samart. 2002. Factors Affecting Managers' Decision to Bribe: An Empirical Investigation. *Journal of Business Ethics* 40: 227–46. [CrossRef]

Prabowo, Hendi Yogi. 2014. To Be Corrupt or Not to Be Corrupt: Understanding the Behavioral Side of Corruption in Indonesia. *Journal of Money Laundering Control* 17: 306–26. [CrossRef]

Rabl, Tanja, and Torsten M. Kühlmann. 2008. Understanding Corruption in Organizations—Development and Empirical Assessment of an Action Model. *Journal of Business Ethics* 82: 477–95. [CrossRef]

Rose-Ackerman, Susan. 1997. The Political Economy of Corruption. In *Corruption and the Global Economy*. Edited by Kimberly Ann Elliott. Washington: Institute for International Economics, pp. 31–60.

Rose-Ackerman, Susan. 2007. *International Handbook on the Economics of Corruption*. Cheltenham: Edward Elgar Publishing.

Rose-Ackerman, Susan. 2010. The Law and Economics of Bribery and Extortion. *Annual Review of Law and Social Science* 6: 217–38. [CrossRef]

Schminke, Marshall, Anke Arnaud, and Maribeth Kuenzi. 2007. The Power of Ethical Work Climates. *Organizational Dynamics* 36: 171–86. [CrossRef]

Schneider, Benjamin. 1975. Organizational Climates: An Essay. *Personnel Psychology* 28: 447–79. [CrossRef]

Schultz, P. Wesley, Jessica M. Nolan, Robert B. Cialdini, Noah J. Goldstein, and Vladas Griskevicius. 2007. The Constructive, Destructive, and Reconstructive Power of Social Norms. *Psychological Science* 18: 429–34. [CrossRef] [PubMed]

Sequeira, Sandra. 2012. Advances in Measuring Corruption in the Field. In *New Advances in Experimental Research on Corruption*. Edited by Danila Serra and Leonard Wantchekon. Cambridge: Emerald Group Publishing Limited, pp. 145–75.

Shover, N., and K. M. Bryant. 1993. Theoretical Explanations of Corporate Crime. In *Understanding Corporate Criminality*. Edited by Michael B. Blankenship. New York: Garland Publishing, pp. 141–76.

Simha, Aditya, and John B. Cullen. 2012. Ethical Climates and Their Effects on Organizational Outcomes: Implications from the Past and Prophecies for the Future. *The Academy of Management Perspectives* 26: 20–34. [CrossRef]

Stachowicz-Stanusch, Agata, and Aditya Simha. 2013. An Empirical Investigation of the Effects of Ethical Climates on Organizational Corruption. *Journal of Business Economics and Management* 14: S433–46. [CrossRef]

Steg, Linda. 2016. Values, Norms, and Intrinsic Motivation to Act Proenvironmentally. *Annual Review of Environment and Resources* 41: 277–92. [CrossRef]

Svensson, Jakob. 2003. Who Must Pay Bribes and How Much? Evidence from a Cross Section of Firms. *Quarterly Journal of Economics* 118: 207–30. [CrossRef]

Svensson, Jakob. 2005. Eight Questions About Corruption. *Journal of Economic Perspectives* 19: 19–42. [CrossRef]

Tanzi, V. 1998. Corruption around the World—Causes, Consequences, Scope, and Cures. *International Monetary Fund Staff Papers* 45: 559–94. [CrossRef]

Tavits, Margit. 2010. Why Do People Engage in Corruption? The Case of Estonia. *Social Forces* 88: 1257–79. [CrossRef]

Transparency International. 2016. Corruption Perceptions Index 2016. Available online: https://www.transparency.org/cpi2015/#results-table (accessed on 9 February 2018).

Treviño, Linda Klebe. 1986. Ethical Decision Making in Organizations: A Person-Situation Interactionist Model. *Academy of Management Review* 11: 601–17.

Treviño, Linda Klebe, Kenneth D. Butterfield, and Donald L. McCabe. 1998. The Ethical Context in Organizations: Influences on Employee Attitudes and Behaviors. *Business Ethics Quarterly* 8: 447–76. [CrossRef]

Treviño, Linda Klebe, Gary R. Weaver, David G. Gibson, and Barbara Ley Toffler. 1999. Managing Ethics and Legal Compliance: What Works and What Hurts. *California Management Review* 41: 131–51. [CrossRef]

Victor, Bart, and John B. Cullen. 1988. The Organizational Bases of Ethical Work Climates. *Administrative Science Quarterly* 33: 101–25. [CrossRef]

Wang, Yau-De, and Hui-Hsien Hsieh. 2012. Toward a Better Understanding of the Link between Ethical Climate and Job Satisfaction: A Multilevel Analysis. *Journal of Business Ethics* 105: 535–45. [CrossRef]

Wang, Yau-De, and Hui-Hsien Hsieh. 2013. Organizational Ethical Climate, Perceived Organizational Support, and Employee Silence: A Cross-Level Investigation. *Human Relations* 66: 783–802. [CrossRef]

Webb, Werner Nicholaas. 2012. Ethical Culture and the Value-Based Approach to Integrity Management: A Case Study of the Department of Correctional Services. *Public Administration and Development* 32: 96–108. [CrossRef]

Wells, C. 2014. Corporate Criminal Liability: A Ten Year Review. *Criminal Law Review* 12: 849–78.

Wikström, Per-Olof H. 2004. Crime as Alternative: Towards a Cross-Level Situational Action Theory of Crime Causation. In *Beyond Empiricism: Institutions and Intentions in the Study of Crime. Advances in Criminological Theory*. Edited by Joan McCord. New Brunswick: Transaction, pp. 1–37.

Wimbush, James C., and Jon M. Shepard. 1994. Toward an Understanding of Ethical Climate: Its Relationship to Ethical Behavior and Supervisory Influence. *Journal of Business Ethics* 13: 637–47. [CrossRef]

Zhao, Xinshu, John G. Lynch, and Qimei Chen. 2010. Reconsidering Baron and Kenny: Myths and Truths about Mediation Analysis. *Journal of Consumer Research* 37: 197–206. [CrossRef]

administrative
sciences

MDPI

Article

Contextualizing Corruption: A Cross-Disciplinary Approach to Studying Corruption in Organizations

Kanti Pertiwi [1,2]

[1] Department of Management, Universitas Indonesia, Jawa Barat 16424, Indonesia; kanti.pertiwi@ui.ac.id or kanti.pertiwi@unimelb.edu.au
[2] Department of Management & Marketing, The University of Melbourne, Parkville VIC 3010, Australia

Received: 27 December 2017; Accepted: 6 April 2018; Published: 10 April 2018

Abstract: This paper aims to establish how organization and management research, an extensive field that has contributed a great deal to research on corruption, could apply insights from other disciplines in order to advance the understanding of corruption, often considered as a form of unethical behavior in organizations. It offers an analysis of important contributions of corruption research, taking a 'rationalist perspective', and highlights the central tensions and debates within this vast body of literatures. It then shows how these debates can be addressed by applying insights from corruption studies, adopting anthropological lens. The paper thus proposes a cross-disciplinary approach, which focuses on studying corruption by looking at what it means to individuals implicated by the phenomenon while engaging in social relations and situated in different contexts. It also offers an alternative approach to the study of corruption amidst claims that anti-corruption efforts have failed to achieve desirable results.

Keywords: organizational corruption; business ethics; management; governance

1. Introduction

'Corruption' has largely been construed as an undesirable and destructive aspect of social life. There are deeply rooted notions about 'corruption' as 'decay' or 'impurity' (Hindess 2012). Consequently, throughout modern Western history, corruption has been deemed to be the enemy of humanity. Many social institutions such as governments, educational and religious foundations, as well as the media, articulately condemn corruption as malignant and align their policies with such a disposition. These policies often include various anti-corruption measures as well as good governance principles, codes and the alike, which are all produced with the aim of abolishing corruption. Yet 'corruption' has made its entrance into the lives of people in different societies and cultures.

'Anti-corruption' arguably entered the scene of international development in the late 1990s in what Naim (1997) called the 'corruption eruption'. There was an overwhelming call, locally and globally at that time, for the eradication of corruption. This call was led by international development agencies, particularly the World Bank (Koechlin 2013). This growing emphasis on the negative effects of corruption led to significant efforts within the research community to unpack the complexities of corruption and identify the ways through which it might be completely eradicated from human interactions. A quick research on the *Web of Science* portal reveals that there was a significant increase in the number of studies on corruption, starting with 1125 articles in the year 2000 but increasing to 18,604 academic articles published by end of year 2017. Scholars in the field of management and organization, like other social scientists, took great interest in examining corruption. Their efforts were prompted by the surge of various scandals involving various business or government organizations around the globe.

Management and organization studies mostly considered corruption as organization misbehaviour (Ackroyd and Thompson 1999), a type of crime (Aguilera and Vadera 2008), the dark side of organizations (Linstead et al. 2014). They also viewed corruption in rationalistic terms in that they perceived corruption as the result of rational agents exercising their rational thinking so as to maximize individual gains. However, this perspective detached the individual from his or her social relations and circumstances. Moreover, it also viewed corruption as an 'objective' fact of life and sought to uncover its true causes and consequences (Sonenshein 2007; Martin and Parmar 2012). A deeper examination of the works of management and organization scholars reveals that there are still debates in the literature pertaining to corruption which need to be addressed. These debates concern whether corrupt behavior should be considered mindful or 'mindless', the extent to which social dimensions influence individuals engaging in corruption and whether ethical issues associated with corruption are 'given' and objectively identifiable or are constructed by individuals in specific social contexts. My analysis of these debates suggests the need for research to look at how corruption is interpreted by actors engaging in social relations and situated in a particular context. It is useful to view these debates by applying insights from anthropological studies on corruption because this approach highlights the need to study corruption using a cross-disciplinary approach outlined in this paper.

This paper is organized as follows: First, it will review some important works on corruption which I label as 'rationalist approaches'; approaches which are often adopted in various fields, including in the area of management and organization. This covers a vast body of literature that has contributed significantly to our understanding of corruption from organization and behavioral perspectives. Second, the paper will then present the three central debates within this particular literature. Third, in addressing these debates, the paper will draw insights from anthropological and related studies to suggest a cross-disciplinary approach to researching corruption. To conclude, it will highlight potential contributions of such an approach.

2. Review of Literature

2.1. Unpacking Corruption: Rationalist Approaches

One dominant approach to studying corruption might be termed 'rationalist'. This includes theory and research that takes both a macro and a micro perspective. The macro (i.e., country-level) view has been adopted by many scholars in law, economics and politics, looking at corruption and its effects on a host of variables such as a country's political processes, economic performance and other measures of development. The micro perspective has been adopted, in particular, by management and organization scholars who discuss corruption as a type of unethical behavior which may be analyzed at individual and organization levels. Both perspectives tend to assume that corruption is in and of itself inherently harmful to society. They also regard it as behaviourally dysfunctional. Central to these rationalist views is the assumption that corrupt individuals are rational actors seeking to maximize their gains. I will describe each of these perspectives and the findings that have been generated from these assumptions.

'Rationalist' research maintains that corruption is in and of itself inherently harmful or dysfunctional to society and many scholars describe it in negative terms (Torsello and Venard 2016) as a generic 'social problem'. They commonly argue that corruption hurts economic growth and retards development. Adopting the World Bank's definition of corruption as the 'abuse of public office power for private gain', they adopt the public-private dichotomy that underpins much of the mainstream corruption research. These scholars assume that there is a similar division in markedly different societies with contrasting cultures between what is considered as public and private goods. Meanwhile other studies have shown that these important factors, rather than being universal, are historically determined and locally specific (Rothstein and Torsello 2014).

The rationalist perspective further maintains that corruption is detrimental to investment, productivity (Lambsdorff 2003) and, therefore, a country's economic growth rate (Mauro 1995). It has been argued that its effects are weaker in the less developed nations, possibly because the scale and type of corruption found there is considered 'more predictable' when corrupt governments behave as expected by those seeking favors. Hence there is less negative impact on investment (Campos et al. 1999). Other rationalists contend that corruption leads to the unfair allocation of resources and a poor quality of infrastructure (Klitgaard 1988). At the same time, they speculate that this hinders a firm's growth because paying bribes increases costs but does not always guarantee an increase in profits (Fisman and Svensson 2007).

Other research has found that corruption is inversely linked to the degree of democracy. Countries which have fully democratized have lower levels of corruption than those only partially democratized because of the lack of competition between political actors (Montinola and Jackman 2002). These authors contend that in fully democratized countries, officials or politicians have lower incentives to engage in bribe-taking because they can be replaced rather easily by their constituents through democratic processes. Countries which are considered more democratic have lighter regulation for entry for start-up firms thus lower levels of corruption (Djankov et al. 2002) due to the assumption that more democratic governments face more pressures to not create burdensome regulations. Finally, when looking at the quality of democratic institutions, which is the extent to which there is competition and openness in the electoral systems, Bhattacharyya and Hodler (2010) maintain that corruption is higher in cases where the quality of democratically controlled institutions is below a certain threshold. They argue that it is inversely lower where these institutions are stronger because they are effective barriers to a government's and politicians' rent seeking activities.

There are some counter-arguments to this negative view of corruption. For example, Lui (1985) proposes that bribery 'greased the wheels' of the economy, therefore benefitting governments. Meon and Weill (2010) also argue that corruption is beneficial in a weakly governed country, particularly where governments are considered ineffective and prone to producing burdensome regulations. Corruption, this argument runs, helps economic growth in these countries but can prove costly in others which do not suffer weak governance. Similarly, a recent study by Huang (2016) which looks at 13 countries in the Asia Pacific using data from 1997–2013 challenges the conventional wisdom that corruption is bad for economic growth. The author contends that corruption plays a positive role in stimulating growth in South Korea while it has had an adverse effect on growth levels in China, suggesting there is not a universally linear relationship between the two variables.

Some researchers stress that corruption can be seen as either 'dysfunctional' or 'functional', depending on the institutional settings. This points to the importance of considering the corresponding political and economic systems as well as the cultural and legal environments (Girling 1997; dela Rama and Rowley 2017). A related body of literature discusses 'state capture'—how businesses capture the state by making private payments in order to influence laws, rules, decrees or regulations. 'State capture'—or corruption—is beneficial for the captor firms' performance but detrimental for the rest of the economy (Hellman et al. 2003; Rijkers et al. 2017). Recent work supports this view by questioning the extent to which corruption harms as opposed to benefits a firm's competitive position. Instead of viewing corruption as inherently destructive, the corporate political strategy literature suggests that corruption benefits corporations by way of developing political ties and exploiting regulatory processes (Galang 2012; Nguyen et al. 2016). For example, some studies have looked at how former politicians or cabinet members are recruited as board members, suggesting that firms are increasingly aware of the benefits of having political ties to influence policy and regulations (Hillman 2005; Lester et al. 2008; Zheng et al. 2015).

As mentioned, rationalist scholars adopting a macro view also believe that corruptors are rational actors in that corruption results from a rationally calculated cost and benefit analysis on the part of the party committing it. As long as the benefit of corruption exceeds the costs, corruption continues. Thus some scholars argue that business-government corruption can be eliminated by increasing competition between firms within markets as this will increase the cost of paying bribes (Ades and Di Tella 1999) although evidence from post-communist countries suggests otherwise (Diaby and Sylwester 2015). In a similar vein, others suggest that government wages must be increased—so that bribe-payers would have to increase their offerings if they are to compete with legitimate earnings (Van Rijckeghem and Weder 2001; An and Kweon 2017).

Overall, despite their contribution, the works cited above have received much criticism. For instance, the rational economic view of corruption has been deemed 'too narrow and too narrowly technical' (Hindess 2012). Moreover, these studies assume that corruption is universally harmful or dysfunctional (Harrison 2006). They also assume that corrupt individuals are rational actors. Therefore, to control corruption, conditions must be created in which the costs of engaging in corruption exceed the benefits. As a result, these views tend to ignore the complexities of norms and cognitions (Misangyi et al. 2008), which is the focus of management and organization scholars whose work I discuss next.

2.2. Rationalist Works in Organization and Management Studies on Corruption

The management and organization literature discusses corruption or unethical behavior both at individual and organization levels. Corruption has been studied as a particular form of unethical behavior, which harms the organization and the society as a whole (Cleveland et al. 2009; Rose-Ackerman and Palifka 2016). Many of these studies are built upon the assumption that corruption occurs due to some kind of moral deficiency located within self-interested individuals (Bracking 2007; Gyekye 2015).

Researchers interested in unpacking corrupt behavior employ a variety of methods, including experiments, interviews of different kinds, and narrative analysis. In so doing, various explanations have emerged either focusing on the idea that corruption arises because of 'bad apples' such as corrupt individuals, or because of 'bad barrels' as in certain types of organizations which encourage corruption. Extending the 'bad barrels' argument, scholars highlighted the importance of understanding the 'bad larder' (Gonin et al. 2012) or the context of the organization and its influence on corruption. I will begin by summarizing the findings from this body of literature under the metaphors of 'bad apples', 'bad barrels' and 'bad larders'. I then identify three emerging debates emanating from these discussions. Finally, I conclude that it is necessary to view corruption through a different lens to properly address the issues raised through these debates.

The 'bad apples' argument stresses that unethical behaviors in organizations are due to the personal characteristics of differing individuals (Brass et al. 1998). In other words, some people are just born 'bad' or raised to be 'bad' and they are unable to stop themselves doing bad things (Fleming and Zyglidopoulos 2009). For example, individuals are more likely to engage in corrupt behavior when they are ambitious (Jackall 1988) or have a stronger external locus of control—the tendency to assign responsibility for a situation to something beyond the control of the individual (e.g., Reiss and Mitra 1998). Others maintain that those who have a relativistic morality (that is situation-dependent) as opposed to idealistic (universal morality) (e.g., Elias 2002); or have low empathy with others' situation (Detert et al. 2008) are more prone to corruption than those who do not. Other findings suggest that better ethical decisions are made by females compared to males, by older people compared to younger people (O'Fallon and Butterfield 2005), and by people who are more religiously committed compared to those who are not (Singhapakdi et al. 2000). Initially, it was also argued that women appear to be less tolerant of corruption than men, especially in Western culture (Alatas et al. 2009) while a more recent study found that women's representation in government reduces corruption (Esarey and Schwindt-Bayer 2017). More recently, using the organization identification perspective, Vadera and Pratt (2013) argue that individuals who over-identify—have a sense of strong attachment to the organization—are more likely to commit corrupt acts with the intention of benefitting the organization. Others observe that people from a certain cultural milieu, such as India, are more tolerant of corruption than others, such as people from Australia, while in the case of Singapore and Indonesia, people are found to be more and less tolerant than expected, respectively (Cameron et al. 2009). Still others suggest that lower levels of perception of corruption are found in more individualistic compared to collectivist countries (Jha and Panda 2017).

While the 'bad apples' argument draws attention to the role of individual attributes, the 'bad barrels' argument highlights features of the organization in facilitating corruption. These arguments complement and, at the same time, challenge the previous 'bad apples' argument. In the first instance, they question the ability of individuals to escape from corruption as well as the role of cognition and ethical reasoning in deciding the agent's responses. Second, they acknowledge the possibility that even 'good apples' might engage in corruption and develop 'mental strategies' to cope with the possible dissonance felt after committing a questionable act (Fleming and Zyglidopoulos 2009). This might, for example, involve producing an account which helps one to feel better about acting corruptly. Instead of viewing corruptors as individuals having perfect agency, the proponents of the 'bad barrel' argument suggest that corruption occurs due to factors within the organization, including the organization's ethical climate, culture and leadership.

Ethical climate is the collective organizational normative structure (Victor and Cullen 1988) which influences ethical decision making. An egoistic climate, for example, correlates positively with unethical behavior (Peterson 2002), and more specifically corruption (Gorsira et al. 2018), while a positive ethical climate has a positive influence on ethical behavior (O'Fallon and Butterfield 2005) through collective empathy—that is caring about others likely to be affected by the behavior, and a sense of a collective efficacy—the belief that the behavior will have the desired effect (Arnaud and Schminke 2012). An ethical culture can also reduce unethical behavior (Schaubroeck et al. 2012). Culture refers to formal (e.g., reward systems, ethics training programs) and informal systems such as peer behavior and identity-building stories (Schaubroeck et al. 2012).

Through practising ethical leadership, a set of traits that will promote the development of a shared understanding of what constitutes an ethical culture, unethical behavior such as corruption can be reduced. This is consistent with the findings that when an organization's leaders are perceived to be ethically positive, there are lower reports of counterproductive employee behavior (Mayer et al. 2009). One of the ways to promote the shared understanding is to tell powerful stories about ethics which others can replicate, or through delivering formal speeches in order to communicate organization's expectations (Schaubroeck et al. 2012). In contrast, when leaders downplay the negative consequences of misconducts, or in other words they become morally disengaged, employees' ethical behaviour is negatively affected (Bonner et al. 2016).

The extension of the 'barrel' allegory is the 'bad larder' (Gonin et al. 2012), which refers to factors outside the organization, such as the industry culture or climate, network relationships, the role of government and societal norms or values. This argument stresses that corruption often occurs due to certain inter-firm practices such as gift-giving (Verhezen 2009), or networking activities between business and government that can potentially turn into corruption (La Porta et al. 1999). Densely connected subgroups—referred to as cliques (Doreian 1971)—are able to develop and sustain distinct subgroup cultures and norms which support corruption (Brass et al. 1998). Furthermore, cliques operate under advance mechanisms in which a dense network of relationships between individuals and organizations facilitate illegal activities covered by legal ones such as using one's expertise and professional knowledge to mask illegal deals and decisions (Jancsics and Javor 2012). Similarly, in the field of political sociology, it was argued that the presence and persistence of informal ties referred to as 'cliques' are associated with potential misconduct or procedural irregularities (Ozierański and King 2016).

Focusing more on relationships, scholars argue that relationships lead to corruption when there is a felt obligation to reciprocate others' treatment (Palmer 2008). Moreover, language becomes an important facilitator in helping individuals understand interactions in reciprocal relations; naming a gift as a 'bribe' signals higher expectation for reciprocity (Lambsdorff and Frank 2010). Other scholars have studied the role of government whereby more intrusive regulations (Treisman 2007) and more ties to government agents increase the likelihood of firms opting to bribe because these ties assist managers in undermining rules regarding questionable practices (Collins et al. 2009). Looking at the influence of social norms on corruption, two norms are particularly relevant: reciprocity and a high achievement orientation. The former makes firms' managers more tolerant to exchanging favors which may have ethical implications (McCarthy et al. 2012), while the latter makes an organization become more prone to bribery (Martin et al. 2007).

Integrating 'bad apples, bad barrels, and bad larders', some scholars argue that corruption or unethical behavior is a result of an individual's deliberation which, in turn, is an outcome of his or her responses to situational factors (Trevino 1986). This explains why moral cognition does not always end in moral action, as certain situations may influence an individual's final decision. Drawing from Kohlberg (1969) and others, Trevino proposed the 'person-situation' model in which an individual's evaluation of right or wrong is moderated by individual moderators such as the strength of their ego, independence in the field and locus of control, as well as the situational moderators arising out of their cultural and job-related context.

Ego strength refers to how strongly a person follows his or her convictions and rejects impulses. Field dependence refers to the degree of reliance on external referents to guide decision-making, and locus of control refers to the general belief of individuals about whether they have control over life events or whether things happen beyond their control (Trevino 1986). Situational moderators include whether the organization has a clear position about right and wrong and which behavior will be rewarded and which will be punished (O'Fallon and Butterfield 2005; Lehnert et al. 2015). In addition, other external pressures such as the pressure to make decisions concerning competitive positions under time constraints, also influence behavior.

Similarly, Jones (1991) argues for an issue-contingent model which regards unethical behavior as issue-dependent. Like Trevino, Jones' model contends that decision making is partly determined by social learning within the organization (Loe et al. 2000; MacDougall et al. 2015). An individual's engagement in (un)ethical behavior is partly influenced by the intensity of the issue in that an issue which is morally more intense will lead to more ethical decisions. Hunt and Vitell's (1986) theory of marketing ethics offers a similar perspective by including not only individual variables but also the environment which consists of organizational, industry, and cultural norms. They argue that norms determined by social consensus or demonstrated by leaders influence individuals' ethical judgment.

The idea that decent people can engage in corruption if they are caught up in a difficult situation or environment can be explained by the concept of rationalization—the 'mental strategy' that individuals develop to cope with any dissonance they might experience in engaging in corruption, which in turn assists in making corruption seem 'normal'— in other words, normalizes corruption (Ashforth and Anand 2003; Lennerfors 2017).

The rationalist literature speaks of corrupt individuals as having a psychological mechanism that allows them to neutralize any negative feelings that result from engaging in corrupt acts. It involves the effort to construct a narrative which justifies an act that would originally be questionable (Fleming and Zyglidopoulos 2009). In his analysis of the accounts of Abramoff, an American lobbyist charged for a wide range of corrupt actions, Gray (2013) discusses several techniques that are used around lobbying activities, namely indirect gifting—giving congressmen money through "fundraisers", revolving doors—which involves the circulation of congressmen to lobbying posts, and devising a situation that supports rationalization on the part of the officials. Rationalization or neutralization strategies (Gray 2013) may seem to emphasize the idea of agency. However, authors in this stream assert that individuals rationalize not in isolation, but in relation to their social settings. Scholars have identified several rationalization strategies (Ashforth and Anand 2003), which includes softening the immorality of their act by using euphemisms or metaphors such as "fighting in a war" to justify questionable actions (Campbell and Göritz 2014). Empirical research supports the idea that euphemisms are used to make corruption more acceptable (Znoj 2007) by putting the blame on others (a strategy called 'denial of responsibility'). This can involve, for example, actors who make corrupt payments labelling these as extortion which had to be paid. Actors may also deny causing any injury by engaging in narratives such as "no one is affected" or "it's a small payment, just for expediency".

Ethical distance (Zyglidopoulos and Fleming 2008)—which refers to the distance between one's act and its consequences—is useful in explaining systemic corruption—the kind of corruption that is said to be common in non-Western societies (Breit and Vaara 2014). Researchers argue for two types of distance: Temporal and structural. In each type, an accompanying rationalization may be activated. In temporal distance, individuals perceive that corrupt acts have no immediate effect because no penalty has ever beset the individual or the organization using in it, therefore engaging in corruption is not so perplexing. The rationalization that may be triggered in this case is, for example, the denial of injury—"it does not hurt anybody". In structural distance, individuals are insulated from the sense of moral obligation of corruption because they see their role in it as a small part of a larger whole. Within the organization, the individuals perceive that moral obligation is distributed amongst the individuals involved, which means the more people involved the easier it is to escape any moral burden. In collective systemic corruption, individuals perceive their practice as no different to others' so it reduces the dissonance that may surface. In this case, the rationalization that is being triggered is, for example, "everybody's doing it".

3. Emerging Debates in Management and Organizational Corruption Research

This review has so far shown how corruption is understood using different concepts and approaches within the 'rationalist' literature. I will now focus on three key debates emanating from the above discussion. The first debate considers whether ethical behavior (or unethical behavior such as corruption) is mindful or mindless, the second examines whether unethical decision makers are discrete individuals or embedded in a social context, and the third explores whether ethical issues such as corruption are objective or constructed. Each will be discussed in turn, starting with an explanation of the debate, followed by relevant theories and empirical support, and concluding with a discussion of how these debates point to the value of bringing in anthropological approaches in studying corruption.

3.1. (Un)ethical Behavior: Mindless or Mindful

The first debate questions the assumptions of the rationalistic approach to corruption and considers whether corruption should be assumed to be a mindful act or whether scholars should consider the possibility that corrupt behavior flows from mindlessness. Mindfulness or heedfulness (Weick and Roberts 1993) refers to the state of being careful, critical, purposeful, attentive and vigilant, akin to the condition required in being rational or using reason: The individual has intent, is putting in effort, and able control the process (Bargh 1994). Mindlessness is characterized as non-conscious processing of repetitive behavior (Ashforth and Fried 1988; Smith-Crowe and Warren 2014), representing "a failure to see, to taken note of, to be attentive to" (Weick and Roberts 1993, p. 61) what is going on. Similarly, intuition is used in describing the psychological process that occurs "quickly, effortlessly, and automatically, such that the outcome but not the process is accessible to consciousness" (Haidt 2001, p. 818).

When individuals act mindlessly, they act "with little or no real problem solving or even conscious awareness" (Ashforth and Anand 2003, p. 14), therefore the corrupt act is not an outcome of moral reasoning, a process which is intentional and effortful (Langer and Moldoveanu 2000). Mindlessness can occur due to social influence and organizational structures (Palmer 2008). Social influence includes the authorization of corruption by leaders, the socialization of corruption itself or an escalation of commitment, in which organization members engage in corruption to reduce dissonance over past decisions which subsequently appear to lack merit (Palmer 2008; Staw 1976). For example, instead of trying to rectify a decision that is later found to be defective, organization members increase their commitment towards the decision in question, simply because they want to avoid continued dissonance (Palmer 2008).

Social influence processes such as general consensus puts pressure on individuals to believe that their decisions are meritorious, while organizational structures limit individual capacity to make the right call concerning ethical issues. Organizational structures refer to how tasks are distributed across different parts of the organization as well as the routines developed to guide these tasks. For example, the recall division at Pinto (the car company which failed to recall faulty products in the 1990s) was separated from its safety test division in such a way that the company's information flow was badly managed, which subsequently impaired decision making. In other words, corruption is enacted mindlessly because people experience pressures from their superiors or peers, or because people are 'locked' in within certain organizational rules, scripts and schemas which make them 'fail' to deliberate and choose a different course of action (Palmer 2008).

Rather than seeing corrupt acts as the outcome of deliberate 'mindful' reasoning, some scholars argue it is more likely to be the result of mindlessness (Sonenshein 2007). Social psychological research notes that "moral reasoning is rarely the direct cause of ethical judgment" (Haidt 2001, p. 815). Individuals' ethical or moral judgment is instead derived from a quick evaluation or intuition, which in turn is influenced by social and cultural factors (Haidt 2001). Scholars question whether rationalization precedes corrupt behavior, as opposed to occurring after the act and there appears to be no relationship between rationalization strategies and the desire or the intention to act corruptly (Rabl and Kuhlmann 2009). If mindlessness really prevails and rationalizations only occur after the fact, implications exist for the way scholars study corruption. Furthermore, Palmer's (2008) thick descriptions of corruption narratives and detailed information of actors' thought and emotions, show that there may be alternative explanations of corruption as a result of mindless as opposed to mindful processing.

3.2. Ethical Behavior: Atomistic or Embedded

The second debate promotes the idea of exploring the notion of the 'barrel' or 'larder' more deeply. It highlights that, instead of treating corruption in isolation from its context, scholars should give more attention to social aspects of corruption as well as to how social relations influence the meanings of corrupt practices (Misangyi et al. 2008). Business ethics researchers in particular tend to overlook the effect of social factors in ethical decision making (Bartlett 2003). Therefore, researchers argue that factors such as business culture, industry characteristics or societal norms demand greater consideration. For instance, unethical practice is influenced by a weak business culture which tends to lead to non-transparent practices and strong potentially corrupt connections between business and politicians) (Vaiman et al. 2011). A market that is characterized by concentrated ownership of firms in the hands of a number of wealthy families similarly encourages rent-seeking behaviors between businessmen and the government (Fogel 2006). Others suggest that high scores in the cultural dimension of power distance (the extent to which people accept an unequal distribution of power) and masculinity (the extent to which people stress materialism and wealth) correlate with corruption (Getz and Volkema 2001).

The above assertions seem to have only scratched the surface of what other scholars refer to as social context. These other scholars suggest that explanations for corruption lie beyond culture or structure and that they are intrinsically bound up with the meanings and identities of people and their practices (Misangyi et al. 2008). These meanings and identities are reproduced in ongoing social relations (Sewell 1992), shaped by interactions between social actors who continuously interpret, carry out and enact them (Zilber 2002). They are also the "way(s) of how a particular social world work" (Jackall 1988, p. 112). In other words, the meanings and identities are the 'driving forces' for behavior and they have rarely been explored by corruption researchers.

Seeing corruption as embedded in meanings and identities is particularly important in the case of systemic or institutionalized corruption (Misangyi et al. 2008), where corruption is widespread and treated as legitimate or no longer questioned. Misangyi and colleagues (Misangyi et al. 2008) argue that in systemic corruption, corrupt practices are interpreted differently by individuals. Therefore, to change an already corrupt system one needs to change the meanings assigned to the practices within that system.

3.3. Ethical Issues: Objective or Constructed

The third debate in the literature questions the claims of rationalist researchers that corruption is objectively identifiable and takes the idea of meaning even further to suggest that (un)ethical or deviant behavior (such as corruption) is socially constructed. Scholars have acknowledged the importance of decision makers' perceptions in deciding to engage in particular actions. For instance, individuals' perception of uncertainty within their environment will have an impact on internal and external networking activities (Sawyerr 1993) which may include ethically questionable practices such as gratuity and bribery (Mele 2009). Similarly, managers' perceptions of financial constraints and of competition intensity in a market influence firms' decision to bribe (Martin et al. 2007). This shows that it is important to account for how firms interpret or perceive their environment.

Aside from arguing that interpretation of decision-making variables varies, some scholars have also acknowledged the importance of actors' perceptions in determining whether the behavior under study constitutes 'misbehavior', 'deviance' or indeed 'corruption'. Scholars who argue for this view make largely objectivist assumptions—that individuals interpret their environment in a similar manner and that they are uncovering cues from their environment as opposed to actively constructing their own situations or problems. Martin and Parmar (2012) further contend that interpretation works in a more complex way than what is described in rationalist studies. Rationalist corruption studies rarely problematize the possibility of a more varied interpretation of the proxies for 'cultural practices', 'financial constraints', 'competition' and 'government intervention' in their survey items.

On the other hand, few corruption studies are convinced that individuals are not passive but active interpretive actors, acknowledging the varied interpretations of human problems and conditions by individuals (Weick 1979; Berger and Luckman [1967] 1971). Sonenshein (2007), for example, questions the rationalist models described above and contends that individuals construct ethical issues in a much more nuanced way, producing "more idiosyncratic interpretations" (Sonenshein 2007, p. 1029), often with very limited information, and make ethical judgments intuitively as opposed to rationally, with less deliberation than scholars have generally believed. Consistent with Haidt (2001), he argues that moral reasoning is used only after decisions are made, partly to help individuals justify the decisions or to explain for the rapid processing beyond their awareness that occurs prior to facing the decisions' outcomes.

In constructing issues, people draw on: (1) Social anchors (communicating with other individuals) to interpret the moral intensity of an issue, and (2) their understanding of others' interpretation of an issue by forming a mental model. These two mechanisms highlight that issue construction is not only individual but also social. Moreover, issues are to be understood in a much more nuanced way, as opposed to being treated as binaries, i.e., 'triggering ethical dilemma' or 'not triggering ethical dilemma'. Individuals do not merely react to stimuli, they construct meanings (Boland and Tenkasi 1995).

This idea that individual construction or interpretation varies is supported by Turgeman-Goldschmidt (2008) who studied the life experiences of a group of computer hackers and illustrated how individuals assigned meanings to practices which did not correspond with the 'unethical' or 'deviant' label used in rationalist research. Commonly perceived as a specific type of computer-related deviance, hackers in their study actively constructed a positive identity for themselves by arguing that, for example, they were creating a 'better world' by 'not letting companies like Microsoft control the market', or perceiving themselves as a 'guardian of the state' by invading computer systems of the state's enemy. Similarly, Walton (2013b) has found that instead of seeing practices of *wantok*—an informal exchange between people from the same clan or family often associated with nepotism as destructive, people in Papua New Guinea see them as "social protection mechanisms" (Walton 2013b, p. 187), because they help pull people out of poverty.[1]

These findings suggest that what outsiders label as 'unethical', 'deviant' or 'corrupt' may not be understood as such by the individuals concerned. This is why scholars have called on researchers to "study the interpretive processes" (Sonenshein 2007, p. 1026) through which individuals interpret or construct (un)ethical behavior such as corruption because of the multifarious and contested nature of the behavior.

Apart from the construction of issues surrounding corruption, the notion of 'ethics'—generally understood as individual's evaluation of good and bad—is also problematic because, similar to corruption, it has often been construed as objective as opposed to subjective and situated in a particular place and time. Recent scholarship argues that in order to understand ethics or morality, one needs to look at how issues pertaining to ethics or morality are constructed in social interactions of everyday life (Tileaga 2012).

In summary, some management and organization scholars have called for a more nuanced way of understanding the environment as part of the process of issue construction (Sonenshein 2007). Issue construction, further referred to as interpretation (Sonenshein 2007), is the process by which individuals create their own meaning by using stories or narratives as social events unfold (Boland and Tenkasi 1995). Because individuals construct an issue based on their expectation (what they expect to see) and motivations (what they want to see). Sonenshein (2007, p. 1026) suggested that researchers "study the interpretive processes that construct ethical issues out of social stimuli in the environment".

The last debate emanating from the literature in particular suggests that 'dysfunctional behavior' such as corruption has multiple meanings as it is socially constructed. Consequently, corruption needs to be studied in a way that can recognize and explore its social and varied construction. In this regard, I have drawn from anthropological research (Haller and Shore 2005; Torsello and Venard 2016) to study corruption which emphasizes its social, multifarious and contextualized meanings, an approach I now explain in more detail.

4. Anthropological Approaches to Corruption

In addition to the dominant rationalist approach to studying corruption, there is a growing and diverse body of research which looks at corruption based on a different set of assumptions. I use the term 'anthropological' approach to describe this work, although it is by no means a clear-cut body of literature and encompasses studies in fields covering not only anthropology but also sociology, human geography, discourse and human ethics.

The anthropology and sociology literature overlap in terms of their treatment of corruption as a social construction. However, further engagement with both literatures shows that they are often different in terms of the focus of their analysis and their theoretical orientation when analyzing corruption. For example, sociologists tend to be more interested in the 'causes and processes' (Hodgkinson 1997, p. 21), the structural elements (institutions, organizations and policy) or the macro-societal context and different scenarios of corruption (Numerato 2009), whereas anthropologists are less so. Instead, they tend to focus more on the meaning-making, also linguistic aspects of experiences of corruption, to which this paper draws attention, among others. As a result, there are more empirical materials from the anthropology literature that speak directly to the mainstream organizational literature, compared to the sociology literature. On the other hand, the field of anthropology itself is vast and can often be classified into two: Cultural and organizational anthropology, which are also different in regards to their level of analysis. Works in cultural

---

[1] Of course readers may also argue that this meaning is mostly relevant to 'small' or 'petty' corruption involving everyday people as opposed to 'grand' corruption which implicates people in top positions in business and government. However, the extent to which certain meanings are only applicable for certain types of corruption has been debated by scholars, for example see Kennedy, D. 1999. The international anti-corruption campaign. *Connecticut Journal of International Law* 14: 455.

anthropology tend to analyze corruption at the level of individual in the context of societies (e.g., Smith 2008; Gupta 1995), whereas works in organizational anthropology often deal with corruption in the context of organizations (e.g., Jackall 1988). Lastly, human geography (particularly the critical strand) is different from anthropology despite its similar treatment of corruption as a social construction, as it focuses more on how different forms of corruption affects the lives of communities in relation to their respective socioeconomic statuses and access to resources (e.g., Walton 2013a).

Adapting and extending the work of Torsello and Venard (2016), the anthropological approach differs from and adds value to the rationalist literature in the economic and management/organization streams in the following ways. First, these studies ignore universal or formal definitions of corruption on the grounds that they fail to capture the complexities of the public and private categories prescribed in those definitions (Torsello and Venard 2016). Furthermore, they subscribe to the idea that the law is plural, it is not an objective entity, free from interpretations of the powerful (Pardo 2004). Consequently, these researchers are more interested in understanding social reality—how local communities define corruption—following the 'emic' approach in social research (Headland et al. 1990). This is consistent with sociological research, which argues that members of organizations or society have varying constructions of existing regulations which results in different ways of responding or complying with them (Gray and Silbey 2014).

The lack of interest in applying a strict definition of corruption has led anthropological scholars to argue that corruption is not inherently dysfunctional as most researchers believed. People may generally associate the word corruption with relatively similar notions like 'decay' or 'impurity' (Hindess 2012), but the practices labelled as such may be understood as something entirely different. In addition, they also problematize that certain definitions do not fit situated experience. Walton (2013b) for example, points out that Western interpretation of corruption obscures the experience of the poor and marginalized people of Papua New Guinea (PNG) insofar they see corruption as functional—it assists in securing their share of state resources.

Second, anthropological studies largely avoid moral evaluation and prefer multiple views of ethics and morality (Torsello and Venard 2016), following a social constructionist approach. They shy away from discussing corruption from an ethical or moral stance (except for few exceptions in which they dispute the objective treatment of the terms 'ethics' or 'moral'), because they are concerned with what they regard as a judgmental approach. The approach, taken by many rationalists, associates corruption with 'underdevelopment', 'poverty' and 'destructive behavior'. A more anthropological approach holds that this prevents an objective view of the socio-cultural complexities of corruption and that a judgmental evaluation of corruption limits the ability to understand certain practices and their local meanings, which need to be analyzed in context. For example, Gray (2013)'s analysis on the variety of techniques used to frame unethical actions as moral or justifiable indicates that there may be specific elements related to people's understanding of ethics or morality which give way to the perpetuation of certain corrupt practices that deserve further attention[2].

The anthropological view is more inclined towards understanding the complexity of ethics and (un)ethical behavior by paying attention to how they are grounded in people's situated experience (Carmalt 2011). This is consistent with the assertion by Shadnam (2014) that a homologous approach—one that treats morality and organization as socially co-constitutive—is important in studying ethics and morality.

Avoiding a moral evaluation resonates with the idea that scholars need to study the ethics and morality of corruption using a relational, grounded and situated approach because it allows researchers to capture the contingent nature of, and the complexities of, the social context involved in topics related

---

[2] What seems to be missing in Gray (2013)'s analysis is, however, the broader socioeconomic and cultural context within which those questionable actions take place, to which some anthropological works give more attention. In addition, the arguments put forward by Gray tends to overlook the kind of 'everyday corruption' (Nuijten and Anders 2017), which involves everyday citizens and the possibility of mindlessness as opposed to careful deliberation in explaining corrupt behavior.

to moral and ethics, including corruption (Clammer 2012). Instead of applying a fixed universal approach to ethics, the anthropological approach appreciates that ethics needs to be understood from the point of view of actors situated in a specific time and place. Adopting such a view has allowed sociologist (Ledeneva 2001) to unpack the complexity of *blat*, the use of personal connections in Russia which is often framed in a negative way because it bypasses formal procedures (Onoshchenko and Williams 2014). *Blat*, commonly labeled as corruption in Russia, is in fact just a different mode of exchange which *does not carry any sense of moral decay* (Ledeneva 2001).

Third, anthropological studies of corruption pay great attention to the processual aspect of corruption, particularly in how corruption is 'constituted' at a specific time and place. Instead of taking a static view, looking to establish whether or not corruption happens, they focus on the detailed processes involved whereby corruption comes about—a more processual view (Torsello and Venard 2016; Ashforth et al. 2008). Unlike rationalist scholars, who tend to reduce or collapse a series of unfolding events into what can be described as corruption into statistical summaries, they focus more on those very details. For example, in exploring corruption processually they elucidate the specific cultural processes and the complexities of people's experience of corruption and of the state in which choice of words plays a role in giving contour to those experiences (Gupta 1995).

Anthropological studies also attend to the interpretive and linguistic aspects of corruption as it views corruption as a "meaningful, culturally constructed, discursively mediated, symbolically saturated, and ritually regulated" (Brubaker and Laitin 1998, p. 441) social phenomenon. This means that researchers adopting an anthropological approach will not look at corruption as an objectively identifiable phenomenon. Nor will they view corruption as merely a set of social practices. Instead, they will also attend to the textual aspects of those practices, following the language and meanings that social actors attribute to it (Torsello 2010). The anthropological approach also resembles many of the features of the homologous view of corruption (Shadnam 2014) as they view corruption as a phenomenon inseparable from the social dimensions of human behavior, and which continues to be defined and re-defined through everyday communicative practices.

Corruption could not and should not be separated from patterns of thought and action which sustain it by way of social regulations and sanctions. An anthropological approach is interested in investigating not the 'effects' of corruption but the 'constitution' of corruption in a specific time and place (Shadnam 2014). In exploring corruption processually, Orjuela (2014) describes how corruption enables people to maintain a sense of ethnic stability and perseverance. Using examples from Nigeria, Kenya and Sri Lanka, she underscores the complexities of corruption beyond cost-benefit calculations, illuminating individual motivations and struggles to fulfil ethnic identity expectations. In paying attention to the language and meanings that people use to describe corruption, she captures the complexity of corruption as a political project through which people strive to be seen as loyal to their community.

Lastly, the anthropological approach draws attention to the role of meanings and identities embedded in social practices, many of which are labelled as corruption (Misangyi et al. 2008). Because of the different assumptions explained previously, anthropological studies of corruption engage more deeply with the understanding of the subjective experience of individuals, their ways of being and doing things, which leads to an exploration of meanings of various practices and role identities of people involved in those practices (Torsello and Venard 2016). Such a view has enabled scholars to demonstrate how role identities shape and are shaped by people's experience of corruption. More importantly, in examining identities, the approach may help explain the normalization of controversial practices which allow "good people do bad things" (Kaptein 2013). Breit (2011), for instance, shows that in the case of an alcohol monopoly scandal in Norway, a country that is relatively free from corruption according to Transparency International, corruption not only allows people to attack controversial business practices, but also to express a critique towards the state's dominant role in the alcohol market and a way of articulating ideas about Norwegian national moral identity. These studies show how the alternative understandings of corruption are achieved by placing the cultural context in the foreground of corruption research. These alternative understandings are important, not only because they help us to rethink about existing anti-corruption efforts, but also because they help us to think about delicate and overarching social and political issues from which corruption cannot be separated.

5. Conclusions

This paper has so far contributed by connecting various important research findings in relation to corruption and recognizing their different approaches. It has discussed the rationalist approaches to studying corruption that tend to treat corruption as universally and inherently 'destructive'. It then identified three central debates within the management and organization literature that concern:

> (1) Whether corruption is a result of mindless or mindful processing; (2) the role of individual's perception or subjectivity and (3) the role of social contexts or environment in influencing their perception. In addressing the debates, the paper has drawn from anthropological studies (Torsello and Venard 2016; Haller and Shore 2005) which emphasize a contextualized understanding of corruption, which eschew formal definitions and moral evaluations, and which focus attention on process, meaning and identity.

Consequently, upon applying insights from anthropological and related studies to address the debates within organization and management works, this paper proposes a cross-disciplinary approach to studying corruption. Such study will focus on the interpretation of corruption by organization members situated in context as well as the various identities and processes through which corruption comes to be experienced by individuals. It will ask, for example, questions such as *"What does corruption mean to people in this particular organization or community?"* and *"How do people construct or interpret different issues in relation to various practices associated with corruption?"*. In exploring identities, it will ask questions such as *"What role identities are being invoked when people discuss their experiences of corruption?"*. With regards to the view of multiple morality, the study will explore the issue by asking questions such as: *"What does it mean to be moral or ethical to people in this specific organization or community?"* and *"How do notions of ethics and morality feature in the constructions of corruption?"*. To allow such an endeavour, researchers will need to adopt a research approach that researchers in anthropology and related field have already been familiar with. For example, they may apply qualitative methodology and methods such as ethnography, interviews or media text analysis, and adopt an interpretive perspective—which takes human interpretation as their starting point for understanding the social world (Burrell and Morgan 1985; Moran 2002). Asking the above basic and open-ended questions on meanings and interpretations would allow researchers to return to the three debates outlined previously.

In addition to addressing the debates, a cross-disciplinary approach will potentially contribute to the literature in at least three ways. First, by asking questions around people's intersubjective meanings and experiences of corruption, researchers are able to explore the perspective of the 'insiders', one that is often silenced in empirical studies on corruption. Mainstream research has largely treated corruption as having a singular, pre-determined and fixed meaning across contexts (Martin and Parmar 2012; Sonenshein 2007). It tends to treat social actors as passive entities and to see their own task as being to uncover this pre-existing meaning and behave accordingly (Martin and Parmar 2012). However, a cross-disciplinary approach treats corruption differently—as a socially constructed phenomenon. In this way, it has the potential to enrich or even challenge existing research by showing the multifarious nature of corruption.

Second, a cross-disciplinary approach that eschews from moral evaluation has the potential of bringing in the views of certain members of society, such as public servants, politicians, the poor and the uneducated, who are often barraged for their 'corruptness'. Clearly, people's understanding of corruption is influenced by their intersubjective experience of the phenomenon (Znoj 2007). A cross-disciplinary approach will address the limited attention paid to the lived experience of corruption, especially in management and organization studies (Sonenshein 2007; Torsello and Venard 2016).

Third, by introducing a cross-disciplinary approach that appreciates individual interpretation of social issues, researchers will expand the conceptual tool box of corruption research in management and organization studies by addressing what some scholars have identified as a limitation of corruption theories in management and organization studies: the lack of "research from a 'local' point of view" (Torsello and Venard 2016, p. 50).

Notwithstanding all of the potential theoretical contributions above, applying anthropological insights into organization research is not without its limitations. Researchers must be aware that the problem of access is one of the first barriers. Given the general moralizing tendency, it is important, but understandably difficult, for researchers to identify potential research participants who would be comfortable sharing their experiences of practices which many often label as corruption. In addition, this type of research brings the risk of researchers being exposed to illegal practices and this posits potentially difficult questions about legal responsibility. This is especially true in the light of a researcher's obligation to protect their participants from harm. Finally, there is also limitation in terms of reporting back the findings to the research community in which books are more preferred compared to journal articles due to the massive amount of data that needs to be presented and analyzed (Torsello and Venard 2016).

Finally, a cross-disciplinary research has important potential contributions for anti-corruption practices. Learning that corruption might be treated as "unwritten rules" (p. 2), a different mode of interpersonal exchange which does not carry any sense of moral decay (Ledeneva 2001), it became evident that there is a wide gap to bridge between those standing on behalf of anti-corruption campaigns and good governance and those whose practice are being scrutinized. Moreover, in light of limited achievements of the global anti-corruption movement, an understanding of the meanings of practices many labelled as corruption in its specific context may help to reveal the limitations of existing approaches. Through exploring meanings in context, anti-corruption and good governance campaigners may begin to evaluate whether their existing strategies speak to the communities they seek to shape or influence.

Acknowledgments: The author acknowledges the support of the Endeavour Awards and the University of Melbourne, which aided the research for this study and would like to thank the editor and the two anonymous reviewers for their helpful comments and suggestions.

Conflicts of Interest: The author declares no conflict of interest.

References

Ackroyd, Stephen, and Paul Thompson. 1999. *Organizational Misbehaviour*. London and Thousand Oaks: Sage Publications.

Ades, Alberto, and Rafael Di Tella. 1999. Rents, competition, and corruption. *The American Economic Review* 89: 982–93. [CrossRef]

Aguilera, Ruth V., and Abhijeet K. Vadera. 2008. The dark side of authority: Antecedents, mechanisms, and outcomes of organizational corruption. *Journal of Business Ethics* 77: 431–49. [CrossRef]

Alatas, Vivi, Lisa Cameron, Ananish Chaudhuri, Nisvan Erkal, and Lata Gangadharan. 2009. Gender, culture, and corruption: Insights from an experimental analysis. *Southern Economic Journal* 75: 663–80.

An, Weihua, and Yesola Kweon. 2017. Do higher government wages induce less corruption? Cross-country panel evidence. *Journal of Policy Modeling* 39: 809–26. [CrossRef]

Arnaud, Anke, and Marshall Schminke. 2012. The ethical climate and context of organizations: A comprehensive model. *Organization Science* 23: 1767–80. [CrossRef]

Ashforth, Blake E., and Vikas Anand. 2003. The normalization of corruption in organizations. *Research in Organizational Behavior* 25: 1–52. [CrossRef]

Ashforth, Blake E., and Yitzhak Fried. 1988. The mindlessness of organizational behaviors. *Human Relations* 41: 305–29. [CrossRef]

Ashforth, Blake E., Dennis A. Gioia, Sandra Lynn Robinson, and Linda Klebe Trevino. 2008. Re-viewing organizational corruption—Introduction. *Academy of Management Review* 33: 670–84. [CrossRef]

Bargh, John A. 1994. The four horsemen of automaticity: Intention, awareness, efficiency, and control as separate issues. In *Handbook of Social Cognition*. Thousand Oaks: SAGE Publications Ltd., vol. 1, pp. 1–40.

Bartlett, Dean. 2003. Management and business ethics: A critique and integration of ethical decision-making models. *British Journal of Management* 14: 223–35. [CrossRef]

Berger, Peter L, and Thomas Luckman. 1971. *The Social Construction of Reality*. London: Allen Lane. First Published 1967.

Bhattacharyya, Sambit, and Roland Hodler. 2010. Natural resources, democracy and corruption. *European Economic Review* 54: 608–21. [CrossRef]

Boland, Richard J., and Ramkrishnan V. Tenkasi. 1995. Perspective making and perspective taking in communities of knowing. *Organization Science* 6: 350–72. [CrossRef]

Bonner, Julena M., Rebecca L. Greenbaum, and David M. Mayer. 2016. My boss is morally disengaged: The role of ethical leadership in explaining the interactive effect of supervisor and employee moral disengagement on employee behaviors. *Journal of Business Ethics* 137: 731–42. [CrossRef]

Bracking, Sarah. 2007. Political Development and Corruption: Why 'Right Here, Right Now!'? In *Corruption and Development: The Anti-Corruption Campaigns*. Edited by Sarah Bracking. Basingstoke: Palgrave Macmillan.

Brass, Daniel J., Kenneth D. Butterfield, and Bruce C. Skaggs. 1998. Relationships and unethical behavior: A social network perspective. *Academy of Management Review* 23: 14–31.

Breit, Eric. 2011. Discursive contests of corruption: The case of the Norwegian alcohol monopoly. *Culture and Organization* 17: 47–64. [CrossRef]

Breit, Eric, and Eero Vaara. 2014. 4 Corruption and the media. *Organizations and the Media: Organizing in a Mediatized World* 30: 48.

Brubaker, Rogers, and David D. Laitin. 1998. Ethnic and nationalist violence. *Annual Review of Sociology* 24: 423–52. [CrossRef]

Burrell, Gibson, and Gareth Morgan. 1985. *Sociological Paradigms and Organisational Analysis: Elements of the Sociology of Corporate Life*. Aldershot: Gower.

Cameron, Lisa, Ananish Chaudhuri, Nisvan Erkal, and Lata Gangadharan. 2009. Propensities to engage in and punish corrupt behavior: Experimental evidence from Australia, India, Indonesia and Singapore. *Journal of Public Economics* 93: 843–51. [CrossRef]

Campbell, Jamie-Lee, and Anja S. Göritz. 2014. Culture corrupts! A qualitative study of organizational culture in corrupt organizations. *Journal of Business Ethics* 120: 291–311. [CrossRef]

Campos, J. Edgardo, Donald Lien, and Sanjay Pradhan. 1999. The Impact of Corruption on Investment: Predictability Matters. *World Development* 27: 1059–67. [CrossRef]

Carmalt, Jean Connolly. 2011. Human rights, care ethics and situated universal norms. *Antipode* 43: 296–325. [CrossRef]

Clammer, John. 2012. Corruption, development, chaos and social disorganisation: Sociological reflections on corruption and its social basis. In *Corruption: Expanding the Focus*. Moorebank: ANU Press.

Cleveland, Margot, Christopher M. Favo, Thomas J. Frecka, and Charles L. Owens. 2009. Trends in the international fight against bribery and corruption. *Journal of Business Ethics* 90 (S2): 199–244. [CrossRef]

Collins, Jamie D., Klaus Uhlenbruck, and Peter Rodriguez. 2009. Why firms engage in corruption: A top management perspective. *Journal of Business Ethics* 87: 89–108. [CrossRef]

dela Rama, Marie, and Chris Rowley. 2017. Future directions for research into corruption and anticorruption practice. In *The Changing Face of Corruption in the Asia Pacific*. New York: Elsevier, pp. 369–377.

Detert, James R., Linda K. Trevino, and Vicki L. Sweitzer. 2008. Moral disengagement in ethical decision making: A study of antecedents and outcomes. *Journal of Applied Psychology* 93: 374–91. [CrossRef] [PubMed]

Diaby, Aboubacar, and Kevin Sylwester. 2015. Corruption and market competition: Evidence from post-communist countries. *World Development* 66: 487–99. [CrossRef]

Djankov, Simeon, Rafael La Porta, Florencio Lopez-De-Silanes, and Andrei Shleifer. 2002. The regulation of entry. *Quarterly Journal of Economics* 117: 1–37. [CrossRef]

Doreian, Patrick. 1971. *Mathematics and the Study of Social Relations*. New York: Schocken Books.

Elias, Rafik Z. 2002. Determinants of earnings management ethics among accountants. *Journal of Business Ethics* 40: 33–45. [CrossRef]

Esarey, Justin, and Leslie Schwindt-Bayer. 2017. Estimating Causal Relationships Between Women's Representation in Government and Corruption. Available online: http://jee3.web.rice.edu/gender-corruption-and-causality.pdf (accessed on 9 April 2018).

Fisman, Raymond, and Jakob Svensson. 2007. Are corruption and taxation really harmful to growth? Firm level evidence. *Journal of Development Economics* 83: 63–75. [CrossRef]

Fleming, Peter, and Stelios C. Zyglidopoulos. 2009. *Charting Corporate Corruption: Agency, Structure and Escalation, Charting Corporate Corruption: Agency, Structure and Escalation*. Cheltenham: Edward Elgar Publishing Ltd.

Fogel, Kathy. 2006. Oligarchic family control, social economic outcomes, and the quality of government. *Journal of International Business Studies* 37: 603–22. [CrossRef]

Galang, Roberto Martin N. 2012. Victim or victimizer: Firm responses to government corruption. *Journal of Management Studies* 49: 429–62. [CrossRef]

Getz, Kathleen A., and Roger J. Volkema. 2001. Culture, perceived corruption, and economics: A model of predictors and outcomes. *Business & Society* 40: 7–30.

Girling, John. 1997. *Corruption, Capitalism and Democracy, Routledge Studies in Social and Political Thought Vol 4*. London: Routledge.

Gonin, Michael, Guido Palazzo, and Ulrich Hoffrage. 2012. Neither bad apple nor bad barrel: how the societal context impacts unethical behavior in organizations. *Business Ethics-a European Review* 21: 31–46. [CrossRef]

Gorsira, Madelijne, Linda Steg, Adriaan Denkers, and Wim Huisman. 2018. Corruption in Organizations: Ethical Climate and Individual Motives. *Administrative Sciences* 8: 4. [CrossRef]

Gray, Garry C. 2013. Insider accounts of institutional corruption: Examining the social organization of unethical behaviour. *British Journal of Criminology* 53: 533–51. [CrossRef]

Gray, Garry C., and Susan S. Silbey. 2014. Governing inside the organization: Interpreting regulation and compliance. *American Journal of Sociology* 120: 96–145. [CrossRef]

Gupta, Akhil. 1995. Blurred boundaries: the discourse of corruption, the culture of politics, and the imagined state. *American Ethnologist* 22: 375–402. [CrossRef]

Gyekye, Kwame. 2015. Political corruption: A philosophical inquiry into a moral problem. *Philosophy and Politics: Discourse on Values, Politics, and Power in Africa* 10: 353.

Haidt, Jonathan. 2001. The emotional dog and its rational tail: A social intuitionist approach to moral judgment. *Psychological Review* 108: 814. [CrossRef] [PubMed]

Haller, Dieter, and Cris Shore. 2005. *Corruption: Anthropological Perspectives*. London: Pluto Press.

Harrison, Elizabeth. 2006. Unpacking the anti-corruption agenda: Dilemmas for anthropologists. *Oxford Development Studies* 34: 15–29. [CrossRef]

Headland, Thomas N., Kenneth L. Pike, and Marvin Harris. 1990. *Emics and Etics: The Insider/Outsider Debate*. Newbury Park: Sage Publications.

Hellman, Joel, Geraint Jones, and Daniel Kaufmann. 2003. Seize the state, seize the day: State capture and influence in transition economies. *Journal of Comparative Economics* 31: 751–73. [CrossRef]

Hillman, Amy J. 2005. Politicians on the board of directors: Do connections affect the bottom line? *Journal of Management* 31: 464–81. [CrossRef]

Hindess, Barry. 2012. Introduction: How should we think about corruption? In *Corruption: Expanding the Focus*. Moorebank: ANU Press, pp. 1–24.

Hodgkinson, Peter. 1997. The sociology of corruption-Some themes and issues. *Sociology* 31: 17–35. [CrossRef]

Huang, Chiung-Ju. 2016. Is corruption bad for economic growth? Evidence from Asia-Pacific countries. *North American Journal of Economics and Finance* 35: 247–56. [CrossRef]

Hunt, Shelby D., and Scott Vitell. 1986. A general theory of marketing ethics. *Journal of Macromarketing* 6: 5–16. [CrossRef]

Jackall, Robert. 1988. Moral mazes: The world of corporate managers. *International Journal of Politics, Culture, and Society* 1: 598–614. [CrossRef]

Jancsics, David, and Istvan Javor. 2012. Corrupt governmental networks. *International Public Management Journal* 15: 62–99. [CrossRef]

Jha, Chandan, and Bibhudutta Panda. 2017. Individualism and Corruption: A Cross-Country Analysis. *Economic Papers: A Journal of Applied Economics and Policy* 36: 60–74. [CrossRef]

Jones, Thomas M. 1991. Ethical decision-making by individuals in organizations—An issue-contingent model. *Academy of Management Review* 16: 366–95. [CrossRef]

Kaptein, Muel. 2013. *Workplace Morality: Behavioral Ethics in Organizations*. Bingley: Emerald Group Publishing.

Klitgaard, Robert E. 1988. *Controlling Corruption*. Berkeley: University of California Press.

Koechlin, Lucy. 2013. *Corruption as an Empty Signifier: Politics and Political Order in Africa*. Leiden: Brill.

Kohlberg, Lawrence. 1969. *Stage and Sequence: The Cognitive-Developmental Approach to Socialization*. New York: Rand McNally.

La Porta, Rafael, Florencio Lopez-de-Silanes, Andrei Shleifer, and Robert Vishny. 1999. The quality of government. *Journal of Law, Economics, and Organization* 15: 222–79. [CrossRef]

Lambsdorff, Johann Graf. 2003. How corruption affects productivity. *Kyklos* 56: 457–74. [CrossRef]

Lambsdorff, Johann Graff, and Bjorn Frank. 2010. Bribing versus gift-giving—An experiment. *Journal of Economic Psychology* 31: 347–57. [CrossRef]

Langer, Ellen J., and Mihnea Moldoveanu. 2000. The construct of mindfulness. *Journal of Social Issues* 56: 1–9. [CrossRef]

Ledeneva, Alena. 2001. *Unwritten Rules*. London: Centre for European Reform.

Lehnert, Kevin, Yung-hwal Park, and Nitish Singh. 2015. Research note and review of the empirical ethical decision-making literature: Boundary conditions and extensions. *Journal of Business Ethics* 129: 195–219. [CrossRef]

Lennerfors, Thomas Taro. 2017. Corruption: Maximizing, Socializing, Balancing, and Othering. In *The Handbook of Business and Corruption: Cross-Sectoral Experiences*. Bingley: Emerald Publishing Limited, pp. 25–48.

Lester, Richard H., Amy Hillman, Asghar Zardkoohi, and Albert A. Cannella. 2008. Former government officials as outside directors: The role of human and social capital. *Academy of Management Journal* 51: 999–1013. [CrossRef]

Linstead, Stephen, Garance Maréchal, and Ricky W. Griffin. 2014. Theorizing and Researching the Dark Side of Organization. *Organization Studies* 35: 165–88. [CrossRef]

Loe, Terry W., Linda Ferrel, and Phylis Mansfield. 2000. A review of empirical studies assessing ethical decision making in business. *Journal of Business Ethics* 25: 185–204. [CrossRef]

Lui, Francis T. 1985. An equilibrium queuing model of bribery. *Journal of Political Economy* 93: 760–81. [CrossRef]

MacDougall, Alexandra E., Zhanna Bagdasarov, James F. Johnson, and Michael D. Mumford. 2015. Managing workplace ethics: An extended conceptualization of ethical sensemaking and the facilitative role of human resources. In *Research in Personnel and Human Resources Management*. Bingley: Emerald Group Publishing Limited, pp. 121–89.

Martin, Kirsten, and Bidhan Parmar. 2012. Assumptions in decision making scholarship: Implications for business ethics research. *Journal of Business Ethics* 105: 289–306. [CrossRef]

Martin, Kelly D., John B. Cullen, Jean L. Johnson, and K. Praveen Parboteeah. 2007. Deciding to bribe: A cross-level analysis of firm and home country influences on bribery activity. *Academy of Management Journal* 50: 1401–22. [CrossRef]

Mauro, Paolo. 1995. Corruption and growth. *Quarterly Journal of Economics* 110: 681–712. [CrossRef]

Mayer, David M., Maribeth Kuenzi, Rebecca Greenbaum, Mary Bardes, and Rommel Bombie Salvador. 2009. How low does ethical leadership flow? Test of a trickle-down model. *Organizational Behavior and Human Decision Processes* 108: 1–13. [CrossRef]

McCarthy, Daniel J., Sheila M. Puffer, Denise R. Dunlap, and Alfred M. Jaeger. 2012. A stakeholder approach to the ethicality of BRIC-firm managers' use of favors. *Journal of Business Ethics* 109: 27–38. [CrossRef]

Mele, Domenec. 2009. The practice of networking: An ethical approach. *Journal of Business Ethics* 90: 487–503. [CrossRef]

Meon, Pierre-Guillaume, and Laurent Weill. 2010. Is corruption an efficient grease? *World Development* 38: 244–59. [CrossRef]

Misangyi, Vilmos. F., Gary R. Weaver, and Heather Elms. 2008. Ending corruption: The interplay among institutional logics, resources, and institutional entrepreneurs. *Academy of Management Review* 33: 750–70. [CrossRef]

Montinola, Gabriella R., and Robert W. Jackman. 2002. Sources of corruption: A cross-country study. *British Journal of Political Science* 32: 147–70. [CrossRef]

Moran, Dermot. 2002. *Introduction to Phenomenology*. London: Routledge.

Naim, Moisés. 1997. The corruption eruption. *Trends in Organized Crime* 2: 60. [CrossRef]

Nguyen, Thang V., Bao D. Ho, Canh Q. Le, and Hung V. Nguyen. 2016. Strategic and transactional costs of corruption: perspectives from Vietnamese firms. *Crime, Law and Social Change* 65: 351–74. [CrossRef]

Nuijten, Monique, and Gerhard Anders. 2017. Corruption and the secret of law: An introduction. In *Corruption and the Secret of Law*. London: Routledge, pp. 13–36.

Numerato, Dino. 2009. The media and sports corruption: An outline of sociological understanding. *International Journal of Sport Communication* 2: 261–73. [CrossRef]

O'Fallon, Michael J., and Kenneth D. Butterfield. 2005. A review of the empirical ethical decision-making literature: 1996–2003. *Journal of Business Ethics* 59: 375–413. [CrossRef]

Onoshchenko, Olga, and Collins C. Williams. 2014. Evaluating the role of blat in finding graduate employment in post-Soviet Ukraine The "dark side" of job recruitment? *Employee Relations* 36: 254–65. [CrossRef]

Orjuela, Camilla. 2014. Corruption and identity politics in divided societies. *Third World Quarterly* 35: 753–69. [CrossRef]

Ozierański, Piotr, and Lawrence King. 2016. The persistence of cliques in the post-communist state. The case of deniability in drug reimbursement policy in Poland. *The British Journal of Sociology* 67: 216–41. [CrossRef] [PubMed]

Palmer, Donald. 2008. Extending the process model of collective corruption. In *Research in Organizational Behavior, Vol 28: An Annual Series of Analytical Essays and Critical Reviews*. Edited by Arthur P. Brief and Barry M. Staw. Bingley: Emerald Group Publishing Limited, pp. 107–35.

Pardo, Italo. 2004. *Between Morality and the Law: Corruption, Anthropology and Comparative Society*. Farnham: Ashgate Publishing.

Peterson, Dane K. 2002. The relationship between unethical behavior and the dimensions of the ethical climate questionnaire. *Journal of Business Ethics* 41: 313–26. [CrossRef]

Rabl, Tanja, and Torsten M. Kuhlmann. 2009. Why or why not? Rationalizing corruption in organizations. *Cross Cultural Management-an International Journal* 16: 268–86. [CrossRef]

Reiss, Michelle C., and Kaushik Mitra. 1998. The effects of individual difference factors on the acceptability of ethical and unethical workplace behaviors. *Journal of Business Ethics* 17: 1581–93. [CrossRef]

Rijkers, Bob, Caroline Freund, and Antonio Nucifora. 2017. All in the family: State capture in Tunisia. *Journal of Development Economics* 124: 41–59. [CrossRef]

Rose-Ackerman, Susan, and Bonnie J. Palifka. 2016. *Corruption and Government: Causes, Consequences, and Reform*. Cambridge: Cambridge University Press.

Rothstein, Bo, and Davide Torsello. 2014. Bribery in Preindustrial Societies: Understanding the Universalism-Particularism Puzzle. *Journal of Anthropological Research* 70: 263–84. [CrossRef]

Sawyerr, Olukemi O. 1993. Environmental uncertainty and environmental scanning activities of Nigerian manufacturing executives—A comparative analysis. *Strategic Management Journal* 14: 287–99. [CrossRef]

Schaubroeck, John M., Sean T. Hannah, Bruce J. Avolio, Steve W. J. Kozlowski, Robert G. Lord, Linda K. Treviño, Nikolaos Dimotakis, and Ann C. Peng. 2012. Embedding ethical leadership within and across organization levels. *Academy of Management Journal* 55: 1053–78. [CrossRef]

Sewell, William H. 1992. A theory of structure—Duality, agency, and transformation. *American Journal of Sociology* 98: 1–29. [CrossRef]

Shadnam, Masoud. 2014. Heterologous and homologous perspectives on the relation between morality and organization: Illustration of implications for studying the rise of private military and security industry. *Journal of Management Inquiry* 23: 22–37. [CrossRef]

Singhapakdi, Anusorn, Janet K Marta, Kumar C Rallapalli, and C. P. Rao. 2000. Toward an understanding of religiousness and marketing ethics: An empirical study. *Journal of Business Ethics* 27: 305–19. [CrossRef]

Smith, Daniel Jordan. 2008. *Culture of Corruption: Everyday Deception and Popular Discontent in Nigeria, Culture of Corruption: Everyday Deception and Popular Discontent in Nigeria*. Princeton: Princeton University Press.

Smith-Crowe, Kristin, and Danielle E. Warren. 2014. The emotion-evoked collective corruption model: The role of emotion in the spread of corruption within organizations. *Organization Science* 25: 1154–71. [CrossRef]

Sonenshein, Scott. 2007. The role of construction, intuition, and justification in responding to ethical issues at work: The sensemaking-intuition model. *Academy of Management Review* 32: 1022–40. [CrossRef]

Staw, Barry M. 1976. Knee-deep in the big muddy: A study of escalating commitment to a chosen course of action. *Organizational Behavior and Human Performance* 16: 27–44. [CrossRef]

Tileaga, Cristian. 2012. The right measure of guilt: Moral reasoning, transgression and the social construction of moral meanings. *Discourse & Communication* 6: 203–22. [CrossRef]

Torsello, Davide. 2010. Corruption and the economic crisis: Empirical indications from Eastern Europe. *International Issues & Slovak Foreign Policy Affairs* 19: 65–75.

Torsello, Davide, and Bertrand Venard. 2016. The Anthropology of Corruption. *Journal of Management Inquiry* 25: 34–54. [CrossRef]

Treisman, Daniel. 2007. What Have We Learned about the Causes of Corruption from Ten Years of Cross-National Empirical Research? *Annual Review of Political Science* 10: 211–44. [CrossRef]

Trevino, Linda Klebe. 1986. Ethical decision making in organizations—A person-situation interactionist model. *Academy of Management Review* 11: 601–17. [CrossRef]

Turgeman-Goldschmidt, Orly. 2008. Meanings that hackers assign to their being a hacker. *International Journal of Cyber Criminology* 2: 382–96.

Vadera, Abhijeet K., and Michael G. Pratt. 2013. Love, hate, ambivalence, or indifference? A conceptual examination of workplace crimes and organizational identification. *Organization Science* 24: 172–88. [CrossRef]

Vaiman, Vlad, Throstur Olaf Sigurjonsson, and Pall Asgeir Davidsson. 2011. Weak business culture as an antecedent of economic crisis: The case of Iceland. *Journal of Business Ethics* 98: 259–72. [CrossRef]

Van Rijckeghem, Caroline, and Beatrice Weder. 2001. Bureaucratic corruption and the rate of temptation: Do wages in the civil service affect corruption, and by how much? *Journal of Development Economics* 65: 307–31. [CrossRef]

Verhezen, Peter. 2009. *Gifts, Corruption, Philanthropy: The Ambiguity of Gift Practices in Business/Peter Verhezen*. New York: Lang.

Victor, Bart, and John B. Cullen. 1988. The organizational bases of ethical work climates. *Administrative Science Quarterly* 33: 101–25. [CrossRef]

Walton, Grant W. 2013a. An argument for reframing debates about corruption: Insights from Papua New Guinea. *Asia Pacific Viewpoint* 54: 61–76. [CrossRef]

Walton, Grant W. 2013b. Is all corruption dysfunctional? Perceptions of corruption and its consequences in Papua New Guinea. *Public Administration and Development* 33: 175–90. [CrossRef]

Weick, Karl E. 1979. *The Social Psychology of Organizing*, 2nd ed. Reading: Addison-Wesley Pub. Co.

Weick, Karl E., and Karlene H. Roberts. 1993. Collectove mind in organizations—Heedful interrelating on flight decks. *Administrative Science Quarterly* 38: 357–81. [CrossRef]

Zheng, Weiting, Kulwant Singh, and Will Mitchell. 2015. Buffering and enabling: The impact of interlocking political ties on firm survival and sales growth. *Strategic Management Journal* 36: 1615–36. [CrossRef]

Zilber, Tammar B. 2002. Institutionalization as an interplay between actions, meanings, and actors: The case of a rape crisis center in Israel. *Academy of Management Journal* 45: 234–54. [CrossRef]

Znoj, Heinzpeter. 2007. Deep Corruption in Indonesia: Discourses, practices, histories. In *Corruption And the Secret of Law: A Legal Anthropological Perspective*. Edited by Monique Nuijten and Gerhard Anders. Aldershot and Burlington: Ashgate.

Zyglidopoulos, Stelios C., and Peter J. Fleming. 2008. Ethical distance in corrupt firms: How do innocent bystanders become guilty perpetrators? *Journal of Business Ethics* 78: 265–74. [CrossRef]

administrative
sciences

MDPI

Article

Organising the Monies of Corporate Financial Crimes via Organisational Structures: Ostensible Legitimacy, Effective Anonymity, and Third-Party Facilitation

Nicholas Lord [1,*], **Karin van Wingerde** [2] **and Liz Campbell** [3]

1   Centre for Criminology and Criminal Justice, University of Manchester, Manchester M13 9PL, UK
2   Erasmus School of Law, Erasmus University Rotterdam, 3000 DR Rotterdam, The Netherlands;
     vanwingerde@law.eur.nl
3   School of Law, Durham University, Durham DH1 3LE, UK; liz.campbell@durham.ac.uk
*   Correspondence: nicholas.lord@manchester.ac.uk

Received: 9 April 2018; Accepted: 17 May 2018; Published: 19 May 2018

Abstract: This article analyses how the monies generated for, and from, corporate financial crimes are controlled, concealed, and converted through the use of organisational structures in the form of otherwise legitimate corporate entities and arrangements that serve as vehicles for the management of illicit finances. Unlike the illicit markets and associated 'organised crime groups' and 'criminal enterprises' that are the normal focus of money laundering studies, corporate financial crimes involve ostensibly legitimate businesses operating within licit, transnational markets. Within these scenarios, we see corporations as primary offenders, as agents, and as facilitators of the administration of illicit finances. In all cases, organisational structures provide opportunities for managing illicit finances that individuals alone cannot access, but which require some element of third-party collaboration. In this article, we draw on data generated from our Partnership for Conflict, Crime, and Security Research (PaCCS)-funded project on the misuse of corporate structures and entities to manage illicit finances to make a methodological and substantive addition to the literature in this area. We analyse two cases from our research—corporate bribery in international business and corporate tax fraud—before discussing three main findings: (1) the ostensible legitimacy created through abuse of otherwise lawful business arrangements; (2) the effective anonymity and insulation afforded through such misuse; and (3) the necessity for facilitation by third-party professionals operating within a stratified market. The analysis improves our understanding of how and why business offenders misuse what are otherwise legitimate business structures, arrangements, and practices in their criminal enterprise.

Keywords: corporate financial crimes; organisational crime; corporate bribery; corporate tax fraud; corporate vehicles; money laundering; illicit finance; proceeds of crime

---

1. Introduction

While it has long been recognised that corporate financial crimes generate financial advantages that substantially exceed those of other serious crimes, such as counterfeiting, illicit drugs, prostitution, and gambling (McGurrin and Friedrichs 2010), research on corporate crimes has mainly focused on their nature and size, their explanations or determinants, their harms and victims, or their regulation and enforcement (for an overview see (Levi and Lord 2017)). The specific issue of how the financial aspects of corporate crimes, in terms of both operational costs and profits generated, are managed remains under-theorised. This is even more apparent as law enforcement authorities in many countries have adopted a 'follow-the-money' approach in the supervision and enforcement of corporate financial crimes (Nelen 2008; Kruisbergen 2017; Kruisbergen et al. 2016) alongside an increasing focus on the financial organisations (e.g., banks) and professionals (e.g., lawyers, accountants) that enable and facilitate such crimes (Middleton and Levi 2015). In this article, we seek to better understand the intersections of organisations and corporate financial crimes with particular focus on the use of otherwise legitimate organisational structures as a means of controlling illicit finances. Furthermore, we explore the theoretical benefits that can be gained by approaching these issues from an integrated criminological and organisational studies perspective.

The misuse of organisational structures and entities in this way notably came to prominence in the 2016 leak of 11.5 million files at the centre of the Panama Papers scandal, though it has been on the international policy agenda since the start of the 21st Century (OECD 2001). This is not to imply that organisational structures have not been misused historically, but the foregrounding of the issue by the OECD in 2001 was the driver of subsequent policy and scientific agendas. The Panama Papers provided insights into the flows of (illicit) monies through the global financial system and the extensive concealment of legally, unethically, and illegally generated wealth. The spotlight in the case of the Panama Papers fell on Mossack Fonseca, a law firm and company service provider (CSP) based in Panama that specialises in creating offshore companies in jurisdictions such as the British Virgin Islands and the Bahamas to act as conduits for the movement of finances. In 2017, the Paradise Papers leak reaffirmed how such financial arrangements endure transnationally, with the CSP Appleby being scrutinised for its role in facilitating the control of questionable wealth. The implication raised in the Panama and Paradise Papers is that these legal structures are being misused and abused for illicit and illegitimate purposes, such as the evasion and avoidance of tax by wealthy individuals, the concealment of corrupt funds by public officials, and other criminal behaviours, such as money laundering.

With the above in mind, this article analyses how the monies generated for, and from, corporate financial crimes are controlled, concealed, and converted via organisational structures. These organisational structures take many forms, and we focus here on what are termed 'corporate vehicles', which are otherwise legitimate corporate structures and arrangements that facilitate illicit money management. Unlike the illicit markets and associated 'organised crime groups' and 'criminal enterprises' that are the normal focus of money laundering studies, corporate financial crimes involve ostensibly legitimate businesses operating within licit, transnational markets. Within these scenarios, the corporate entity can be the primary offender, an agent of the crime, and/or a facilitator of the management of illicit finances. We focus here on the opportunities presented by these organisational structures in the management of illicit finances that individuals alone cannot access but which require some form of third-party assistance and/or collaboration.

This article is structured as follows. First, we explain what we mean by organisational structures and vehicles, and elaborate on their significance to organisational studies before going on to concretise the intersections of 'corporate crime' and the misuse of otherwise legitimate organisations and organisational structures in corporate financial crimes. Second, we expand on our methodology. Methodologically, there has been no other attempt (that we are aware of) to integrate the identification and assessment of existing empirical materials on the misuse of corporate vehicles using a Rapid Evidence Assessment with insights gained through interview data and case study analysis. Third, we present two case studies from the research—corporate bribery in international business and corporate tax fraud—to ground the nature of the research phenomenon. We use these cases to demonstrate how the findings here are not limited to the idiosyncrasies of specific corporate financial crime types (e.g., corruption and fraud) or specific jurisdictions (e.g., the U.K. and the Netherlands) but have broader global relevance. For instance, corporate financial crimes can differ in terms of their inherent and central processes but all can misuse legitimate organisations to their advantage. Fourth, we analyse three main findings: (1) the ostensible legitimacy created through the misuse of otherwise legitimate business arrangements; (2) the effective anonymity and insulation afforded through such misuse; and (3) the necessary role of third-party professionals that operate within a stratified market. In terms of our substantive contribution to the literature, while the misuse of corporate vehicles has been discussed in the context of organised crime and corruption, it has not been sufficiently analysed in relation to corporate and white-collar crimes and we begin to address this gap here. Finally, we conclude by arguing that this analysis improves our understanding of how business offenders misuse what are otherwise legitimate business structures, arrangements, and practices in their criminal enterprise.

2. Corporate Financial Crimes and Organisational Structures

Conceptually, the focus in this article is on what has been traditionally referred to as 'corporate crime'. That is, those offences, whether criminal, civil, or administrative, that are undertaken by corporate officials (variously dispersed, but representative of the corporate entity) or the corporate entity itself (Clinard and Yeager 1980) or otherwise articulated as offences 'for a firm by the firm or its agents in the conduct of its business' (Hartung 1950, p. 25). That otherwise 'respectable' organisations and corporations are regularly implicated in criminal behaviours is not new; major scandals, such as the LIBOR rigging involving financial institutions including Barclays and UBS, or accounting frauds as with Tesco Plc, or the facilitation of money laundering as with HSBC and Deutsche Bank, give us insight into how the corporation and its environment can be conducive to an array of illicit behaviours for corporate and individual gain at the expense of public and private actors. Empirical evidence has reinforced the widespread, pervasive, and extensive nature of corporate crimes (Sutherland 1983; Clinard and Yeager 1980; Braithwaite 1985; Tombs and Whyte 2015).

It has long been recognised that corporate crimes are also 'organised', both formally and informally (Sutherland 1983, pp. 229–30), and are incentivised and made possible through otherwise legitimate business structures (Levi and Lord 2017). It is this latter point that is of most importance here given our interest in the organisation of the finances of corporate crimes through organisational structures. For instance, it is necessary to understand how corporate offenders confront problems, such as managing the finances for, and from, their criminal behaviours, and the legitimate business structures that shape how, why, and under which conditions they are able to do this over time and place (Edwards and Levi 2008; Lord and Levi 2017). An interesting and important feature of these crimes is that the business offenders have legitimate access to the offending environment (i.e., the organisation and its structures), have spatial separation from likely victims (e.g., market investors), and involve criminal behaviours that appear common and routine within occupational practice providing a superficial appearance of legitimacy and straightforward concealment (Benson and Simpson 2018). Thus, the organisation, or corporation, in addition to providing opportunities and conducive environments for offending behaviours, can be (a) a primary offender, (b) an agent, weapon, conduit, tool, or location for offending, and (c) a facilitator of third party criminality. (Of course, the organisation can also be the victim as well the 'cure' for its own ailments (see Meerts 2018, in this Special Issue)).

The misuse of legitimate organisational structures, and corporate vehicles specifically, has received more academic attention in relation to the concept of 'organised crime' (Ruggiero 2017a) as opposed to corporate and white-collar crimes. For instance, it has been evidenced that organised crime groups may use corporate vehicles to launder illegal profits (e.g., from the drugs trade), to generate income (e.g., boiler room frauds), to avoid personal liability (e.g., as in bankruptcy frauds), or to legitimise other activities (e.g., using a business as a 'front' for illicit market trade) (see Van de Bunt et al. 2007). Additionally, cases of 'blackwashing' or 'reverse money laundering', where legally acquired assets are used to fund criminal activities, have also been analysed (see for example Zabyelina 2015). Money laundering, tax evasion, and bribery in which we see the misuse of 'corporate vehicles' are typically phenomena that transcend the categorical distinctions between corporate and organised crime (see also Ruggiero 2017b). Corporate and organised criminals adopt similar techniques and structures to commit their crimes. At the same time, however, the distinction between the two may inform different institutional responses. Ruggiero (2017a) therefore argues to analyse similarities and differences between the techniques used in corporate and organised crimes. Analysing and comparing the misuse of corporate vehicles in 'organised crime' and 'corporate crime' is a worthy subject for inquiry, and an issue we explore as part of our Partnership for Conflict, Crime and Security Research (PaCCS) project.

However, our focus here is on the opportunities presented by organisational structures in the context of corporate crimes that individuals alone would not be able to realise. These structures enable individuals to manage, conceal, and transfer their illicit finances. This phenomenon, with particular focus on corporate financial crimes, necessitates an analysis of how legitimate business practices and structures facilitate these criminal behaviours by employees internal to and representative of corporations that engage in financial crime in 'glocal', often deterritorialised, markets over time. These organisational structures take many forms (e.g., limited companies, foundations, charities, partnerships) and we focus here specifically on what have been termed 'corporate vehicles' as one organisational form.

3. Methodology and Data

The findings are based on data generated as part of a broader comparative project funded by the PaCCS investigating the use of corporate structures in the organisation of serious and organised crimes, including corporate financial crimes. The research is being undertaken in the U.K. and the Netherlands. While the focus is often on offshore financial centres, mainland U.K. and the Netherlands also provide secrecy: the creation of such structures are not the sole prerogative of overseas territories.

We used a mixture of methods to generate data and insights into understanding how, why, and under which conditions those involved in corporate financial crimes misuse corporate vehicles for the concealment, conversion, and control of illicit finance. First, we undertook a Rapid Evidence Assessment (REA) of the available academic literature. Our REA took place between June 2017 and August 2017 and involved an overview of existing scholarship on the topic of 'corporate vehicles and illicit finance'. The purpose of the REA was to develop a 'state of the art' synthesis of the academic literature in the context of an array of 'serious crimes', covering both white-collar and corporate crimes but also behaviours more commonly associated with organised crime, such as money laundering and corruption. Table 1 provides an overview of the REA focus, key primary and alternative concepts, and databases searched. Key words included a mixture of analytical concepts and crime types. Three databases engines were utilised: ProQuest, Scopus, and Web of Science.

Table 1. The Rapid Evidence Assessment (REA).

Topic Statement	The Misuse of Corporate Vehicles in the Organisation of Serious Crimes
Time Period	Not restricted
Geographical Scope	Global (English speaking)
Primary Concepts	'corporate vehicle', '(offshore) trust', 'limited company', '(offshore) foundation', 'listed company', '(offshore) partnership', 'shell-company', 'shell firm'
Secondary Concepts	'illicit finance', 'serious crime', 'white-collar crime', 'crime proceeds/proceeds of crime', 'dirty money', 'money laundering', 'fraud', 'criminal enterprise', 'organised crime', 'corporate crime', 'financial crime', 'tax evasion', 'offshore'
Databases searched	- ProQuest (44 Databases: see website) - SCOPUS - Web of Science

Primary and *secondary inclusion criteria* were then applied to the search query hits. Table 2 provides an overview of the search queries and hits in addition to the sources that met the inclusion criteria. The search included only peer-reviewed journal articles that had 'full text' availability and that were written in English. There was no date range restriction. All hits were then manually examined to determine their relevance to the topic statement. As a consequence, many hits from the search queries were omitted. This resulted in a total of 132 relevant academic publications following the application of the primary inclusions criteria. The application of the secondary criteria involved a further manual sift of the hits to identify only those publications based on empirical research and of direct relevance to the REA question. These stringent criteria narrowed the number of relevant hits substantially to 21 articles with an empirical underpinning of relevance for our research question.

Table 2. REA Search Hits Following Primary and Secondary Inclusion Criteria.

Primary Concept	Query	Secondary Concepts	Primary Inclusion Criteria	Secondary Inclusion Criteria
"corporate vehicle"			28	7
"trust"		("illicit finance" OR "serious crime" OR "white-collar crime" OR "white collar crime" OR "crime proceeds" OR "proceeds of crime" OR "dirty money" OR "money laundering" OR "fraud" OR "criminal enterprise" OR "organised crime" OR "organized crime" OR "corporate crime" OR "financial crime" OR "tax evasion" OR "offshore")	N/A	N/A
"offshore trust"			13	1
"limited company"			14	3
"foundation"	AND		N/A	N/A
"offshore foundation"			0	0
"listed company"			20	1
"partnership"			N/A	N/A
"offshore partnership"			4	0
"shell company"			47	9
"shell firm"			6	0
			132	21

N/A = not applicable.

The texts of all publications were imported into NVivo.[1] All texts were then read by each of the investigators and analysed in terms of their methodological quality and rigour and the relevance of the empirical findings for answering our research question.

Second, semi-structured interviews were conducted with 35 actors from law enforcement, public authorities, financial institutions, non/inter-governmental organisations, professional services, and academia primarily in the Netherlands and the U.K. This included an expert group meeting with 11 key actors from enforcement authorities, professional services (law firms), and academia in July 2017. The interviews and expert group meeting were designed to understand when and why the use of corporate vehicles might be problematic, the definitional and legal landscape surrounding corporate vehicles, the nature and organisation of the misuse of corporate vehicles for financial gain, and regulation and enforcement of the misuse of corporate vehicles and possible obstacles inhibiting successful enforcement. All interviews lasted on average an hour and were thereafter transcribed. All interviews were analysed using NVivo. The interviews were analysed iteratively, meaning that there were constant shifts between the data and the literature and regular meetings were held to discuss and interpret the data.

Our analysis below (see 'Discussion') is directly informed by the literature identified in our REA and our interview data. We arrange our discussion around three prominent themes that emerged during the analysis of the literature and during our interviews, and draw on these sources to build our conceptual and theoretical insights into the nature and purpose of misuse. In this sense, we triangulate our data to corroborate our core findings. We do not include all literature identified as part of the REA as some was not directly relevant to the organisational aspects of corporate crimes but was concerned with 'organised crime'. Our analysis does not include direct quotes from our interviews but is arranged to discuss core themes in a more integrated, narrative style.

---

[1] NVivo is analysis software designed for managing qualitative data but can also be utilised in the coding of literature.

4. Case Studies

Corporate financial crimes take many forms. In order to concretise the nature of how organisational structures can be misused, we present two cases from our analysis concerned with corporate bribery in international business (i.e., corruption in commerce) and corporate tax fraud (i.e., intentional dishonesty at the expense of public funds). These cases were selected to provide an illustrative account of *how* organisational structures can be misused in corporate financial crimes. In these terms, the cases are not necessarily representative of all cases we encountered but are useful as heuristics to stimulate further investigation. First, we discuss the BAE Systems bribery case. We used open sources in our description and analysis of the case; specifically, court documents and media reports. The second case was derived from the Dutch Organised Crime Monitor, an ongoing systematic analysis of closed large-scale police investigation into organised crime in the Netherlands. It has existed since 1996 and aims to gain insight into the nature of organised crime in the Netherlands and its developments and to use this knowledge to optimise the prevention and fight against organised crime.[2] We chose a case of corporate tax fraud that illustrates how these corporate structures are being misused.

4.1. Corporate Bribery in International Business

When organisations, and corporations in particular, are implicated in bribery in international business, it means those actors operating within the organisation (i.e., employees or senior managers), or on behalf of the organisation (e.g., intermediaries, subsidiaries, or agents), have engaged in an illicit relation of exchange with a foreign public official (or their agent), either as instigator or on request, to win or maintain a business advantage for their organisation (Lord 2014a; Lord and Doig 2014). Bribery in business is a core focus of international conventions such as the OECD Anti-Bribery Convention 1997 and the UN Convention against Corruption, with such behaviours now constructed as universal social bads, particularly in those countries with large shares of world exports (i.e., key players in international commerce, though some remain absent, such as China and India) (Lord 2014b, 2015). Consequently, enforcement and regulation domestically is a priority concern for nation states seeking to communicate an image of active enforcement of such criminality (and perhaps normative superiority) to those international moral entrepreneurs, such as Transparency International, that scrutinise how they respond to their corporations that bribe. The misuse of 'corporate vehicles' is common in, and at the centre of, the organisation of many cases of corporate bribery and related finances.

The Case of BAE Systems

In 2010, BAE Systems (BAES), the U.K.'s largest arms manufacturer, agreed to pay criminal fines in the U.S.[3] ($400 million) and U.K.[4] (£0.5 million) to settle charges related to failures in accounting and bookkeeping but in connection to allegations of bribing foreign public officials in Saudi Arabia, Tanzania, the Czech Republic, and Hungary to win or maintain arms contracts.

In the case of Saudi Arabia, bribes totalling over £6 billion were allegedly paid to Saudi officials as part of a series of defence contracts signed between the U.K. and Saudi Arabian governments. In 1985, the initial al-Yamamah I arms deal (al-Yamamah II was signed in 1988) involved the provision of defence equipment, such as Tornado and Hawk aircraft, in exchange for up to 600,000 barrels of oil a day. The deal was worth around £43 billion. However, finances for the bribes were created by inflating prices to enable 'kickbacks' to be paid which covered extravagant expenses, such as yachts, sports cars, a private jet, and cash payments. The finances for these inducements were organised through shell

---

2   The second author had access to these cases through a previous commissioned study in anticipation of legislative changes in the Netherlands with regard to the supervision and control of corporate vehicles (Van de Bunt et al. 2007).
3   https://www.justice.gov/opa/pr/bae-systems-plc-pleads-guilty-and-ordered-pay-400-million-criminal-fine.
4   https://www.caat.org.uk/resources/companies/bae-systems/r-v-bae-sentencing-remarks.pdf.

companies located in offshore locations and bank accounts in more secretive jurisdictions. For instance, according to court documents, BAES made a series of substantial payments to shell companies and third-party intermediaries that were not sufficiently scrutinised but were used to conceal the use of 'marketing advisors' and the provision of 'support services':

> BAES contracted with and paid certain advisors through various offshore shell companies beneficially owned by BAES. BAES also encouraged certain advisors to establish their own offshore shell companies to receive payments from BAES while disguising the origins and recipients of these payments. (DoJ 2010, para. 8)

Figure 1 provides a visualisation of these organisational arrangements. In one such instance, BAES established a shell company called *Red Diamond Trading International Ltd.* in the British Virgin Islands (BVI) in order to: (i) conceal its marketing advisor relationships (identity and payments); (ii) create obstacles for investigating authorities; (iii) to circumvent laws prohibiting such relationships; and (iv) to assist advisors in avoiding tax liabilities for payments from BAES. Through *Red Diamond*, BAES made payments of more than £135 million despite being aware the funds would be used to influence contract decisions in foreign governments. In another instance, in one 20-month period, BAES paid over £8 million to a front company called *Robert Lee International (RLI)* created by BAES to entertain top Saudi officials[5] with payments transferred via intermediary-owned bank accounts in Switzerland. Payments were also concealed through other front companies created by BAES.[6]

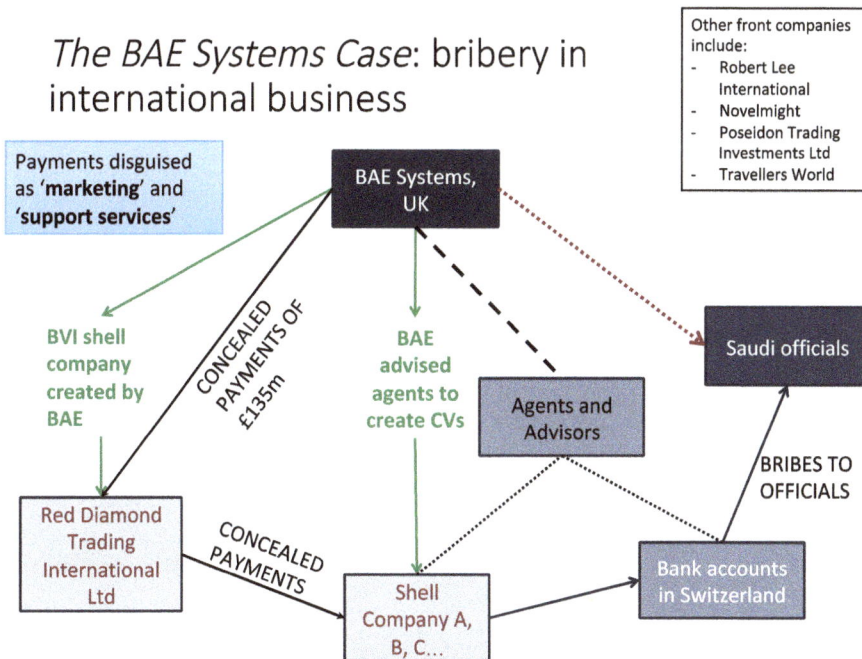

Figure 1. Corporate vehicles (CVs) and BAE Systems Bribery Scandal.

5 https://www.theguardian.com/world/2003/sep/11/bae.freedomofinformation.
6 https://www.theguardian.com/baefiles/page/0,,2095840,00.html.

The use of organisations as structures for illicit finance in this way in cases of corruption is common. An analysis of 213 'grand' corruption cases between 1980 and 2010 identified that over 70% (150) involved the use of at least one corporate vehicle that concealed, at least in part, beneficial ownership. In total, 817 corporate vehicles were used in those 150 cases and the U.K. and its crown dependencies and overseas territories had the second highest number of registered corporate vehicles behind the U.S. (Van der Does de Willebois et al. 2011).

4.2. Corporate Tax Fraud

Tax fraud covers a range of behaviours that involve deception and/or dishonesty for financial gain, such as tax evasion and other forms of non- or under-payment of tax liabilities. A broader conceptualisation that is not limited by criminal law doctrine might focus on tax non-compliance, where we see tax avoidance and aggressive tax planning, particularly by large multi-national corporations. These behaviours are characterised by an improper transfer of money to those evading tax and away from public funds (Leighton 2010, p. 526). Tax frauds reduce tax performance that in turn can increase the tax burden for those who are compliant (Torgler 2010, p. 535). The creation of offshore corporate vehicles through which to conceal, convert, and control finances generated through tax fraud is a common modus operandi. Offshore secrecy havens and the use of corporate vehicles enable rich individuals and corporate elites to pay small amounts of tax and facilitate the concealment of tax fraud schemes and associated proceeds (Levi 2010, p. 495).

The Case of Jansen BV

This case illustrates the combination of tax fraud and the laundering of its proceeds using various corporate vehicles. This case revolves around the Dutch textile wholesale company Jansen BV[7] that had been importing textiles from China and Hong Kong for many years. Mr. Jansen was the CEO of the company and its only shareholder. In order to pay less tax, the following simple but effective construction was set up. First, Mr. Jansen bought the shares of two corporate vehicles abroad. The first vehicle is Wemax Ltd., an offshore company established and based in Hong Kong. The other company is Tejeko NV, which was established in the Dutch Antilles. Mr. Jansen was the sole shareholder of both companies and has full control over both companies. The management of these companies was, however, based in local trust offices in Hong Kong and Curacao.

Wemax Ltd. was placed between Jansen BV and the supplier of textiles in Hong Kong. On paper, Wemax Ltd. purchased the textiles and then sold them to Jansen BV who paid its dues on Wemax's foreign bank account. Consequently, the original supplier of the textiles in Hong Kong had now been concealed for the Netherlands Tax and Customs Administration and it had been made to look as if Jansen BV only did business with Wemax Ltd. Wemax Ltd. then fictitiously doubled the price for the textiles: the original purchase price of €750,000 was raised on paper to €1,500,000. The invoices were addressed to Jansen BV that paid these and included the invoices in its annual reports and tax returns. Wemax Ltd. thus received €1,500,000. Of this, €750,000 was paid to the original supplier of the textiles and the remaining €750,000 was actually 'saved' on the bank account of Wemax Ltd. On paper, the origin of the money is legitimate—from the sale of textiles—and could be withdrawn from the company without actual taxes being paid. After a few years, Jansen had saved approximately €3,000,000 on Wemax Ltd.'s bank account in Hong Kong.

In order to actually use this money, Jansen needed the second corporate vehicle, Tejeko NV, based in the Dutch Antilles. Jansen wanted to use this money to buy a new office building in the Netherlands. Jansen's financial advisor recommended him to take out a loan from Tejeko NV for the amount of €3,000,000. As the money was still in the bank account of Wemax Ltd. in Hong Kong, the advisor also suggested to take out the money in cash as a bank transfer is easily traceable for the authorities.

---

7   Names are fictitious.

Therefore, Jansen flew to Hong Kong repeatedly and took out €3,000,000 in cash from Wemax Ltd.'s bank account. After the cash had been deposited on Tejeko NV's account, Tejeko NV provided a loan of €3,000,000 to Jansen BV in order to purchase the office building. The loan then appeared as a debt on Jansen BV's balance sheet. The following schematic illustrates this structure (Figure 2):

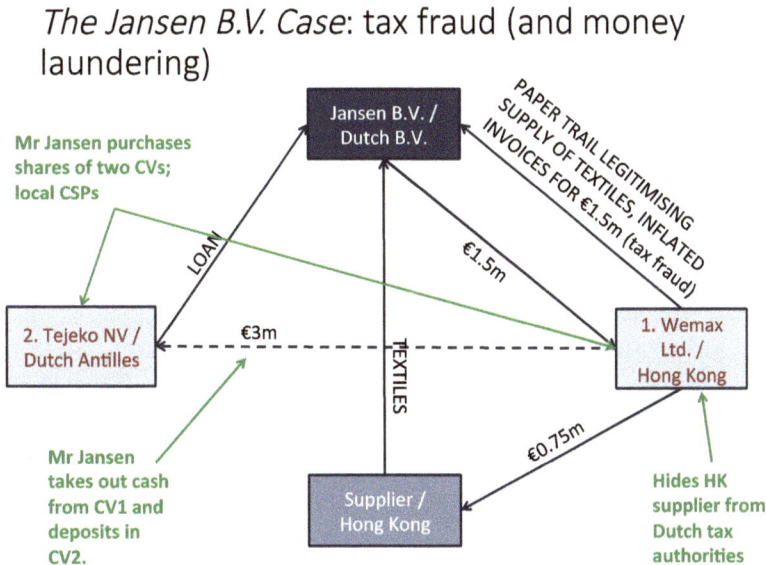

Figure 2. CVs and the Jansen BV tax fraud.

Through this scheme, Jansen has washed the money that he obtained criminally by tax fraud. After all, on paper, the money has been given a legitimate origin, namely a loan from a corporation in the Dutch Antilles. At the same time, he concealed the fact that he actually lent his own money. The result of this scheme is that the profit of Jansen BV was reduced artificially, which means that he had to pay less tax per year. Moreover, Jansen was withdrawing money from his company with which he created a pot of black money abroad that he could freely use afterwards. Also, in this case, the corporate vehicles have been specifically created or purchased for this purpose and their characteristics are attractive for misuse. The creation of the vehicles in Hong Kong and the Dutch Antilles does not require any minimum capital, which makes the setup relatively cheap. Offshore companies from Hong Kong are further characterised by the ability to guarantee anonymity of shareholders. Finally, this combination of vehicles in different jurisdictions, especially Hong Kong, creates problems for law enforcement authorities. Requesting information from these jurisdictions is extremely time-consuming and often fails.

5. Discussion

In this section, we integrate varied data sources to discuss three key findings in the organisation of illicit finances through organisational structures and *corporate* vehicles specifically. In particular, we focus here on (1) the ostensible legitimacy created through the misuse of otherwise legitimate business arrangements and practices in the use of organisational structures; (2) the anonymity and insulation afforded through such misuse; and (3) the necessary role of third-party professionals as (witting/unwitting) facilitators that operate within a stratified market. These three features are interconnected and overlap, as ostensible legitimacy and virtual anonymity cannot be accessed without third party assistance.

5.1. Ostensible Legitimacy: The Misuse of Legitimate Business Arrangements

The first key finding is that the misuse of certain organisational structures provides a veneer of legitimacy. This allows actors involved in corporate financial crimes to give their illicit behaviours a superficial appearance of legitimate action given the close proximity of these financial arrangements to normal business practice. Thus, the illicit practices are concealed. We use the term 'ostensibly' to reflect that while the structures misused are, technically, both legitimate and lawful, in the context of criminal misuse they have only an illegitimate purpose. (Though they could also be used for legitimate purposes). This is important to recognise as it is the ostensible nature provided, rather than the criminal misuse of something legitimate, that is the attractive feature.

According to the OECD (2001, p. 13), corporate vehicles can be defined as 'legal entities through which a wide variety of commercial activities are conducted and assets are held'. These vehicles include a range of organisational forms, often referred to as shell companies, and often have limited liability features. Furthermore, these legal structures permit businesses to incorporate companies in low- or no-tax regimes, provide flexibility in global markets, and reduce the level of regulation, particularly when set up in offshore financial centres that offer great secrecy, either by concealing the origin of the money or the identity of—what has become known as—the ultimate beneficial owner.[8] In these terms, the use of sophisticated corporate vehicles and structures 'to hide the origins of investments or to conceal beneficial ownership of property are legitimate' (Nelen 2008, p. 755). Thus, large flows of money, wealth, and assets move through or are controlled via the global financial system in this way, with (offshore and onshore) financial centres and companies enabling rich global elites, both individuals and companies, to manage their finances for varied legal (and illegal) purposes.

However, while their creation could be primarily for licit purposes, '[t]ransactions processed through the corporate account of a "shell company" become effectively untraceable and thus very useful for those looking to hide criminal profits, pay or receive bribes, finance terrorists, or escape tax obligations' (Sharman 2010a, p. 129). Since 2001, a number of intergovernmental and nongovernmental organisations have highlighted concerns over corporate vehicles being used to conceal criminal monies (OECD 2001; FATF/OECD 2006; Van der Does de Willebois et al. 2011; Otusanya and Lauwo 2012; Global Witness/Christian Aid 2012; Transparency International 2014). Thus, while corporate vehicles predominantly are used for legitimate purposes (e.g., transnational commerce and associated practices, such as mergers and acquisitions or tax planning), they also present opportunities for those involved in criminal enterprise to conceal and control illicit funds whilst maintaining anonymity through the obscuring of 'beneficial ownership' (FATF/OECD 2006, p. 1). Corporate financial crimes, such as bribery and tax frauds, generally involve finances that are already embedded within legitimate financial arrangements (e.g., contractual relations) and contexts (e.g., in bank accounts). This necessitates the use of other organisational structures to transfer the money, as moving such large amounts is improbable via cash or other value systems, although a company could provide credit cards or cash cards for use by perpetrators or beneficiaries both domestically and internationally.

That business offenders portray a pretence of respectability to disguise their underlying deviant behaviour has long been recognised in the criminological literature (Ross 1907; Sutherland 1983). This inherent duplicity and superficial appearance of legitimacy has emerged as a key feature in how most white-collar and corporate criminals realise opportunities for crime and remain undetected (Benson and Simpson 2018). For instance, the use of corporate vehicles as conduits for finance in itself

---

[8]   The Fourth EU Anti-Money Laundering Directive (2015) defines beneficial ownership as 'any natural person(s) who ultimately owns or controls the customer and/or the natural person(s) on whose behalf a transaction or activity is being conducted' (see also FATF/OECD 2016 and FATF/OECD and CFATF 2010). Thus, a 'beneficial owner' is 'a natural person—that is, a real, live human being, not another company or trust—who directly or indirectly exercises substantial control over the company or receives substantial economic benefits from the company' (Global Witness 2013, p. 3). Thus, key features are the control exercised and the benefit derived by those people that own the company (Van der Does de Willebois et al. 2011, p. 3).

does not indicate misuse. Similarly, in normal economic trade, it is perfectly legitimate not to act in one's own name but to take on another 'identity'. Business offenders are able to misuse these otherwise genuine financial arrangements as they construct ostensibly legitimate arrangements to obscure their underlying criminality. Organisational cultures can be conducive to those looking to rationalise such behaviours, making generating pro-social and ethical climates within corporations essential to reduce potential criminal behaviours (see Gorsira et al. 2018, in this Special Issue).

Licit corporate entities provide opportunities to act as structures for the concealment, conversion, and control of illicit finance by offering an external appearance of legitimacy to the 'beneficial owners' of these entities and/or the clients who use them to transfer funds. The hiding of true beneficial ownership in this way has been identified as the most significant feature of the misuse of corporate vehicles (FATF/OECD 2006, p. 2), and this is borne out in our interviews. This ostensible legitimacy is constructed in three primary ways:

- *Organisational forms*: business offenders are able to set up various organisational forms (e.g., limited companies, shell corporations, etc.), usually with assistance from third-party specialists (see below), to construct an ostensibly legitimate ownership arrangement. For instance, individual 'A' can be the beneficial owner of companies 'X', 'Y', and 'Z' and use these to conceal their own involvement.
- *Organisational relations*: business offenders can construct fabricated trading relations between those structures that have been arranged. For instance, individual 'A' can enter companies 'X', 'Y', and 'Z' into contractual or service arrangements that have no substance but enable falsified records to be generated.
- *Organisational practices*: once structures and relations are in place, business offenders can generate fictitious invoices and paper trails to enable finances to transfer via these structures (or appear to) in order for the true underling illicit monies to be concealed and legitimised. For instance, company 'X' can send electronic invoices to company 'Z' that acts as an interlocutor to company 'Y'. This layering approach can further obscure beneficial ownership and illicit finance.

Key to most cases of misuse is that the relationship between the natural persons (i.e., the ultimate beneficial owners) and the corporate vehicles is either concealed or proposed differently than in reality. In most cases of misuse, shell companies are used to conceal or convert the finances or the identity of the ultimate beneficial owners. Their life cycle strongly depends on the fictitious role that they play in the structure. Central to this fiction are practices of falsification, such as through fake invoices (i.e., inflated prices to reduce tax liabilities) or fabricated services (i.e., 'marketing' and 'support services' to disguise monies for bribery). In these cases, we see the parasitical nature of such occupational and organisational deviance as the business offenders implicated hide their criminality behind practices that have an appearance of legitimacy (Benson and Simpson 2018). This creates obstacles to detection for enforcement authorities.

5.2. Effective Anonymity (and Insulation)

The second key finding is that of effective anonymity. This allows those individuals involved in corporate financial crimes to conceal their identity, and offset possible intervention or enforcement of the law, providing a layer of insulation. Thus, the illicit actors themselves are *effectively*, but not entirely, concealed as there will always be some level of connection between the actors and the finances even where this is well-obscured. Corporate vehicles are attractive for criminals and unethical individuals and groups as they are set up in secretive jurisdictions that provide anonymity to their owners and the transactions processed through them effectively become untraceable. Thus, anonymity is a central purpose of using a corporate vehicle. In questioning why request anonymity, rather than a complex legal trail, Sharman (2010a, p. 133) states that '[e]ven if the legal trail is complex, as long as the service provider has proof of the identity of the ultimate beneficiary of a firm, the veil of secrecy is vulnerable to being pierced [despite it being difficult, time-consuming, and expensive to investigate]

. . . However, if no information is collected by the service provider in the first place, nothing can be disclosed later'. With this effective anonymity in mind, as Findley et al. (2013, p. 658) note, '[s]hell companies that cannot be traced back to their real owners are the standard vehicle of choice for those looking to hide illicit financial flows'. By using shell corporations as nominal account holders, extra layers of secrecy between bank accounts and beneficial owners can be created, essentially making such accounts equivalent to numbered accounts that now are prohibited by anti-money laundering regulations (Johannesen and Zucman 2014, p. 85).

The creation and misuse of corporate vehicles is often associated with so-called offshore financial centres and offshore tax havens. However, this may not necessarily be the reality. Sharman states that, in contradiction to conventional wisdom, his findings 'cast strong doubt on the proposition that the problem of financial opacity is caused by palm-fringed tropical islands, rather than large higher-income economies like the United States and Britain' (Sharman 2010a, p. 134). Indeed, our interviewees emphasised the misuse of companies and Scottish limited partnerships in the U.K. to maintain illicit assets (Campbell 2018a). While nearly all offshore centres regulate CSPs, the U.S. and Britain have chosen not to. Thus, 'powerful states are choosing to profit by not following the standards they have imposed on others' (Sharman 2011, p. 984). More generally though, the use of financial centres or tax havens, whether offshore or onshore, represents the pursuit of a 'calculated ambiguity' (Sharman 2010b, p. 2) as it permits obscurity to those looking to conceal (illicit) wealth. They also permit actors involved in criminal behaviour to separate themselves jurisdictionally from the victims of their crimes and from the enforcement and regulatory authorities, creating insulation to offenders.

Making transparent the true beneficial owner anonymised through offshore corporate structures has been identified as central to responding to 'a range of high-priority international problems: the drug trade, organised crime, terrorism, money laundering, tax evasion, corruption, corporate crime, and systemic financial instability' (Sharman 2010a, p. 129) and is at the core of the E.U.'s Fourth Anti-Money Laundering Directive (Campbell 2018b).

In Pursuit of Increased Transparency

Given concerns over the identification of the ultimate beneficial owners and the anonymity they can permit, companies are now required to register any owners with at least 25% stake in the company, and this may well be reduced to 10% in the future (Campbell 2018a, 2018b). However, arbitrary ownership thresholds are straightforward to circumvent as ownership can be split to fall within the threshold limit, ensuring continued anonymity. In other words, actors are able to structure ownership creatively in order to evade being registered as 'beneficial owners'. Similarly, data analysed from the first submission to the U.K.'s Public Register indicates that many requirements are not being met. Analysis by Global Witness indicated that '[a]lmost 3000 companies listed their beneficial owner as a company with a tax haven address, something that is not allowed under the rules', amongst other concerns about data inputting.[9] Thus, such registers may be 'utopian' and ineffective in the current environment given it depends on if and how they will be monitored and enforced. The key question therefore is who polices and monitors these registers and how inaccurate or opaque materials can be challenged. Enforcement of the rules is fundamental to pursuing transparency. This is further corroborated by the U.K.'s public authorities we interviewed, which pointed that out there is a 'compliance cost' to investigating misuse. For instance, obstacles are created as corporate vehicles may be set up in the U.K. but trade overseas. A further major stumbling block remains over the transparency of companies registered in overseas U.K. territories although in 2018 the U.K. government committed to ensuring these territories implement public registers by the end of 2020.

---

[9] https://www.globalwitness.org/en/blog/what-does-uk-beneficial-ownership-data-show-us/.

5.3. Third-Party Facilitation and Market Stratification

Our third finding is that the ostensible legitimacy and effective anonymity provided to individuals using corporate vehicles as structures for illicit finance almost always requires the involvement and facilitation of expert or professional third-party collaborators. Corporate vehicles can be relatively straightforwardly created and/or dissolved in onshore and offshore locations without proof of identity followed by establishing bank accounts for these entities (Sharman 2010a; Van de Bunt et al. 2007). Ownership structures can take many forms, with shares being issued to natural or legal persons in registered or bearer form, and they can have single or multiple purposes (FATF/OECD 2006; OECD 2001). Our research indicates that third-party legitimate actors (e.g., accountants, lawyers, other professionals) are necessary relations in the organisation of illicit finances in cases of corporate financial crimes. These actors can become witting, or unwitting (or wilfully blind), facilitators in particular when acting as CSPs to set up, service, and sell corporate vehicles and other shell companies (Ruggiero 2017a; Chaikin and Sharman 2009, p. 75; FATF/OECD and CFATF 2010; Lankhorst and Nelen 2005; OECD 2001). Such CSPs enable those engaged in illicit market and commercial enterprise to engage in legitimate business transactions and relations and to obscure the provenance and ownership of income, wealth, and assets by exploiting legal/regulatory lacunae and differences in legal/enforcement regimes.

A central issue for criminal actors is that in order to conceal their finance, some form of collusion and/or cooperation with external, professional actors, such as accountants, lawyers, and other professionals, may be required, though informational shielding and distortion may reduce the risks for them. As Levi (2015, p. 10) notes, 'this involves trust in a particular person or persons—perhaps a member of one's close or extended family or ethnic/religious group—or trust in an institution, such as a bank or a money service business (MSB) or a lawyer who may be a trustee of a corporate entity, to an extent sufficient to defeat whatever level of scrutiny will actually be applied'. A key question to ask therefore is how are these third-party actors recruited and how much do CSPs and facilitators actually know (or should do all they can to know) about the misuse of the companies that they create and are they complicit in their misuse for illicit purposes?

Empirical research has identified that 'more than one in four providers (26.2%) worldwide is willing to violate international standards by offering incorporation without certified proof of customer identity, meaning that in practice anonymous shell companies are readily available' (Findley et al. 2013, p. 660). Consequently, Findley et al. (2013) conclude that 'there is a substantial level of noncompliance with the international standards mandating that providers obtain certified identification documents from beneficial owners when forming shell companies' (p. 681) and that 'service providers are no more likely to comply with international rules when they are prompted about the existence and content of the rules' (p. 681). Similarly, in Sharman (2010a) audit study of compliance with the prohibition of anonymous shell companies, 45 providers responded to offer their services, of which 17 offered to set up an anonymous vehicle. Thirteen of the 17 successful approaches were to company service providers in OECD countries compared with only 4 in 28 countries labelled as 'tax havens'. In both studies, a key limitation was that they sought to enlist CSPs available publically but it can be expected that those global corporate and individual elites access CSPs via social network, making insights into these hidden connections difficult.

In these terms, our research indicates that a stratified market exists whereby CSPs that offer services publically online form only one segment. Other, more esoteric, CSPs do not advertise but rather involve introductions through personal networks or relations established at high-level events for elite clientele. Gaining access to these hidden service providers is problematic. In policy terms, increased attention to and responsibility of third-party intermediaries and actors who, whether knowingly, with willful blindness or through incompetence, facilitate the concealment of illegal behaviours is needed. Increased oversight of and intervention with these third party legal and accounting professionals is vital, not least as some seem to operate with impunity.

The Specific Role of Banks and Financial Institutions

Banks and financial institutions have a necessary role in enabling these illicit arrangements and as Ruggiero (2017a) notices offer a number of disconnects between the act committed and the beneficiaries of the crime. First, for illicit finances to be transferred via corporate vehicles, bank accounts need to be established. Second, banks also provide the infrastructure to allow monies to be transferred across the accounts of individual entities and for transactions to take place. Thus, banks and financial institutions are essentially the entry points to the financial system. Without banks and the financial system, the management of illicit finance cannot function. Given this central role, they are required to implement strict anti-money laundering requirements in relation to the 'onboarding' of new corporate and individual clients and the monitoring of suspicious transactions.

In terms of 'onboarding', our research has indicated that corresponding due diligence and client checks can be time-consuming and pervasive, in some cases up to eight months because of extensive checks, which in turn create pressures for financial institutions. Banks face internal and economic pressures not to lose clients and this is exacerbated when clients threaten to move to other providers where difficult questions are in some way circumvented. For instance, one concern for established financial institutions is the emergence of 'Challenger Banks' that promise clients to undertake due diligence processes much quicker but in doing so allow for more risk. While it is unclear whether or not there will be less oversight and more blind spots within challenger banks, it can be expected that it will be difficult for challenger banks to find the balance. However, as they tend to be innovative, they may find solutions to the 'problem'. As a consequence, there are cases whereby financial institutions, such as banks, are 'far too willing to do business with anonymous companies' (Global Witness 2013, p. 7). Banks are required to implement sufficient internal systems to identify and then report suspicious transactions and money laundering, but risk-based approaches to anti-money laundering are not consistent across the banking sector. Furthermore, 'the identification of "suspiciousness" by professionals and others with a legal responsibility to combat money laundering is often a judgment that the people and/or transactions are "out of place" for the sort of account they have and the people they purport to be' (Levi 2015, p. 10). We must question how, in cases such as BAES and Jansen BV, those involved are able to conceal their illicit behaviours from others.

6. Conclusions

Our core argument in this article is that organisational structures, and corporate vehicles in particular, provide opportunities to individuals involved in corporate financial crimes to enjoy and be insulated by an ostensible legitimacy and effective anonymity for the criminal behaviours and the criminal actors, respectively. Without the use of these organisational structures, individual actors would not be able to access such concealment opportunities in the course of their criminal behaviours.

For instance, corporate vehicles can be used to launder illegal profits. In the case of Jansen BV, a structure was created whereby Jansen retained anonymous control over the money generated through the tax fraud. The structure was aimed at misuse, since the corporate veil legitimised investing money from tax fraud into legitimate assets. However, corporate vehicles can be used to legitimise other activities. This is not primarily aimed at financial gain and includes situations in which the natural person does not hide behind the corporate veil, but rather uses it to disguise illegitimate activities. For example, in the case of BAES we see how corporate vehicles are created to provide an appearance of transactional legitimacy in the concealment of finances used for bribery. In both scenarios, these arrangements have been used to avoid personal liability. In the BAES case, for example, agents and advisors hid behind corporate vehicles constructed for illicit purposes with any commissions attached to bank accounts in the name of the corporate entity but under the control of those individual actors.

Of course, organisational structures can facilitate corporate crimes in more ways than organising finance. For example, in his research on the Madoff scandal, Van de Bunt (2010) shows that Madoff used the organisational structure of his firm to create isolation and to conceal the fraud from non-complicit employees. Madoff's Ponzi scheme originated from a separate department which was located on a separate floor. Thus, large and complex organisations may provide cover for corporate crimes through the division of tasks, decentralisation of decision-making, and specialisation of work. This stresses the importance of research into how corporate crimes are organised and facilitated through complex business structures. These arrangements are able to endure and withstand intervention as enforcement asymmetries, obstacles to cross-border information exchange, and cultures of corporate non-compliance globally create barriers to regulatory responses (Sharman 2010a, p. 138). For instance, our project's Expert Group Meeting attended by informed actors from public authorities, amongst other key organisations, identified tensions between (political and economic) openness to foreign investments/investors and the prevention of crime. Governments must seek to protect national economic interests whilst also communicating an image of enforcing strict international standards. Furthermore, the issue of information exchange and actually receiving relevant information from offshore jurisdictions was highlighted as a primary obstacle, demonstrating notable imbalances in enforcement structures and capabilities across jurisdictions.

By integrating criminological insights into the dynamics of the financial aspects of corporate financial crimes with an appreciation of the significance of the study of organisations and their features and associated practices, we have been able to gain theoretical insights into how and why the organisational form can provide opportunities for crimes that individuals alone cannot access. However, we recognise the need for further empirical research in this area to illuminate the connections between the location of individual and corporate criminality within an organisation and their place within more enduring financial arrangements and systems.

Author Contributions: All authors contributed to the design of the research, data collection and analysis and co-wrote the article. All authors read and approved the final manuscript.

Funding: This research was funded by the Partnership for Conflict, Crime and Security Research (PaCCS) grant number [ES/P001386/1].

Conflicts of Interest: The authors declare no conflict of interest.

References

Benson, Michael L., and Sally S. Simpson. 2018. *White-Collar Crime: An Opportunity Perspective*. London: Routledge.

Braithwaite, John. 1985. White-Collar Crime. *Annual Review of Sociology* 11: 1–25. [CrossRef]

Campbell, Liz. 2018a. Dirty Cash (Money Talks): 4AMLD and the Money Laundering Regulations 2017. *Criminal Law Review* 2018: 102–22.

Campbell, Liz. 2018b. The organisation of corruption in commercial enterprise: Concealing (and revealing) the beneficial ownership of assets. In *Corruption in Commercial Enterprise: Law, Theory and Practice*. Edited by Liz Campbell and Nicholas Lord. Oxon: Routledge.

Chaikin, David, and Jason C. Sharman. 2009. *Corruption and Money Laundering*. New York: Palgrave MacMillan.

Clinard, Marshall B., and Peter C. Yeager. 1980. *Corporate Crime*. New York: Free Press.

DoJ (Department of Justice). 2010. BAE Systems PLC Pleads Guilty and Ordered to Pay $400 Million Criminal Fine. DoJ, Office of Public Affairs. Available online: https://www.justice.gov/opa/pr/bae-systems-plc-pleads-guilty-and-ordered-pay-400-million-criminal-fine (accessed on 18 May 2018).

Edwards, Adam, and Michael Levi. 2008. Researching the organization of serious crimes. *Criminology and Criminal Justice* 8: 363–88. [CrossRef]

FATF/OECD. 2006. *The Misuse of Corporate Vehicles, Including Trust and Company Service Providers*. Paris: FATF/OECD.

FATF/OECD. 2016. *FATF Report to the G20: Beneficial Ownership*. Paris: FATF/OECD.

FATF/OECD, and CFATF. 2010. *Money Laundering Using Trust and Company Service Providers*. Paris: FATF/OECD, Port of Spain: CFATF.

Findley, Mark G., Daniel L. Nielson, and Jason C. Sharman. 2013. Using Field Experiments in International Relations: A Randomized Study of Anonymous Incorporation. *International Organization* 67: 657–93. [CrossRef]

Global Witness. 2013. *Anonymous Companies: How Secretive Shell Companies Are a Major Barrier in the Fight against Poverty and What to Do about It.* London: Global Witness.

Global Witness/Christian Aid. 2012. *Company Ownership: Which Places Are the Most and Least Transparent?* London: Global Witness/Christian Aid.

Gorsira, Madelijne, Linda Steg, Adriaan Denkers, and Wim Huisman. 2018. Corruption in Organizations: Ethical Climate and Individual Motives. *Administrative Sciences* 8: 4. [CrossRef]

Hartung, Frank E. 1950. White-Collar Offenses in the Wholesale Meat Industry in Detroit. *American Journal of Sociology* 56: 25–34.

Johannesen, Niels, and Gabriel Zucman. 2014. The End of Bank Secrecy? An Evaluation of the G20 Tax Haven Crackdown. *American Economic Journal: Economic Policy* 6: 65–91. [CrossRef]

Kruisbergen, Edwin W. 2017. Combating Organized Crime. A Study on Undercover Policing and the Follow-the- Money Strategy. Ph.D. dissertation, Vrije Universiteit Amsterdam, Amsterdam, The Netherlands. Available online: https://www.wodc.nl/onderzoeksdatabase/ov-201701-combating-organized-crime.aspx (accessed on 18 May 2018).

Kruisbergen, Edwin W., Edward R. Kleemans, and Ruud F. Kouwenberg. 2016. Explaining attrition: Investigating and confiscating the profits of organized crime. *European Journal of Criminology* 13: 1–19. [CrossRef]

Lankhorst, Francien, and Hans Nelen. 2005. Professional services and organised crime in the Netherlands. *Crime, Law, and Social Change* 42: 163–88. [CrossRef]

Leighton, Paul. 2010. Fairness matters—More than deterrence. Class bias and the limits of deterrence. *Criminology & Public Policy* 9: 525–33.

Levi, Michael. 2010. Serious Tax Fraud and Noncompliance. *Criminology and Public Policy* 9: 493–513. [CrossRef]

Levi, Michael. 2015. Money for Crime and Money from Crime: Financing Crime and Laundering Crime Proceeds. *European Journal on Criminal Policy and Research* 21: 275–95. [CrossRef]

Levi, Michael, and Nicholas Lord. 2017. White-Collar and Corporate Crimes. In *Oxford Handbook of Criminology*, 6th ed. Edited by Alison Liebling, Shadd Maruna and Lesley McAra. Oxford: OUP.

Lord, Nicholas. 2014a. *Regulating Corporate Bribery in International Business: Anti-Corruption in the UK and Germany.* Farnham: Ashgate Publishing.

Lord, Nicholas. 2014b. Responding to transnational corporate bribery using international frameworks for enforcement. *Criminology and Criminal Justice* 14: 100–20. [CrossRef]

Lord, Nicholas. 2015. Establishing enforcement legitimacy in the pursuit of rule-breaking "global elites": The case of transnational corporate bribery. *Theoretical Criminology* 20: 376–99. [CrossRef]

Lord, Nicholas, and Alan Doig. 2014. Corporate bribery of public and private officials. In *Encyclopedia of Criminology and Criminal Justice.* Edited by Gerben Bruinsma and David Weisburd. New York: Springer Verlag.

Lord, Nicholas, and Michael Levi. 2017. Organizing the finances for and the finances from transnational corporate bribery. *European Journal of Criminology* 14: 365–89. [CrossRef]

McGurrin, Danielle, and David O. Friedrichs. 2010. Victims of Economic Crime—On a Grand Scale. *International Journal of Victimology* 8: 147–57.

Meerts, Clarissa. 2018. The organisation as the cure for its own ailments: corporate investigators in the Netherlands. *Administrative Sciences* 8. forthcoming.

Middleton, David, and Michael Levi. 2015. Let Sleeping Lawyers Lie: Organized Crime, Lawyers and the Regulation of Legal Services. *British Journal of Criminology* 55: 647–68. [CrossRef]

Nelen, Hans. 2008. Real estate and serious forms of crime. *International Journal of Social Economics* 35: 751–62. [CrossRef]

OECD. 2001. Behind the Corporate Veil. Using Corporate Entities for Illicit Purposes. Available online: http://www.oecd.org/corporate/ca/43703185.pdf (accessed on 18 May 2018).

Otusanya, Olatunde J., and Sarah Lauwo. 2012. The role of offshore financial centres in elite money laundering practices: Evidence from Nigeria. *Journal of Money Laundering Control* 15: 336–61. [CrossRef]

Ross, Edward. 1907. The criminaloid. *The Atlantic Monthly* 99: 44–50.

Ruggiero, Vincenzo. 2017a. Networks of Greed. *Justice, Power and Resistance* 2: 3–23.

Ruggiero, Vincenzo. 2017b. *Dirty Money. On financial delinquency.* Oxford: Oxford University Press.

Sharman, Jason. 2010a. Shopping for Anonymous Shell Companies: An Audit Study of Anonymity and Crime in the International Financial System. *Journal of Economic Perspectives* 24: 127–40. [CrossRef]

Sharman, Jason. 2010b. Offshore and the new international political economy. *Review of International Political Economy* 17: 1–19. [CrossRef]

Sharman, Jason. 2011. Testing the Global Financial Transparency Regime. *International Studies Quarterley* 55: 981–1001. [CrossRef]

Sutherland, Edwin H. 1983. *White Collar Crime: The Uncut Version*. New Haven: Yale University Press.

Tombs, Steve, and David Whyte. 2015. *The Corporate Criminal: Why Corporations Must Be Abolished*. London: Routledge.

Torgler, Benno. 2010. Serious tax noncompliance. *Criminology & Public Policy* 9: 535–42.

Transparency International. 2014. *Hiding in Plain Sight: How UK Companies Are Used to Launder Corrupt Wealth*. London: Transparency International.

Van de Bunt, Henk G. 2010. Walls of secrecy and silence. The Madoff case and cartels in the construction industry. *Criminology & Public Policy* 9: 435–53.

Van de Bunt, Henk G., Jan van Koningsveld, Maarten J. Kroeze, Benny van der Vorm, Jan-Berend Wezeman, Karin van Wingerde, and Amber Zonnenberg. 2007. *Misuse of Corporate Vehicles in The Netherlands [Misbruik van buitenlandse rechtspersonen]*. Rotterdam: EITC.

Van der Does de Willebois, Emile, Emily M. Halter, Robert A. Harrison, Ji Won Park, and Jason C. Sharman. 2011. The Puppet Masters: How the Corrupt Use Legal Structures to Hide Stolen Assets and What to Do about It. Available online: https://star.worldbank.org/star/sites/star/files/puppetmastersv1.pdf (accessed on 18 May 2018).

Zabyelina, Yuliya G. 2015. Reverse money laundering in Russia: Clean cash for dirty ends. *Journal of Money Laundering Control* 18: 202–19. [CrossRef]

administrative
sciences

MDPI

Article

The Organisation as the Cure for Its Own Ailments: Corporate Investigators in The Netherlands

Clarissa Annemarie Meerts

Faculty of Law, Criminal Law and Criminology, VU University Amsterdam, 1081 HV Amsterdam,
The Netherlands; c.a.meerts@vu.nl

Received: 7 March 2018; Accepted: 6 June 2018; Published: 27 June 2018

Abstract: Public/private relations in the field of security attract considerable academic attention. Usually, the state is central to the analysis, focusing on the diminishing role of a previously dominant state. The role that organisations themselves play in the investigation and settlement of their internal norm violations is, however, much less researched. An emphasis on the role of the state downplays the importance of such actions. This research paper, based on qualitative data from the Netherlands, highlights the role of the organisation as the principal actor in corporate investigations and corporate settlements. The legal constraints upon and day-to-day activities of corporate investigators are considered and the consequences of the distance between public law enforcement actors and corporate security are reflected upon. The paper arrives at the conclusion that the limited insight into the measures taken by organisations in response to internal norm violation can be considered problematic from a democratic, rule-of-law point of view. The freedom of action enjoyed by organisations within the private legal sphere makes oversight and control quite challenging.

Keywords: corporate investigations; corporate settlements; internal norm violations; private justice

---

1. Introduction

In a case of theft and fencing of company property, multiple reactions were chosen against the people involved. There have been two reports to the police and two civil actions. In addition, assets were seized through civil measures, settlement agreements were used for the repayment of damages, twelve employees lost their job and eight employees received an official warning. [Case study 11—Meerts 2018]

It is not uncommon for instances of corporate and white-collar crime to be settled without the interference of criminal court (see for example Beckers 2017). Organisations tend to take their own measures—either with or without a criminal prosecution or settlement. These 'corporate settlement measures' are often based on corporate investigations, conducted by specialised investigators (Meerts 2018). With corporate settlement measures are meant those "solutions to norm violations, which may be derived from public law (criminal law), private law (contract law, tort or labour regulations) or internal regulations (of specific organisations)" (Meerts 2018, p. 22). This definition of corporate settlement is quite broad and contains both measures that are completely internal to the organisation (such as the official warnings in the case cited above) and measures that are external to the organisation (such as the criminal cases against the two employees in the case cited above). Although the criminal case itself is not a corporate settlement measure—the decision whether or not to prosecute lies with the prosecution office, not with the organisation—the decision to officially report to law enforcement authorities is. Reporting to law enforcement authorities is one of the options available to an organisation faced with internal crime.

The aim of this paper is to examine corporate security as an avenue of control exercised by organisations over their employees. The corporate security sector is under-researched: not much is known about the day-to-day activities of corporate investigators. This is an important gap in our knowledge, especially when we take into account the large and growing involvement of private parties in responding to undesirable behaviour (Walby and Lippert 2014). The paper thus aims to fill the gap in our empirical knowledge about corporate investigations, and to place this in the context of a recurring debate: that of public/private bifurcation (see Section 2 for more on this). The corporate security sector is defined here as a highly specialised market for corporate investigation services.[1] Although corporate investigators may be involved in additional activities (such as pre-employment screenings and drafting and implementing integrity codes), the investigative activities of corporate investigators are the focal point of this paper.[2] Investigative activities are mainly constituted by forensic accountancy, (private) investigations more generally, IT investigations, asset tracing, and (assistance with) settlement and prevention tactics (Williams 2005; Meerts 2013). Clients of corporate security may be both commercial and (semi-)public organisations.[3] This last category of organisations is an important source of clients for corporate investigators: in the Netherlands, the 25 largest municipalities have, over the last five years, ordered the investigation of more than 1900 internal norm violations.[4] In this research the following groups are considered to be part of the corporate security sector: private investigation firms, in-house security departments, forensic accountants and forensic (departments of) legal firms.[5]

This paper considers the role of corporate investigations in the identification and settlement of internal norm violations within organisations. The fact that the norm violation is internal to the organisation is important, since it provides the organisation with more possibilities to act upon the behaviour than when there is only external involvement. 'Norm violation' is a broad-scope concept, which may be used for all types of employee behaviour deemed problematic by an organisation. This 'problematic behaviour' may concern (alleged) criminal behaviour such as fraud, but it may just as well be about behaviour that is considered undesirable from the point of view of owners and managers of organisations, for example behaviour that is non-compliant to internal regulations (Richards 2008). All kinds of undesirable behaviour may be investigated by corporate investigators (see also below); however, many incidents that are investigated by corporate investigators have an economic background (theft, fraud, favouritism in the granting of contracts, and the like) (Williams 2006a).[6]

As a result of the employment relationship between the organisation and the person who is the subject of investigation, corporate investigators have extensive access to information. Although corporate security actors do not possess the formal *powers* of investigation enjoyed by law enforcement, their *possibilities* of investigation are extensive: through the (property) rights of the organisation as an employer, they are able to use much information about employees (for example by accessing internal systems). Additionally, the professional backgrounds of corporate investigators makes them adept in investigating open source data and in using investigative tactics (such as interviewing involved persons[7]). After investigations are concluded, corporate investigators may assist organisations

---

[1] Corporate security is a term that is often used in a much wider sense. In such a definition, all security-related activities of (mostly) in-house security are within the scope. Investigations are then part of corporate security but so are surveillance and other activities relating to physical security. In this paper, the focus is on investigations.

[2] Corporate investigators may also be involved in compliance functions. Although compliance may involve investigations, the main aim of compliance is prevention: measures and procedures are put in place to ensure compliance to rules. Corporate investigations, by contrast, focus on the situation in which prevention has failed and norm violations have occurred.

[3] In the case of an in-house corporate security department, the 'client' and investigator are part of the same organisation: for example the organisation's management.

[4] See NRC 28-02-2018 (https://www.nrc.nl/nieuws/2018/02/28/meer-onderzoek-naar-integriteit-door-gemeenten-a1594055).

[5] Forensic accountants and forensic legal investigators (lawyers) differ from regular accountants and lawyers with regard to their main activity. Regular accountants audit the financial administration of an organisation as part of their legally defined task, and regular lawyers are hired to represent their client in legal procedures. Forensic accountants and forensic legal investigators, by contrast, are hired to investigate as a result of a suspicion of a norm violation.

[6] This is not to say that corporate investigations are only conducted with regard to matters of economic crime. Other categories of behaviour which are often investigated internally include, for example, privacy violations and data leaks.

[7] An 'involved person' or 'subject' is what in the context of a criminal justice procedure would be called a 'suspect'. However, because corporate investigators lack formal powers of investigation and the formal procedural guarantees available in

in finding a solution, either by 'going public' (reporting to law enforcement) or 'staying private' (for example settling the incident as a labour dispute).

One of the characteristics of corporate investigations and 'corporate justice' is the emphasis on confidentiality. This, together with the view held by organisations and corporate investigators that the criminal justice system is inefficient and in most cases will not provide a suitable solution, means that most white-collar crimes that have been investigated by corporate investigators never reach the criminal justice system. It follows that the knowledge of the state about such internal investigations is fairly limited.

The above considerations culminate in the following research question: *What is the role of corporate investigators in the investigation and settlement of norm violations within organisations?* To answer this question, we need to examine (1) the legal frameworks within which corporate investigators operate (sub-question 1), (2) the investigative methods corporate investigators may use (sub-question 2) and (3) the settlements that are possible as a response to the corporate investigations (sub-question 3). These questions are answered with the help of empirical material collected in the context of this research.

The theoretical framework that provides the context for the discussion of the empirical findings is discussed in the next section of this paper. This is followed by the explication of the research methods that have been used to collect data. Section 4 examines the legal frameworks within which corporate security actors operate (sub-question 1), followed by Sections 5 and 6, which discuss the activities of organisations and corporate investigators in this context (sub-question 2 and 3). The paper is concluded by a discussion of some ethical issues and governance limitations of current practices in corporate security. It is concluded that the market for corporate investigations can be seen in the framework of a private/public demarcation: corporate investigators operate quite independently from the criminal justice system. While this situation has its advantages, it is argued that from a democratic, rule-of-law point of view it may be considered problematic.

2. The Theoretical Framework—Public/Private or Private/Public?

Traditionally, governments are tasked with the prevention and repression of crime (Van de Bunt and van Swaaningen 2005). The monopoly over legitimate use of force is commonly seen as the essential tool for governance by states (Weber 1946).[8] However, it is now widely recognised that from a historical perspective this situation is rather new (Garland 2001). This realisation has gained much academic attention under the banner of the shift from 'government' to 'governance' (see for example Lea and Stenson 2007). State actors, private actors and non-governmental organisations are now commonly seen as governing (global) society (see for example Willetts 2011). When it comes to the governance of criminal behaviour, however, the scientific community still seems mostly concerned with state action against crime (Hoogenboom 2007). Over the years, a wide range of publications has emerged, focusing on regulatory agencies (see for example Mascini and van Erp 2014), civilians (see for example Van Steden 2009) and private security professionals (see for example South 1988). Security provision is no longer seen as being the sole responsibility of law enforcement agencies: even within the context of the state, regulatory agencies, special investigative units within ministries and the input of local government are all seen as contributing to the provision of security (Van de Bunt and van Swaaningen 2005).

Academic attention for the contribution of private actors usually does not focus on the investigation of norm violations by the organisation within which the norm violation occurred. Rather, the preventative function of private security is researched. In this context, public/private relationships

---

a criminal justice procedure are not present in corporate investigations and settlements, criminal justice terminology is avoided here (see also Meerts 2018).

8   With this is meant not just the actual use of force but police powers in general.

are often conceptualised along the lines of a private sector complementing a dominant state.[9] In this line of reasoning, concepts such as privatisation and responsibilisation are used to indicate that the state involves private parties, either by privatising some of its activities, or by mobilising private actors to get involved in the provision of security (Garland 2001). Relations between the public sector and private security are, then, mostly conceptualised in the context of private parties' utility within the state agenda through cooperation (Hoogenboom and Muller 2002; Hoogenboom 2009; Dorn and Levi 2009; Cools et al. 2010). A popular theory in this line of reasoning is the junior partner thesis, first introduced by Kakalik and Wildhorn. According to this theory, public actors may use private security actors as a junior partner to advance the goals of the state (Hoogenboom 1988). In this view, private actors fill the void that was created by the inability of law enforcement actors to meet security demands. Private actors are considered to be complementary to public actors and to focus on preventative action.

An alternative perspective on public/private relations in this field may be derived from the work of James Williams, who sees the corporate investigations market as a commodification of internal norm violations, through the marketing of a professional service which is directly responsive to organisations' needs (Williams 2005; see also Meerts 2016). Corporate investigators provide organisations with the means to investigate and settle a norm violation without involving public law enforcement (Meerts 2018). Instead of thinking in terms of public/private relations, with private security serving as a subsidiary to the state, we should, therefore, take the private sector as our point of departure.

This research takes this last approach: the activities of corporate investigators are examined as an independent professional activity, not as a subsidiary of the state. Such an approach sensitises us to the context in which corporate investigators work and opens up a field of research, in which corporate investigations and settlements are considered as distinct and separated from criminal justice investigations and solutions. Insofar as it becomes necessary to bring the state back into the analysis, this may invoke what Dorn and Levi (2009) once referred to as private/public relations, reflecting the leading role of providers of private justice. The empirical data is considered along the lines of the private/public model, in which the state is seen as a supplement to the efforts of the private sector, instead of the other way around (such as is the case in junior partner theory). This does not imply a normative judgement at the onset, either in favour or critical of the corporate security market—although the need for such judgement may present itself once such analysis is done.

3. Methodology

The research question posed in the introduction of this paper is answered based on qualitative data gathered between October 2012 and March 2016.[10] The main source of information for the research consists of 59 semi-structured interviews that have been conducted among corporate investigators, clients and law enforcement professionals. This type of interview can be defined as an expert interview (Baarda et al. 1996). One advantage of an expert interview is that respondents are generally well-informed and, as a result, the interview should provide rich information. Additionally, the interview process may be more efficient. A challenge might be that experts, and especially those in management and higher positions, are often pressed for time and difficult to reach because they are shielded by administrative staff. However, the use of gatekeepers mitigated these issues in this research. Respondents were approached through gatekeepers and snowball sampling, making use of previous contacts and previous research by the author. For each group of respondents, a slightly modified topic list was used, so as to take full advantage of the knowledge of the respondent. However, to ensure that the research question and sub-questions can be answered, the following topics were part of every interview: professional background of the respondent; types of cases in which corporate investigators are involved; reasons for corporate investigations/settlements; process

---

9   This can also be discerned in the literature on the compliance functions of corporate security (see for example Verhage 2015).
10   This research was funded by a NWO (Netherlands Organisation for Scientific Research) Research talent grant.

of the investigations; process of settlements; regulation; public/private relations; and general opinion regarding the existence of corporate security. At the conclusion of each interview the question was posed whether the respondent felt any important subject had been neglected and whether he or she had suggestions for prospective respondents. The purpose of this is to minimise the possibility that important subjects and respondents are ignored. Interviews had an average duration of one hour and eleven minutes, with outliers of 23 min (the shortest interview) and two hours and fifteen minutes (the longest interview). All interviews were conducted face-to-face. The majority of the interviews was with a single person, however, four were conducted with two respondents at a time. When possible, the interviews were recorded to be transcribed verbatim at a later point in time. Some respondents did not consent to being tape-recorded, in these cases extensive notes were taken.

The minority of respondents in this research was female (10), the rest were male (49). Most respondents fall into the age group 40 to 60 years old and have substantial (more than 5 years) work experience in the field of financial crime (this is not the case for the clients, who have, however, substantial work experience with regard to corporate settlements). Most of the professional activities of respondents were conducted in the *Randstad*, which consists of the four largest Dutch cities (Amsterdam, Rotterdam, The Hague and Utrecht) and their surrounding areas. The activities are not limited to this geographical space, though, as respondents execute their work all over the Netherlands (and abroad). Respondents had a high average education level (academic education), with the exception of police respondents, who generally had a lower education level (being trained within the police organisation itself).

Table 1 provides an overview of the respondents of this research. Respondents are found among three main groups of professionals: corporate investigators (33), law enforcement professionals (16), and clients (10). Within these groups we can further differentiate. Within the group of corporate investigators, ten respondents work for private investigation firms, eighteen for an in-house security department, five for a forensic accounting department and three for a forensic (department of a) legal firm. As can be derived from Table 1, the forensic legal investigators had a double role, as respondents were investigators in some cases and clients in other cases.[11] The corporate investigators who have been respondents for this research were employed within 22 different organisations. The law enforcement professionals who participated in this research worked for the police (eight), the prosecution office (five) and the investigative department of the Dutch revenue authority, FIOD (three). All law enforcement respondents had a background in financial crime. Clients, finally, were HR personnel (one), labour lawyers within the organisation (four), external lawyers (three) or general management (two). All clients interviewed in this research were employed by a different organisation (ten). These numbers show that respondent groups are not represented to the same extent in this research. The decision was made to focus on corporate investigators for two reasons. First, this group is most important for the research question since the activities of corporate investigators are central to it. Secondly, the wide variety of backgrounds among corporate investigators made it necessary to include more corporate investigators in the research than other respondents.

---

[11] These respondents were approached and interviewed as clients. For this reason, they are counted in this category (which is why the numbers of investigators do not add up to 33). The fact that these respondents switched between the roles of investigator and client in different cases has provided useful insights to this research. At the time of interviewing, the Dutch corporate security sector did not contain many legal investigators, which is why so few legal investigators have been interviewed. Only during the research did this group emerge from the other interviews.

Table 1. Overview of interviews.

Number of interviews	59			
Average duration interviews	1 h 11 min		*Gender*	
	Number of people	*Number of organisations*	*Male*	*Female*
Corporate investigators	**33**	**22**	**31**	**2**
Private security firms	10	7	8	2
In-house security	18	12	18	0
Forensic accountants	5	3	5	0
Legal investigators	3 *	3 *	3	0
Law enforcement professionals	**16**	**10** [i]	**11**	**5**
Police	8	6	7	1
Prosecution	5	3	1	4
FIOD	3	1	3	0
Clients	**10**	**10**	**7**	**3**
HR, labour lawyers, management	7	7	4	3
Clients/legal investigators	3 *	3 *	3	0

* These are the same respondents/organisations. They are only 'counted' in this table as clients; [i] There were three law enforcement organisations involved in this research (police, the prosecution office and FIOD), but respondents were part of 10 different parts of these organisations.

Respondents indicate that corporate investigators are used to investigate a wide variety of norm violations (both criminal and non-criminal). Many of these have a financial component such as fraud, theft, corruption or embezzlement.[12] Corporate investigators are, however, also enlisted to investigate norm violations that provide no direct financial gain, such as data leakage, breach of privacy, breach of trust, sexual harassment and unauthorised ancillary activities. The norm violations that are investigated by corporate investigators range from small (petty theft or the leakage of minor information) to substantial (millions of euros in fraud). The corporate investigators included in this research work for a wide variety of clients. In addition to (semi-)public organisations (including charities, municipalities and schools), clients may be active in all economic sectors (for example: the financial sector, telecommunications or logistics). Respondents do indicate, however, that most of their clients are medium to large-scale organisations, which respondents attribute to the costs of investigations. All data[13] gathered are treated with utmost confidentiality and have been anonymised to ensure that no information can be traced back to any respondent or his or her employer. No parts of this research were covert and informed consent has been attained at every step (Laenen and O'Gorman 2016). The paper should not be regarded as generalising to the Netherlands as a whole; the statements made are indicative of the respondents in the research (who, however, do suggest that their statements are more generally applicable).

4. Legal Frameworks and Supervision over the Corporate Security Sector

To gain insight into the corporate investigations industry, it is important to start with an examination of the legal frameworks within which the market operates, as specified in sub-question 1 of this research. Respondents indicate that the state has very little insight into what happens in the corporate security sector. One of the reasons for this is the highly fragmented nature of the sector. Multiple actors, all with their own regulations and processes of control, combine to form a 'corporate security sector' which is used by organisations to react to norm violations. The most prominent of these

---

[12] For interesting work on corruption and corruption studies, see *inter alia* Pertiwi (2018) and Gorsira et al. (2018).
[13] This research was part of a larger project, in the context of which the additional research methods of observation and the use of case studies were used. Because the information gathered through these methods is not used in this paper, they are not explicated here. However, information about the observations and case studies can be found in (Meerts 2018).

are private investigation firms, in-house security departments, forensic accountants and, added most recently, investigative (departments within) legal firms. The various investigators use the conceptual differences between them as a commercial advantage over other investigators.

> You know, an investigation has different dimensions, you have a financial part, a technical part, an operational part. And sometimes you need one type of investigator because he is better at that particular part than others because of his background and experience. [Respondent 13—corporate investigator]

This quote of respondent 13 shows that certain investigators are better equipped to investigate a specific matter than others. An in-house investigator may for example be a good choice when complicated internal processes within an organisation are involved, since the in-house investigator knows the organisation. On the other hand, when it is deemed important that an independent party investigates the matter, external investigators may be more suitable. In complicated financial cases a forensic accountant will be the obvious choice. When multiple (international) jurisdictions are involved, a legal investigator with extensive legal knowledge might be chosen. There is, however, a tendency in the market to diversify the background of staff. In this way, corporate investigators may make use of multiple specialisms, according to the specific demands of the case at hand. Most corporate investigation units are, therefore, a mixture of professional backgrounds.

Seen in this light, the fragmentation of legal frameworks regulating corporate investigative activities might become somewhat problematic. The legal framework that applies is dependent on the label an investigator wears. Some regulation applies to all: no corporate investigator is allowed to break the (criminal) law during his investigations and all have to take the Data Protection Act[14] into account. As there are no private formal powers of investigation, the Code of Criminal Procedure, regulating the use of powers of investigation by law enforcement agencies, does not apply. This limits investigative possibilities (corporate investigators may not, for example, enter premises without explicit consent) but it also creates opportunities and flexibility. Within the limits of what is proscribed by law, corporate investigators have considerable room of manoeuvre.

The legal framework that is applicable is dependent on the type of investigator. Of the four groups—in-house investigation departments, private investigation firms, forensic accountants and forensic (departments within) legal firms—only private investigation firms need a permit under the law regulating private security and private investigation firms (*Wpbr*). The control over this permit is located with the police but this is now a purely administrative process (Klerks 2008). As a result of this law, private investigation firms need to implement a Privacy Code of Conduct similar to the one issued by the representative organisation for the Dutch security market (*NVb*) and declared binding by law to all private investigation firms. The Privacy Code of Conduct provides the most specific regulation for investigative activities.

Although forensic accountants and legal investigators are regulated by a general legal framework, these laws are not constructed to deal with investigative activities—rather, they are focused on traditional accounting activities and the traditional role of the lawyer. Both these professional groups do have disciplinary proceedings and in the case of forensic accountants, these disciplinary proceedings are specific to investigative activities (Meerts 2018). For accountants, some general guidelines for person-oriented investigation have been issued, and although these may be used in disciplinary proceedings, they are *guidelines* and as such not legally binding (NIVRA/NOvAA 2010). When it comes to in-house investigators, these professionals only have the internal guidelines of their company to follow (in addition to the generally applicable laws on criminal behavior and dada protection, as cited above).

---

[14] Per 25 May 2018 the Dutch Data Protection Act (WBP) is replaced by the European General Data Protection Regulation. The effects of this change on the legal requirements for data protection on the corporate security sector are, as of yet, not entirely clear.

In spite of the differences in legal frameworks, fieldwork does suggest that all groups tend to adhere to the Privacy Code of Conduct for private investigation firms. In the case of forensic accountants, the guidelines for person-oriented investigation specifically refer to the Privacy Code of Conduct to be used as a guideline by forensic accountants (NIVRA/NOvAA 2010). Respondents indicate that they are focused on legal principles, such as proportionality and subsidiarity—principles that are central to the abovementioned guidelines as well. However, as this is largely on a voluntary basis, compliance is not guaranteed. The diversification in the corporate investigations arena and in legal frameworks and control create a fragmented field in which the state has very little knowledge about actual activities. Democratic control over the corporate security sector is very limited. Control over corporate investigations is, for an important part, reliant on the ethics of individual investigators and on the client. This places much responsibility on organisations using the services of corporate investigators (Meerts 2018).

5. Corporate Investigations

For an important part, the influence of the organisation is exerted at the start of the investigative process and at its conclusion (by deciding on a settlement), and much less during the investigations. Investigations commonly start with an assignment letter by the organisation that is faced with the norm violation.[15] The client organisation can assert much control over the investigations by framing the assignment in a certain way. Although corporate investigators endeavour to be independent and objective, they are reliant in a large degree on their clients. Partly, this is created by the fact that the investigative possibilities of corporate investigators rely heavily on the rights an organisation has to exert control over its employees (Schaap 2008). Through the employers' (property) rights in relation to, for example, employees' work computers, corporate investigators have access to the information stored on these devices.

The way in which the assignment is framed determines the scope of the investigations. Respondents indicate that they are aware of the possibility that their investigations could be used for improper purposes and they try to avoid such situations. However, this is not always easy to determine in practice.

> Imagine that a CEO comes to you and says, 'look I have Mr. Jones here and he's in his late fifties, rather expensive, we would like to get rid of him but firing him would be expensive so could you have a look at his expense account and see whether you can't find something or other'. Well, no, sorry, we don't do that. [But] it's not always that straightforward because if the same person contacts us, saying 'we think that Mr. Jones is fiddling with expense accounts for this or that reason ...' The story is the same, it's just told differently. So it's not always possible to know exactly but you have to try. That's why an intake [conversation between client and investigator about the case] is so important, to get an impression of the context of the case, what kinds of signals are there, how were they discovered, is it specific enough to warrant investigation? [Respondent 2—corporate investigator]

The possibility to have a measure of control over the investigations and over the information that might flow to the public realm is one of the reasons for organisations to enlist the services of corporate investigators (Williams 2005). This means corporate investigators have to find a balance between the interests of clients and their own objectivity and independent position. One way in which corporate investigators try to prevent organisations from unduly influencing the investigations is to

---

[15] In the case of an in-house investigations department, the report of the norm violation is usually enough—the assignment is implied here in the mission statement of the in-house department. In case of in-house departments, the alleged norm violation may also be reported directly to this in-house department by concerned employees or through whistle-blower arrangements (for the latter, see (Loyens and Vandekerckhove 2018).

not communicate with the client about preliminary findings. However, clients are commonly notified about the general progress of the investigations.

The investigative possibilities of corporate investigators are substantial, and with technological progress, constantly expanding. For the purposes of this paper, it suffices to discuss the four main sources of information: documents; (internal) systems; open sources and personal contact (Meerts 2016). Inspection of the internal documentation is often used as a starting point for investigations: financial administration, invoices, contracts and other documents are used to form an indication of the issue at hand. As a corporate investigator explains:

> We usually start with the records. And that is a very broad concept of course. There are financial records, digital but also hard copy. Digital is for example the books and hard copy the invoices, source documents, everything that the books are based on. [Respondent 5—corporate investigator].

Apart from (financial) documentation, much information may be derived from the internal systems at place in an organisation. Typically, these systems are not created for investigative purposes, but they may nevertheless be used in the context of an investigation. Personnel log files, camera systems and track-and-trace systems are examples; communications systems (such as email and phone records) and data carriers (such as computers, external memory-drives and smart phones) also fall within this category. As long as the organisation is the owner, these sources may be accessed by corporate investigators (Schaap 2008). Respondents indicate that they are hesitant to use more intrusive investigative measures, such as accessing the content of emails or audio-taping telephone conversations conducted on employer premises or via an employer mobile phone. Although allowed by law, the weighing of the widely-used principles of proportionality and subsidiarity often means that investigators use less far-reaching alternatives, such as analysis of phone records to see with whom the person has been in contact.

> The thing is, people's actions in the context of the company are done with company means, during working hours, regarding the company's clients. So they have some right to privacy but this is not absolute. People need to know that. These key cards—they register attendance and we're not here to check whether or not you came in on time or left early. But if there happens to be a situation in a certain room, money's missing or something like that, of course we will check who has been there. [Respondent 39—corporate investigator]

Much additional information is, furthermore, provided by desk research into open sources. 'Open' sources may be easily accessible for everyone, but this type of information source may also be 'on-subscription', for example, databases collecting Chamber of Commerce information or name and address data. They are open in the sense that they are open to everyone who is willing to pay a fee for access. Free open sources are, for example, social media and traditional media.[16]

Interviews with the 'subject' or 'involved person'[17] are usually done only at the end of investigations. In this way, investigators may confront the subject with other information which has been gathered. Other interviews with, for example, colleagues or managers of the involved person, are often less formalised and may be done at an earlier stage of the investigation process. For a subject, the interview process is formalised to a higher degree, although it should be noted that a subject does not have the procedural protections a suspect has in the context of criminal investigations. People who are interviewed do, however, have the right to be assisted by a representative (such as a lawyer) and

---

[16] The growing attention for privacy on social media is an interesting development in this context, which may prove to make the use of this kind of open source data more difficult in future. Growing awareness may drive social media users to protect their social media profiles better, making access through legal means more difficult.

[17] The language used here is important. As mentioned before, in line with the absence of powers of investigation, criminal justice terminology, such as 'interrogation' and 'suspect', is usually avoided by corporate investigators.

respondents also indicate that they inform the interviewee that his cooperation is voluntary and he is not obliged to cooperate.

> His statement is made freely, I mean if during our conversation he decides not to want to talk about it, ok that's his story. I'm not sure he's going to be better off with that [action] but when someone walks out the door, he walks. I'm not going to grab him by the neck and say, ok now you're going to talk. [Respondent 15—corporate investigator]

Following the widely-used adversarial principle, interviewees are given the opportunity to read their statement and to correct factual errors.[18] After a final interview report has been drafted, the person who has been interviewed is asked to sign the interview report together with the interviewers, which he or she may refuse to do. Interviews are generally conducted by two investigators for reasons of transparency and reliability.

Many corporate investigations remain entirely in the private realm, as the investigative possibilities are often enough to provide the necessary information without having to resort to the formal powers of investigation of law enforcement (which could be mobilised through a report to the authorities). After investigations are finalised and subjects have had the opportunity to react to the draft report, a final report is made and presented to the client. Based on the findings in this report, a client may decide on one of several possible courses of action.

This section has discussed the second sub-question as defined in the introduction to this paper. We now follow the course of the investigation process further, by seeking an answer to the third sub-question about corporate settlements, in the following section.

6. Corporate Settlements

Corporate investigations and solutions may remain entirely private, but law enforcement agencies may be involved as well. Under certain circumstances this involvement may be sought at an early stage of, during, or prior to the corporate investigations (Meerts 2018). Such involvement is, for example, highly likely in the minority of cases in which media coverage has already exposed the matter (and not reporting to the authorities would create the image that the incident is being swept under the rug). Alternatively, the police may be brought in because corporate investigators cannot obtain the necessary information (see also Van de Bunt et al. 2013). "Sometimes you know in advance, if you don't involve the police you won't be able to do the full investigations. For some information you just need the police" [Respondent 13—corporate investigator]. Apart from any conscious action by corporate investigators or clients, law enforcement may already be involved at an early stage, as a result of their own efforts.

However, in most instances in which law enforcement agencies are involved, this happens only *after* corporate investigations have been finalised. Respondents suggest that this is important, in the sense that a well-substantiated report increases the likelihood that law enforcement authorities will indeed investigate. In addition, it is often rather unclear in the early stages of investigations whether the behaviour actually qualifies as a crime. Some corporate investigations are necessary then: "Let's take theft as an example. It starts with a missing item. But that doesn't mean that this item has been stolen. If we immediately go to the police and we have to tell them later on, never mind we found it—that doesn't really reflect well on us does it?" [Respondent 15—corporate investigator]. Another reason to report would be that it is necessary for the insurance claim or it may be a moral consideration—of all the solutions available to corporate investigators, only the criminal procedure has a distinctive punitive side.

---

[18] The adversarial principle is derived from (forensic) accountancy principles but is generally complied with by corporate investigators with all kinds of backgrounds. Private investigation firms and forensic accountants are obliged to do so, but fieldwork indicates that all types of investigators seem to adhere to this rule. The adversarial principle refers to the process in which someone is given the opportunity to reply not only to investigators' verbal queries but also to check and comment upon the notes of the interview and parts of the report while still in draft.

Whatever the reason for a report to the authorities, it is hardly ever the only action taken: a report to public law enforcement may prove useful in many ways, but it does nothing to solve the problem in the labour relationship (Meerts and Dorn 2017). In addition, restitution of damages may be obtained much faster through other channels, since the criminal justice system is a slow process—and even then there is no guarantee that the person will be punished or will be obliged to repay damages. Therefore, a report to law enforcement authorities is usually combined with other settlement options. In addition to a criminal trial, organisations may use a civil suit as a means to arrive at a solution. One reason to use civil proceedings is that they are faster and less publicised. Another may be that the standard of evidence is lower in civil cases than in criminal cases. Information presented in civil court is considered a fact when neither party contests its accuracy. Information that may be considered circumstantial in criminal court may serve as evidence in civil court. A civil procedure may take multiple forms: the employer or employee may bring a civil claim for damages based on breach of contract or tort but it may also involve the termination of the labour contract. When the employee does not consent to termination of the contract, a ruling of a labour judge is usually necessary.

Although a civil court case does produce less publicity than a criminal case, it is still a court proceeding and therefore fairly 'out in the open' and this may conflict with the organisations' interests. "There are certain tensions you know. An organisation wants the money back but they don't want to have a lot of publicity. They want it done quietly." [Respondent 6—client]. A more private way to settle the matter is through a settlement agreement. This may be a contract in which parties agree on an amount payable by the involved person and it may also include conditions, such as the termination of the labour contract. "In this case, there were two people involved and we struck a deal with the one and the other is paying a monthly amount" [Respondent 6—client]. A settlement agreement in the context of the labour agreement is a termination with mutual consent (article 7:900 Civil Code).

Respondents suggest that non-disclosure clauses are fairly standard to settlement agreements: parties commit themselves to the confidentiality of the agreement and the circumstances of termination. "You come to terms with each other about what you will and will not make public. You make a settlement agreement and a non-disclosure is usually in there—well, then we won't talk about it anymore. From either side." [Respondent 19—corporate investigator]. A non-disclosure agreement is not unique to settlement agreements, however data suggest that its use is highly prevalent here. Compared to other private settlements, which are largely based on action by the organisation, the person subjected to investigations has more influence on the process in case a settlement agreement is used. This influence should not be overstated though—through threats of criminal charges or civil seizure, (s)he may be forced to comply with the agreement. A settlement agreement does have advantages over other solutions for an employee: in this case, the right to unemployment benefits may be preserved and many settlement agreements include some sort of severance payment to the employee.

Alternatively, internal sanctions may follow corporate investigations. Large organisations usually have internal regulations, and measures to be taken in response to the infringement of these rules are often formalised as well. These sanctions may be very mild—an (official) warning—or severe—summary dismissal (dismissal on the spot). Many other possibilities are available. Within the range of sanctions an employee may for example be passed over for a raise or demoted, certain types of access (to for example the financial administration) might be denied, the employee may be removed from a certain position, and benefits may be taken away.

Termination of the labour contract may be seen as the ultimate internal sanction, simultaneously bringing an end to the fact that someone is indeed internal to the organisation. Sometimes involvement of a judge is necessary for termination, but there are many instances in which this is not the case. In addition to the already discussed settlement agreement, a fixed term contract may simply not be renewed or the employee may (be persuaded to) initiate the separation. In 'urgent circumstances', the employer may resort to a summary dismissal (Article 7:677 Civil Code). What may be seen as an urgent circumstance is not defined; however a criminal offence or non-compliance with internal rules falls within this category. If a summary dismissal is to be used, there is a condition of 'immediacy', which means that the employer has to act as soon as the facts are clear. Corporate investigations are, thus, allowed to obtain a clear overview of the facts. Respondents suggest that an employee is often suspended from active duty pending the investigations, so as to make sure the condition of immediacy is complied with.

It is important to note that although corporate investigators may be involved in an advisory capacity in the decision making process regarding corporate settlements, it is the organisation itself (in the form of Human Resources and management) that takes the decision.

> We do the investigations and that's it. Two of my colleagues have a different opinion, [they think that] when they say someone's guilty he should be fired, [but other colleagues] have a more nuanced view. Our job is the investigation, getting the evidence and building a case that would hold up in court if necessary. The decisions are up to the involved manager and HR. [Informal conversation with a corporate investigator]

Corporate investigators may exert influence over this decision, by providing the organisation with advice. The extent and depth of this advice differs among investigators, most notably because forensic accountants are wary of drawing legal conclusions from the investigations (whereas legal investigators see their added value specifically in drawing legal conclusions and providing advice on how to proceed) (Meerts 2018). If the decision is made to report to law enforcement authorities, this report is usually done by the investigators.

> And eventually you will come to the point that you write your report and explain your findings but also draw conclusions based on that. That could be that there must be measures taken against certain persons or that the structure of the organisation should be changed. And it could also lead to the question whether or not the incident should be reported to the police. [Respondent 30—corporate investigator]

7. Conclusions

This research paper highlights the role of the organisation as the principal actor in corporate investigations and corporate settlements. The legal constraints upon and day-to-day activities of corporate investigators have been considered above. In this conclusion, the consequences of the distance between public law enforcement actors and corporate security are reflected upon. The present work permits us to make some critical comments about the industry, its governance and the ways this research frames these issues. As noted in the introduction, private/public relations in the field of security have generally been approached via consideration of the supposedly diminishing role of a previously dominant state (privatisation, responsibilisation and the growth of mass private property as distinct from public goods). That point of departure implies that private security actors have either filled a gap in security provision left by the state (acting as a supplement to public law enforcement) or that they have replaced the state in this area (becoming a substitute for public law enforcement).

To the contrary, this paper argues that the role of the state in the investigation and settlement of internal norm violations within companies, is better conceptualised in terms of *absence* (Williams 2005; Meerts and Dorn 2009). The emphasis on the role of the state, furthermore, downplays the importance of the actions taken by organisations themselves against internal norm violations.[19]

Taking the private sector, then, as our point of departure, we may discern that, in the social reality of corporate security, it is the state that is the supplement to the solution provided by corporate investigators: the state is the 'junior partner' here, to be called upon selectively, as and when needed.

---

[19] The same can be said about the role of non-government organisations such as Transparency International. The argument that the state has diminished in importance is not limited to the field of security provision but can rather be seen in the context of a general shift from 'government' to 'governance'. See for more on this topic: (Börzel and Risse 2005).

A report to public law enforcement is made when it serves a purpose for corporate investigators and organisations. When this is not the case, corporate investigations and settlements largely remain in the private legal sphere. We may, then, conclude that the short answer to the research question is that the role of corporate investigators in the investigation and settlement of norm violations within organisations is substantial and that it exceeds involvement by state agencies. In theoretical terms, the private/public demarcation identified by Williams (2005) can be found in the context of the investigation of norm violations within Dutch organisations.

As a consequence, little is known about the way in which organisations deal with internal norm violations (Meerts 2018). While this has the advantage for the state that the criminal justice system is not flooded by cases it is not very well equipped to deal with, a negative consequence is limited public control over the ways in which organisations deal with internal norm violations. As mentioned in this paper, in the Dutch case there is a permit system available for corporate investigators, however, this is only applicable to private investigation firms. This means that most investigators are not caught by the 'regulatory gaze' of the state (White 2014.). In light of the question of how to frame public/private relations in the field of corporate security, it would be interesting to explore whether and how legal frameworks, roles and activities of corporate investigators may differ between countries. The UK, for example, does not have a permit system for private investigators (see for example Meerts 2018). Interestingly, minor fieldwork conducted in the UK in the context of this research suggests that the way in which investigations are done, and the issues that may be identified (for example with regard to private/public cooperation), are broadly similar in the UK and the Netherlands. Interesting work in specific national jurisdictions by for example Williams (2005, Canada), Gill (2013, UK) and Gottschalk (2015, Norway) seems to point in the same general direction. However, more (specifically comparative) research is necessary on this topic.

This relative invisibility, together with other characteristics of the sector, make comprehensive control over, or even insight in, the way organisations deal with internal norm violations very challenging (Williams 2006b). Much is left to the individual investigator and the client organisation. Seen from the perspective of the values of democracy and the rule-of-law, this is problematic. Corporate investigations may have considerable impact on the lives of employees. In addition, there is a marked power imbalance between the organisation and the person who is subjected to the investigations. Even when no rules are broken by investigators or organisations that hire them, the involved person may be pressured into a disadvantageous situation; at the very least he may be upset.

In principle corporate investigations have a 'downwards gaze'. Since the organisation determines the assignment, most investigations are focused on individuals (lower-level management and employees) instead of on the organisation itself (Williams 2014).[20] The legal person of the organisation is often part of the investigations only *as context*, and faulty processes may be identified in order to be corrected. However, blame is hardly ever put on the organisation, although there are many examples of organisations acting as a perpetrator or facilitator (see Gorsira et al. 2018; Van Rooij and Adam 2018; Lord et al. 2018). In this way, corporate investigations have an inherent bias towards 'rotten apples'. The barrel is taken into account but often not held accountable.

Funding: The research underlying this paper was funded by a grant from the Netherlands Organisation for Scientific Research (NWO).

Acknowledgments: I would like to thank the anonymous respondents who participated in this research, as well as Nicholas Dorn, an anonymous reviewer and the editors of this special issue for their helpful comments on earlier drafts of this paper.

Conflicts of Interest: The author declares no conflicts of interest.

---

[20] Respondents stress their independence within the limits of the assignment, however the way an assignment is delineated by the client has much impact on the investigations.

References

Baarda, Ben, Martijn P. M. de Goede, and A. G. E. van der Meer-Middelburg. 1996. *Basisboek Open Interviewen. Praktische Handleiding voor het Voorbereiden en Afnemen van Open Interviews*. Groningen: Stenfert Kroese.

Beckers, Joep Johannes Hubertus. 2017. *Tussen Ideaal en Werkelijkheid. Een Empirische Studie naar de Strafrechtelijke Aanpak van Organisatiecriminaliteit in Nederland*. Rotterdam: Erasmus universiteit Rotterdam.

Börzel, Tanja A., and Thomas Risse. 2005. Public-Private Partnerships: Effective and legitimate tools for international governance? In *Complex Sovereignty: On the Reconstitution of Political Authority in the 21st Century*. Edited by Edgar Grande and Louis W. Pauly. Toronto: University of Toronto Press, pp. 195–216.

Cools, Marc, Dusan Davidovic, Hilde DeClerck, and Eddy De Raedt. 2010. The international private security industry as part of the European Union security framework: A critical assessment of the French EU presidency White Paper. In *EU and International Crime Control. Topical Issues*. Edited by Marc Cools, Brice De Ruyver, Marleen Easton, Lieven Pauwels, Paul Ponsaers, Gudrun Vande Walle, Tom Vander Beken, Freya Vander Laenen, Gert Vermeulen and Gerwinde Vynckier. Antwerpen: Maklu, pp. 123–36.

Dorn, Nicholas, and Micheal Levi. 2009. Private–Public or Public–Private? Strategic Dialogue on Serious Crime and Terrorism in the EU. *Security Journal* 22: 302–16. [CrossRef]

Garland, David. 2001. *The Culture of Control; Crime and Social Order in Contemporary Society*. Chicago: University Press.

Gill, Martin. 2013. Engaging the corporate sector in policing: Realities and opportunities. *Policing* 7: 273–79. [CrossRef]

Gorsira, Madelijne, Linda Steg, Adriaan Denkers, and Wim Huisman. 2018. Corruption in Organizations: Ethical Climate and Individual Motives. *Administrative Sciences* 8: 4. [CrossRef]

Gottschalk, Peter. 2015. Private Investigations of White-Collar Crime Suspicions: A Qualitative Study of the Blame Game Hypothesis. *Journal of Investigative Psychology and Offender Profiling* 12: 231–46. [CrossRef]

Hoogenboom, Bob, and Erwin R. Muller. 2002. *Voorbij de Dogmatiek: Publiek-Private Samenwerking in de Veiligheidszorg*. Den Haag: COT.

Hoogenboom, Bob. 1988. *Particuliere Recherche: Een Verkenning van Enige Ontwikkelingen*. 's-Gravenhage: SDU Uitgeverij.

Hoogenboom, Bob. 2007. Grijs gebied tussen publiek en privaat bedreigt veiligheid. *Christen Democratische Verkenningen* 2007: 58–65.

Hoogenboom, Bob. 2009. *De publiecke Saeck; Politie en Veiligheid in een Verwilderde Wereld*. Den Haag: Boom Juridische Uitgevers.

Klerks, Peter. 2008. Terughoudend toezicht op omvangrijke private recherche. *Tijdschrift voor Veiligheid* 7: 9–19.

Laenen, Freya Vander, and Aileen O'Gorman. 2016. Ethische aspecten van het kwalitatief onderzoek. In *Kwalitatieve Methoden en Technieken in de Criminology*. Edited by Tom Decorte and Damian Zaitch. Leuven: Acco, pp. 555–86.

Lea, John, and Kevin Stenson. 2007. Security, Sovereignty, and Non-State Governance "from Below". *Canadian Journal of Law and Society/Revue Canadienne Droit et Société* 22: 9–27. [CrossRef]

Lord, Nicholas, Karin van Wingerde, and Liz Campbell. 2018. Organising the Monies of Corporate Financial Crimes via Organisational Structures: Ostensible Legitimacy, Effective Anonymity, and Third-Party Facilitation. *Administrative Sciences* 8: 17. [CrossRef]

Loyens, Kim, and Wim Vandekerckhove. 2018. Whistleblowing agencies around the world: A comparative case study. *Administrative Sciences* 8. (Forthcoming).

Mascini, Peter, and Judith G. van Erp. 2014. Regulatory governance: Experimenting with new roles and instruments. *Recht der Werkelijkheid* 35: 3–11. [CrossRef]

Meerts, Clarissa Annemarie. 2013. Corporate security–private justice? (Un)settling employer-employee troubles. *Security Journal* 26: 264–79. [CrossRef]

Meerts, Clarissa Annemarie, and Nicholas Dorn. 2009. Corporate security and private justice: Danger signs? *European Journal of Crime, Criminal Law and Criminal Justice* 17: 97–111. [CrossRef]

Meerts, Clarissa Annemarie, and Nicholas Dorn. 2017. Cooperation as mantra: Corporate security and public law. In *Over de Muren van Stilzwijgen—Liber amicorum Henk van de Bunt*. Edited by René van Swaaningen, Karin van Wingerden and Richard H. J. M. Staring. Den Haag: Boom Criminology, pp. 503–15.

Meerts, Clarissa Annemarie. 2016. A world apart? Private investigations in the corporate sector. *Erasmus Law Review* 9: 162–76. [CrossRef]

Meerts, Clarissa Annemarie. 2018. *The Semi-Autonomous World of Corporate Investigators. Modus Vivendi, Legality and Control*. Rotterdam: Erasmus Universiteit Rotterdam.

NIVRA/NOvAA. 2010. *NBA-Handreiking 1112. Praktijkhandleiding Persoonsgerichte Onderzoeken voor Accountants-Administratieconsulenten/Registeraccountants*. Amsterdam: Koninklijke Nederlandse Beroepsorganisatie voor Accountants.

Pertiwi, Kanti. 2018. Contextualizing Corruption: A Cross-Disciplinary Approach to Studying Corruption in Organizations. *Administrative Sciences* 8: 12. [CrossRef]

Richards, James. 2008. The many approaches to organisational misbehaviour: A review, map and research agenda. *Employee Relations* 30: 653–78. [CrossRef]

Schaap, Cees D. 2008. *De Private Forensisch Fraudedeskundige. Een Feitelijke en Juridische Positionering*. Nijmegen: Wolf Legal Publishers.

South, Nigel. 1988. *Policing for Profit: The Private Security Sector*. London: Sage.

Van de Bunt, Henk G., and René van Swaaningen. 2005. Privatisering van de veiligheidszorg. In *Privatisering van Veiligheid*. Edited by Laurens C. Winkel, Sjaak Jansen, Hendrik O. Kerkmeester, Rob J. P. Kottenhagen and Vincent Mul. Den Haag: Boom Juridische Uitgevers, pp. 5–19.

Van de Bunt, Henk G., Judith G. van Erp, Roland J. J. Eshuis, Nina L. Holvast, and Thy Pham. 2013. Bestuurdersaansprakelijkheid in de praktijk. Motieven voor het intern aansprakelijk stellen van bestuurders. In *Capita Civilologie*. Edited by Willem H. van Boom, Ivo Giesen and Albert J. Verheij. Den Haag: Boom Juridische Uitgevers, pp. 907–28.

Van Steden, Ronald. 2009. Burgerparticipatie in lokale veiligheidsnetwerken: Over 'nodale sturing' en 'verankerd pluralisme'. *Justitiële Verkenningen* 35: 29–42.

Van Rooij, Benjamin, and Fine Adam. 2018. Toxic Corporate Culture: Assessing Organizational Processes of Deviancy. *Administrative Sciences* 8. (Forthcoming). [CrossRef]

Verhage, Antoinette. 2015. Global governance = global compliance? The uneven playing field in ant-money laundering. In *The Routledge Handbook of White-Collar and Corporate Crime in Europe*. Edited by Judith G. Van Erp, Wim Huisman and Gundrun vande Walle. Abingdon: Routledge, pp. 471–85.

Walby, Kevin, and Randy Lippert, eds. 2014. *Corporate Security in the 21st Century: Theory and Practice in International Perspective*. Basingstoke: Palgrave Macmillan.

Weber, Max. 1946. Politics as a Vocation. In *From Max Weber: Essays in Sociology*. Edited by Hans H. Gerth and Charles Wright Mills. New York: Oxford University Press, pp. 77–128.

White, Adam. 2014. Beyond the regulatory gaze? Corporate security, (in) visibility, and the modern state. In *Corporate Security in the 21st Century. Theory and Practice in International Perspective*. Edited by Kevin Walby and Randy Lippert. Basingstoke: Palgrave Macmillan, pp. 39–55.

Willetts, Peter. 2011. *Non-Governmental Organizations in World Politics. The Construction of Global Governance*. Abingdon: Routledge.

Williams, James W. 2005. Reflections on the private versus public policing of economic crime. *British Journal of Criminology* 45: 316–39. [CrossRef]

Williams, James W. 2006a. Private legal orders: Professional markets and the commodification of financial governance. *Social and Legal Studies* 15: 209–35. [CrossRef]

Williams, James W. 2006b. Governability matters: The private policing of economic crime and the challenge of democratic governance. *Policing and Society* 15: 187–211. [CrossRef]

Williams, James W. 2014. The Private Eyes of Corporate Culture: The Forensic Accounting and Corporate Investigation Industry and the Production of Corporate Financial Security. In *Corporate Security in the 21st Century. Theory and Practice in International Perspective*. Edited by Kevin Walby and Randy Lippert. Basingstoke: Palgrave Macmillan, pp. 56–77.

administrative sciences

MDPI

Article

Whistleblowing from an International Perspective: A Comparative Analysis of Institutional Arrangements

Kim Loyens [1,*] and Wim Vandekerckhove [2]

[1]   School of Governance, Utrecht University, Bijlhouwerstraat 6, 3511 ZC Utrecht, The Netherlands
[2]   Department of Human Resources and Organisational Behaviour, University of Greenwich,
      London SE10 9LS, UK; W.Vandekerckhove@greenwich.ac.uk
*   Correspondence: k.m.loyens@uu.nl

Received: 27 April 2018; Accepted: 2 July 2018; Published: 5 July 2018

Abstract: While there appears to be consensus amongst policy makers that legislation to protect whistleblowers is needed, the emerging policy question addresses what institutional framework is most fit to implement whistleblowing legislation. However, the institutions to whom whistleblowers report—which are in the literature addressed as internal or external recipients of whistleblowing concerns—have been given limited scholarly attention. Research has instead focused on motives, behaviour, and experiences of whistleblowers on the one hand, and whistleblowing legislation on the other. Particularly the role of external agencies, like ombudsmen, anti-corruption agencies, and Inspector General offices, in dealing with whistleblowing concerns has been under-studied. With the aim of starting to fill this research gap, this paper reports the findings of a comparative study of governmental whistleblowing agencies (other than courts) and non-governmental whistleblowing protection organizations (NGOs), as important examples of external recipients of whistleblowing concerns, in 11 countries with whistleblowing legislation. The study aimed to find similarities and differences between these agencies, and to identify challenges and dilemmas that the installation of whistleblowing agencies bring about. Data collection was done by means of 21 interviews with academic experts and high-ranking officials within the selected countries, and in-depth analysis of available (policy) documents and reports. This paper finds that in the studied countries, there is a trend to install governmental whistleblowing agencies that combine various tasks to implement whistleblowing legislation (e.g., advice, psychosocial care, investigation of wrongdoing or retaliation, and prevention of wrongdoing). When such agencies are absent or considered weak, NGOs may step in to fill the need. Whereas most governmental whistleblowing agencies have investigative tasks, in Belgium and in the Netherlands, investigations of wrongdoing and retaliation are done within the same department for the reason that these issues cannot be easily separated. Other agencies have separated these tasks to avoid conflict of interest or because different expertise is claimed to be needed for both. Further research is needed to analyze the effects of each institutional approach, and how to avoid conflict of interest, particularly the risk of partial investigations of wrongdoing. Our study also shows that while not many countries provide government funds for specific psychosocial care for whistleblowers, most governmental whistleblowing agencies do give advice to whistleblowers and invest in the prevention of wrongdoing or training of those who implement whistleblowing legislation. While providing important insights into the role of whistleblowing agencies in 11 countries, this study also develops questions for further research.

Keywords: whistleblowing; institutions; reporting wrongdoing; comparative study

1. Introduction

Many scholars have studied the motives and experiences of whistleblowers (e.g., Ayers and Kaplan 2005; De Graaf 2010; Loyens 2012; Miceli et al. 1991; Near and Miceli 1996; Roberts 2014; Rothschild and Miethe 1999). Whistleblowing policies and legislation in different countries have also been studied extensively either by scholars using a comparative law perspective (see e.g., Dworkin and Brown 2013; Fasterling and Lewis 2014; Lewis and Trygstad 2009; Morvan 2009; Vaughn 2012), or by international organisations (BluePrint for Free Speech 2015; OECD 2011; Osterhaus and Fagan 2009; PACE Parliamentary Assembly of the Council of Europe; UNODC 2015). However, the agencies that receive reports made by whistleblowers—in the whistleblowing literature referred to as internal or external recipients 'who can effect action' (Miceli and Near 1992, p. 16)—have been given much less attention in academia (Brown et al. 2014; Moberly 2014). Several scholars (Miceli and Near 1992; Miceli et al. 2008) have argued that it is important to study the role of internal and external recipients of whistleblowing concerns. Their responsiveness and how that is perceived by would-be whistleblowers can affect the decision to report or not. This study focuses on external recipients, particularly on (1) government agencies (other than courts) that receive reports about alleged wrongdoing in other organisations and/or alleged retaliation against those who blew the whistle—which may include Ombudsmen, anti-corruption agencies, Inspector General offices, and the Securities and Exchange Commission (Moberly 2014; Roberts and Brown 2010); and (2) civil society organisations or non-governmental organisations (NGOs) that receive whistleblower disclosures and—often in a more activist way—try to enhance whistleblower protection. We do not focus on the media in their role as an external recipient of concerns (Bosua et al. 2014; Vandekerckhove 2010).

Research suggests that whistleblowing reports are an important source of information to uncover wrongdoing within organizations (Brown, Mazurski and Olsen 2008, cited in Lewis et al. 2014). External recipients of concerns are considered crucial for effectively ending the wrongdoing, because internal recipients (like a supervisor) may be more inclined to cover up or ignore the problem (Dworkin and Baucus 1998; Mesmer-Magnus and Viswesvaran 2005; Moberly 2014). At the same time, organisations often prefer whistleblowers to use internal reporting channels (see also Meerts, THIS ISSUE), as to avoid possible damage to reputation and disruption of employer-employee relations if concerns are discussed outside the organisation (Moberly 2014). The few studies that have analyzed the role of external recipients have focused on the effectiveness of whistleblowers to stop the wrongdoing (Miceli and Near 2002) and recipients' satisfaction with whistleblowing processes linked to procedural and distributive justice of whistleblowing channels (Near et al. 1993). However, not much empirical evidence is available about the actual role and tasks of these recipients in practice (Brown et al. 2014). The Australian 'Whistling While They Work' (WWTW) study is one of the very few examples in which valuable insight into the role of external recipients is presented. Based on an analysis of a number of different agencies, like ombudsmen, auditor generals, and public service commissions, Annakin (2011) found that the common approach of these agencies to not investigate the wrongdoing independently, but instead referring it back to the whistleblower's own department (similar to the approach in citizen complaint investigations), decreases the effectiveness of these agencies in stopping the wrongdoing or indeed forcing organizations to start detoxing their organizational cultures (see Van Rooij & Fine, THIS ISSUE). Moreover, this practice leads to the identity of the whistleblower—who often wants to remain anonymous—being revealed within his or her organization. Other problems include the lack of expertise and skills of staff in dealing with whistleblowing cases, and the lack of coordination between the various external recipients, resulting in agencies shoving responsibility onto others.

Given the rather little empirical data available for external recipients—compared to internal recipients—Moberly (2014, p. 295) calls for more research to "better understand the role external recipients can play in the whistleblowing process", not only in investigating wrongdoing, but also in protecting whistleblowers. Likewise, Brown and colleagues (Brown et al. 2014, pp. 489–90) express "the strong need for the study of whistleblowing protection efforts to shift beyond comparative legal

Adm. Sci. **2018**, *8*, 30

studies or attempts to identify good and bad features of whistleblowing laws and procedures, in the abstract, to also include [...] data on how the systems established under those laws are operating in practice". Although this study does not go as far as examining whether whistleblower concerns are effectively resolved by external agencies, as further suggested by Moberly (2014), this paper will provide a descriptive analytic comparison of the various roles whistleblowing agencies have in the studied countries, which is a first step towards bringing these agencies (and not just the legislations) to the forefront, and providing insights into their role in whistleblowing protection. In this sense, the current study is a first step to broadening the disciplinary lens on whistleblowing institutions beyond legal scholarship towards cross-disciplinary study, similar to what Perwati (THIS ISSUE) argues for in the context of corruption. This study more precisely aims to address a gap in the literature by analyzing the role of whistleblowing agencies in 11 countries, focusing on their advisory, psychosocial care, investigative, and preventive tasks. The central research question is: "What are the most important similarities and differences between whistleblowing agencies that perform advisory, psychosocial care, investigative, and/or preventive tasks?" Based on the experiences in these whistleblowing agencies, we will also identify the dilemmas and challenges that the installation of these agencies bring about, in addition to the lessons that can be drawn from that.

By answering this question, the current paper not only commences to fill a research gap; its contribution is also of practical importance. The driving question for policy makers is no longer whether whistleblowing legislation is needed, nor what key aspects such legislation must encompass (Devine 2015, 2016). Rather, the growing number of countries with whistleblowing legislation suggests that the emerging policy question for the next decade will be through what institutional framework whistleblowing legislation can best be implemented (Council of Europe 2014; European Commission 2018). Our paper lays the groundwork for further research to answer this policy implementation question, by presenting a comparative study of external recipients of concerns that provide services to whistleblowers in different countries.

In the next section, this paper will describe the research design, sampling of the cases, data collection methods, and analysis. Then, the main findings will be discussed, which respectively relate to the legal framework, the existence of government agencies and/or NGOs that support whistleblowers, investigative tasks of governmental whistleblowing agencies and NGOs (focusing on wrongdoing and retaliation investigations), ways in which governmental whistleblowing agencies and NGOs provide psychosocial care and advice for whistleblowers, and to what extent such agencies invest in the prevention of wrongdoing. The final part concludes the paper with a discussion and recommendations for future research.

2. Methods

This paper reports the results of a comparative study of whistleblowing agencies in 11 different countries that was conducted in the period of June 2017 to February 2018. The research was carried out as part of a broader project (Loyens and Vandekerckhove 2018) commissioned by the Dutch Whistleblowing Authority ('*Huis voor klokkenluiders*'), established in July 2016. The sampling was carried out at the country level. By means of a purposeful maximum variation sampling technique (Patton 1990), we started with a selection of countries within the Council of Europe and G20 with designated whistleblowing legislation and with institutions that have a certain level of comparability with the Dutch Whistleblowing Authority (being the commissioner of this study), mainly shown in the combination of advisory, psychosocial, investigative, and/or preventive tasks. Given that the Dutch Whistleblowing Authority is an external recipient of disclosures, we focused on those institutions. We aimed for a mix of early-movers and late-movers to include both countries with established institutional frameworks around whistleblowing and countries that are undergoing institutional rearrangements. During the study, some countries on our initial list were omitted (Slovakia and Sweden, respectively because of non-cooperation with key stakeholders and perceived lack of implementation of the law). We later added Australia and Israel, mainly because of their recent efforts to further develop the institutional framework to implement the whistleblowing legislation. This resulted in the final sample shown in Table 1 below.

Table 1. Final sample of countries included in this study.

Country	Whistleblowing Legislation Dates
Council of Europe countries	
UK	1998 (2013)
Belgium	2004; 2013
France	2004; 2016
Norway	2007
Serbia	2014
Ireland	2014
The Netherlands	2016
G20, but not CoE countries	
USA	1978 (2012); 2010
Republic of Korea	2001 (2014); 2011 (2015)
Australia	2004; 2009; 2013
Other countries	
Israel	1997; 2008

Within these countries, we studied both government agencies and NGOs that perform advisory, psychosocial care, investigative, and/or preventive tasks concerning whistleblowing. Data collection methods included: (1) analysis of policy and legislative documents concerning whistleblowing in the selected countries;[1] (2) analysis of existing research reports about agencies within the selected countries and implementation of whistleblowing legislation; and (3) 21 semi-structured interviews (17 by telephone and four face-to-face) with whistleblowing professionals, being high ranking officers working in the studied agencies, and academic experts who study whistleblowing in their country and who have been involved in recent legislative or institutional rearrangements. An interview protocol was used during the interviews (consisting topics like tasks, institutional arrangements, whistleblower protection, and implementation challenges), while remaining open for additional topics that interviewees considered relevant to discuss. Given the sensitive topic and to avoid social desirability bias, confidentiality of the respondents' identity was guaranteed and interviews were not recorded. During the interviews notes were made, which were written out in full detail shortly after the interview. Data were collected by two researchers who had regular discussions to increase the comparability of data collection. Data analysis was done by first summarizing the data per country in Excel tables and structuring them in general categories like 'institutional characteristics' and 'tasks' (further subdivided in 'advice', 'psychosocial care', 'investigation', and 'prevention'). The findings were then visualized in infographics (as shown in Figures 1 and 2 below), after which a comparison was made between agencies in the selected countries. To increase the validity of the findings, the interviewees reviewed the country summaries and infographics (as a form of member-checking), and their suggested revisions were taken into account. These revisions mainly consisted of providing further detail, and correcting omissions on our part.

3. Findings

This part will start with a brief comparison of the whistleblowing legislation in the selected countries, which (although not the focus of this paper) is the framework within which the studied external recipients of whistleblowing concerns operate. The following four sections will discuss the main findings of this study, along the lines of four subthemes. First, while there is a clear

---

[1] In the federal countries in our study, we focused on agencies at the state level, and only included regional agencies if interviewees referred to important differences between state and regional arrangements.

trend to install governmental whistleblowing agencies that deal with individual whistleblowing cases, this is more common for public sector than private sector whistleblowing. In countries with no or weak governmental whistleblowing agencies or with a fragmented institutional landscape, NGOs sometimes step in to provide whistleblowing protection. Second, we find that, in most countries, the investigation of alleged wrongdoing and the investigation of alleged retaliation are done by separate agencies to avoid conflict of interest, because the investigation of wrongdoing is considered to require more neutrality towards the whistleblower than retaliation investigations. Nevertheless, some whistleblowing agencies combine both investigative tasks. Third, only in a few of the selected countries are government funds available to provide specific psychosocial support for whistleblowers. While most whistleblowing agencies advise whistleblowers about the procedure and the decision to report, only the Dutch Whistleblowing Authority gives continuing support through the entire procedure, not unlike whistleblower protection by NGOs in some of the studied countries. Fourth, most whistleblowing agencies invest in the prevention of wrongdoing in public and/or private sector organizations, but only a few of them have the ambition to perform as a center for knowledge and expertise. The main findings are summarized in Table 2.

3.1. Legal Framework in Selected Countries

When comparing whistleblowing arrangements in the selected countries, two important differences can be observed, respectively relating to the sectoral scope of the legislation and the type of wrongdoing for which the legislation offers protection if reported by whistleblowers. With regard to sectoral scope, whilst some countries have separate whistleblowing regulations for the public and private sector (Australia, Israel, the Republic of Korea, and the USA) or whistleblowing provisions that only cover the public sector (Belgium), there is a clear trend to install stand-alone whistleblowing legislation covering both public and private sectors (Ireland, France, The Netherlands, Serbia, Norway, and the UK). Federal countries like the USA and Australia tend to have a fragmented legal framework, with not only separate pieces of whistleblowing legislation for the public and private sector, but also different regulations and agencies at various levels of the public sector. This has, in the USA, resulted in "a patchwork of more than 60 laws in different states, at different levels, for different sectors (including the private sector), and for different purposes" (Loyens and Vandekerckhove 2018, p. 25). The situation in Australia is similar (albeit with a lower number of whistleblowing laws), but discussions about unifying the legislation to cover both the public and the private sector are ongoing. Recently, Ireland and France made the shift from fragmented whistleblower protection towards a unified stand-alone legislation, which has the advantage that protection measures and whistleblowing statutes are the same for both public and private sector whistleblowers (Loyens and Vandekerckhove 2018).

Table 2. Summary of whistleblowing arrangements concerning external recipients of concerns in 11 countries.

Countries	Sectoral Scope	Whistleblowing Agency	Investigation	Care & (Legal) Advice	Prevention (Which Agency)
Australia	Separate for public and private sector	Government: ombudsman	Wrongdoing or referral	Government: information	Ombudsman (government)
Belgium	Only public sector	Government: ombudsman	Wrongdoing and retaliation	Government: information, advice	/
Ireland	Public and private sector	Government: prescribed persons	No investigative agency	NGO: advice, legal assistance	Integrity@Work (NGO)
Israel	Separate for public and private sector	Government: ombudsman	Wrongdoing and retaliation in separate units	Government: information, advice	/
France	Public and private sector	Government: ombudsman	Retaliation	/	/
The Netherlands	Public and private sector	Government: Dutch Whistleblowing Authority	Wrongdoing and retaliation	Government: psychologist, advice	Dutch Whistleblowing Authority (government)
Norway	Public and private sector	Government: clinic (only psychosocial support)	No investigative agency	Government: psychosocial care clinic	/
Republic of Korea	Separate for public and private sector	Government: ACRC	Retaliation	NGO: advice, legal assistance	/
Serbia	Public and private sector	NGO: Pistaljka	Only investigative journalists (Pistaljka)	NGO: advice, legal assistance	Pistaljka (NGO)
UK	Public and private sector	Government: prescribed persons & National Guardian Office (NHS)	No investigative agency	NGO: advice, legal assistance	NHS (government); Public Concern at Work (NGO)
USA	Separate for public and private sector	Government: OSC, SEC, OWB, MSPB; NGO: GAP	Retaliation (OSC, MSPB) & wrongdoing in separate units (SEC); investigative journalists (GAP)	Government: information, advice (OWB)	OSC (government); GAP (NGO)

When comparing the type of wrongdoing for which whistleblowers receive protection if they report it, we find much variation in the wording and definitions used in the selected countries. Despite the differences, we can observe some patterns. First, most legislation covers all of the following types of wrongdoing: (1) breaches of law, (2) danger to the health and safety of people, and to the environment, and (3) integrity violations. In the third type, there is huge variation in the wording and scope. Some examples include: 'shortcoming of public service duty' (Belgium), 'abuse of public trust' (Australia), 'abuse of authority' (Republic of Korea, USA), 'breaches of ethical codes' (Norway), 'gross mismanagement' (Ireland, USA), and 'violation of administration' (Israel). Moreover, this category is omitted in the whistleblowing legislation in France and the UK. Some countries add other types of wrongdoing to broaden the scope of the legislation. Norway stands out by also including "negative culture, corruption, illegality and unethical or harmful incidents" (Lewis and Trygstad 2009, p. 382). A noteworthy observation is that the scope of wrongdoing in private sector legislation tends to be less broad than the scope in public sector legislation (see e.g., Australia and USA), although the Republic of Korea is a possible exception. Only in a few countries does the legislation explicitly state that the wrongdoing should be in the public interest. In 2013, a 'public interest test' was introduced in the UK: a judge at an Employment Tribunal hearing considers whether the whistleblower had 'a reasonable belief the disclosure was in the public interest'. Given the very broad and imprecise definition of wrongdoing in the Norwegian whistleblowing law (see above), the legislative committee that will suggest revisions to the law is considering introducing a public interest test as well. Although in the Netherlands no public interest test is installed, the Dutch law explicitly stipulates that whistleblowers can only be protected if they report wrongdoing that may harm the public interest.

Of course, in all countries, whistleblowing legislation makes it possible for whistleblowers to make claims in court with regard to the wrongdoing they have observed and retaliation they have experienced. How these courts function is, however, outside of the scope of our research. In this paper, we concern ourselves with organisations other than courts that may facilitate successful whistleblowing (i.e., effective in stopping wrongdoing and safe for the whistleblower).

3.2. Governmental Whistleblowing Agencies and NGOs

Particularly in countries with separate whistleblowing legislation for the public sector, there is a trend to install governmental whistleblowing agencies that advise or support whistleblowers, investigate alleged wrongdoing and/or alleged retaliation, offer protection, and promote the prevention of wrongdoing. In our study, six countries have already installed such an agency,[2] but the combination of tasks differs (as shown in Figure 1). In four of the selected countries, this role is mandated to the Ombudsman (Australia,[3] Belgium,[4] Israel, and France). In the USA, the Office of Special Counsel (OSC) is the authorized whistleblowing agency for the public sector. Other whistleblowing agencies, such as the Securities and Exchange Commission (SEC) that implements the Dodd-Frank Act, offer protection for all whistleblowers who report security law violations. Within the SEC, the Office of the Whistleblower (OWB) investigates alleged retaliation, gives advice to whistleblowers, and promotes the prevention of wrongdoing. So far, only in the Republic of Korea and the Netherlands is a government agency installed to deal with both public and private sector whistleblowers. Since its establishment in 2001, the mandate of the Anti-Corruption and Civil Rights Commission (ACRC) in the Republic of Korea has grown from dealing with anti-corruption to dealing with whistleblowing cases on a broader range of wrongdoing in the public and private sector (covered by two separate pieces of legislation).

---

[2] In France, the new legislation had mandated the ombudsman for the investigation of whistleblowing cases, but the executive decree implementing these new tasks for the ombudsperson had not been signed at the time of writing this paper (June 2018). Therefore, France is not included in Figure 1.

[3] As for Australia, this study focused on the Commonwealth Ombudsman at the national level.

[4] As for Belgium, this study focused on the Flemish and Federal level. At both levels, the Ombudsman operates as the whistleblowing agency for the public sector.

Hence, only the Netherlands has a governmental whistleblowing agency that operates under a stand-alone whistleblowing legislation for both the public and the private sector. Other countries in our sample are exploring the same option (France, Norway, and Australia).

Although the UK has the longest experience of a whistleblowing law that covers the public and private sector, it does not have a central whistleblowing agency linked to that law, which is also the case in Ireland. The legislations in both of these countries only provide a list of 'prescribed persons' that receive reports and investigate alleged wrongdoing. For Ireland, there is no information available as to how pro-active these regulating bodies are concerning whistleblowing cases. But in the UK, the National Audit Office recently conducted an audit (in 2015) that showed that staff within these 'prescribed person' bodies were often unaware that they were mandated as a recipient of whistleblower concerns. Specifically for the National Health Service (NHS) in the UK, a whistleblowing agency was established in 2016 (see below).

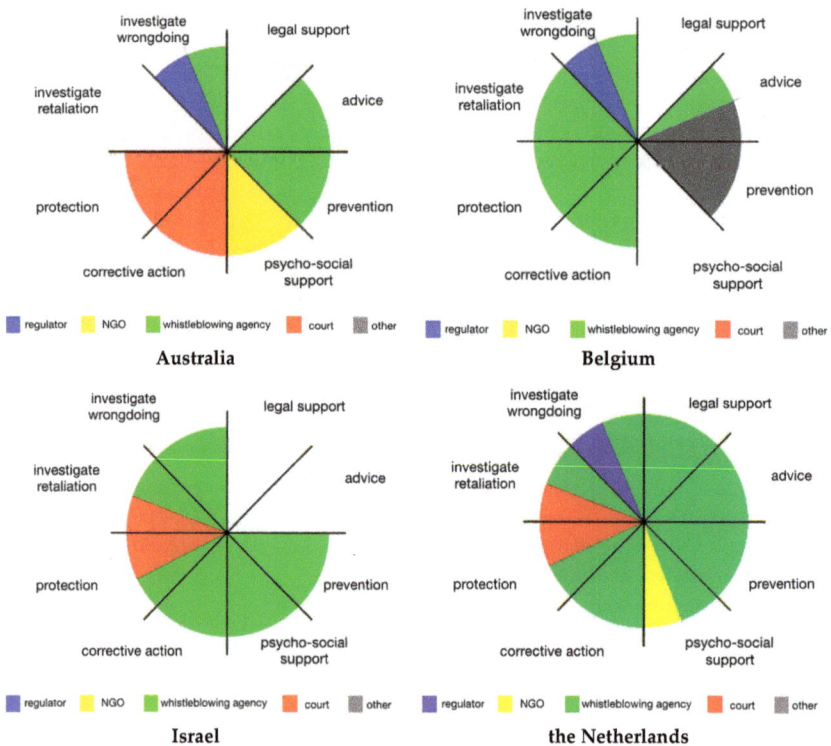

Figure 1. *Cont.*

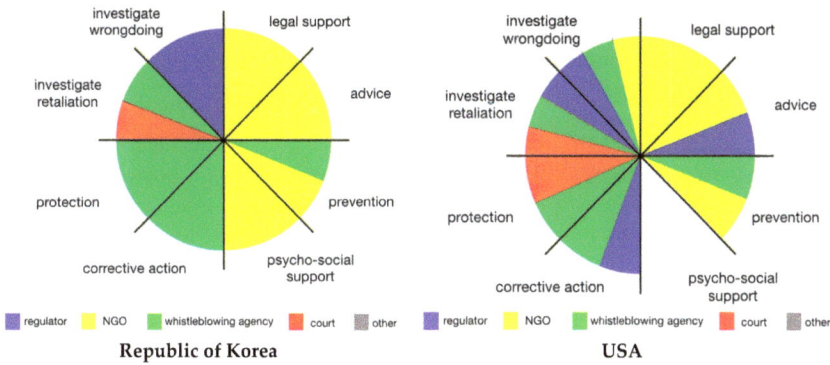

Figure 1. Various tasks of governmental whistleblowing agencies in this study.

In some countries, specific NGOs have been created that conduct some of the tasks of the governmental whistleblowing agencies described above. Sometimes the role of NGOs is complementary to that of governmental whistleblowing agencies (like the Government Accountability Project (GAP[5]) in the USA), while in other countries, these NGOSs have stepped in because no government agency has been installed (yet) (like Pistaljka[6] or 'The Whistle' in Serbia) (see Figure 2).

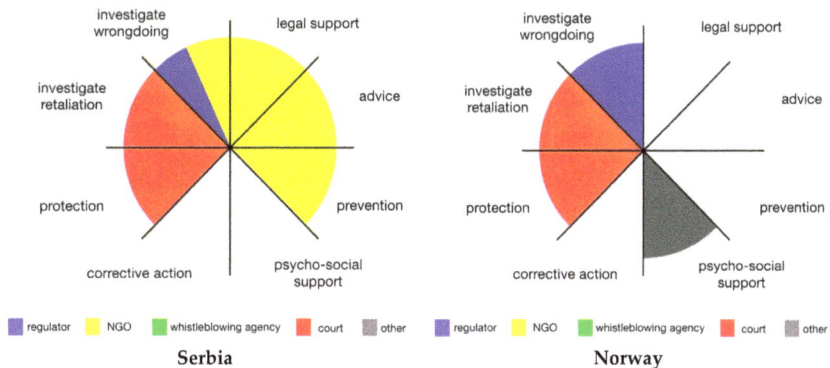

Figure 2. Agencies involved in whistleblowing in Serbia and Norway.

Particularly in countries without either a governmental whistleblowing agency or NGOs that support whistleblowers (as in Norway, see Figure 2), whistleblowers find themselves in a precarious situation, as has been shown in research of the Fafo Institute of Labour and Social Research in Oslo. The researchers of Fafo conclude that since 2010, whistleblowing has become more difficult in Norway: in surveys, whistleblowers increasingly report being retaliated against, resulting in a decrease of the willingness to report (Bjørkelo 2017; Fafo 2016), and qualitative studies show negative consequences of whistleblowing like "job loss [and] the stigma of association of even being seen as a friend or an associate of a current or previous employee that has reported about wrongdoing at work" (Bjørkelo 2017, p. 8). An interviewee states that the situation seems particularly problematic in the Norwegian public sector, but research to support that statement has yet to be conducted.

---

⁵ See: https://www.whistleblower.org/.
⁶ See: https://pistaljka.rs/.

3.3. The Investigation of Reported Wrongdoing and Alleged Retaliation

Most whistleblowing agencies in our sample either investigate reported wrongdoing (Australia), or alleged retaliation (France, USA OSC, USA Merit Systems Protection Board (MSPB), Republic of Korea). However, how these agencies operate in practice has not remained uncriticized. The Merit Systems Protection Board (MSPB), for example, which is a court-like government agency to which federal whistleblowers in the USA can appeal with retaliation claims (or because they believe to have experienced other Prohibited Personnel Practices), has received severe criticisms from GAP (Devine 2017) and some of our interviewees. Several whistleblowing experts in our study explain that the administrative judges in general have a hostile attitude towards the whistleblowing legislation, which may explain the 95–98% rulings against whistleblowers, and are prone to informal political pressure, which reduces their (perceived) independence in practice. Their lack of expertise in dealing with whistleblowing cases in practice is also mentioned in several interviews, as are the delays that result in final decisions only being made after three to six years. Combined, these factors negatively influence the already vulnerable position of whistleblowers within the American federal government. As for Australia, our study confirms the finding of Annakin (2011) that in practice, the Ombudsman often does not investigate the disclosed wrongdoing, but refers it to the department of the whistleblower for investigation. The Ombudsman must be informed by these agencies of decisions not to investigate and may extend time limits for such investigations.[7] On its own current interpretation of the legislation, the Ombudsman cannot investigate retaliation against whistleblowers. However, some experts and whistleblowers think the Ombudsman can, which illustrates the lack of clarity of the current legislation. In practice, the Ombudsman thus only investigates whether agencies applied the procedural requirements of the whistleblowing legislation in dealing with the disclosure. If the Ombudsman concludes that an agency has erred, recommendations are made and reported to the Prime Minister and to the Parliament if the department decides not to implement them. Given the risks of the decentralized investigative approach in which "the Principal Officer and Authorised Officer within each agency [are held] responsible for receiving, assessing, allocating, investigating and responding to each disclosure" (Moss 2016, p. 26) and the lack of experience of the Commonwealth Ombudsman in employer-employee disputes, it has been suggested that whistleblowing protection be taken away from the Commonwealth Ombudsman and moved to a new Whistleblower Protection Authority (Moss 2016; Parliamentary Joint Committee on Corporations and Financial Services 2017).

In some countries, the governmental whistleblowing agencies investigate both the alleged wrongdoing and retaliation claims (Belgium, Israel, The Netherlands, SEC USA). For the Israeli Ombudsman[8] and the SEC (USA), these tasks are performed by separate departments within the same agency. Interviewees could not always give clear reasons as to why these investigative tasks are separated. Some referred to the different types of expertise needed for both types of investigations, or the risk of conflicting interests because investigating wrongdoing may require more neutrality towards the whistleblower than retaliation investigations. In departments combining both investigative tasks, there is (in their opinion) an increased risk of partiality in wrongdoing investigations. Only in Belgium (for the public sector) and the Netherlands (for public and private sector) are investigations of wrongdoing and retaliation done within the same department. However, because in Israel no 'Chinese walls' are installed between both investigative departments, resulting in elaborate and easy information sharing that is not regulated with protocols, we see no substantial difference from the Belgian and Dutch situation. Interviewees in these countries explained that combining these investigative tasks

---

[7]   In 2016–2017, 684 disclosures were made to all Commonwealth agencies, of which only 60 were made directly to Ombudsman. Of these 60 disclosures, only 40 PID's were accepted and 23 of those were referred to the Agency concerned to be investigated. Furthermore, the Ombudsman received 34 complaints about how PID's were dealt with in agencies, and finalized 44 complaint investigations (Commonwealth Ombudsman 2017).

[8]   In Israel, the State Comptroller investigates the alleged wrongdoing, and the Ombudsman investigates retaliation against whistleblowers and provides protection. The Ombudsman is part of the State Comptroller in Israel.

(or exchanging information about it) is advisable, because the issues that are investigated cannot be easily separated in practice.

Some NGOs also have a role in the investigation of wrongdoing, but obviously their (perceived) independence in practice is different than that of governmental whistleblowing agencies. Both GAP (USA) and Pistaljka (Serbia) employ journalists who investigate the charges whistleblowers make and publish the results in articles and reports. By doing so, these organisations help to expose wrongdoing in the government and other agencies to the public. Unlike some governmental whistleblowing agencies (see above), these NGOs do not investigate alleged retaliation against whistleblowers.

3.4. Psychosocial Care and Advice to Whistleblowers

In our sample, government funds for specific psychosocial care for whistleblowers are only available in the Netherlands and in Norway. In Norway, a psychosocial care clinic was established in 2012—funded by the Ministry of Health—for whistleblowers who have suffered retaliation. More than 200 whistleblowers have already been given psychosocial care in the past six years. Nevertheless, the program will probably be closed down. The official reason is money-related, but an interviewee explains that an additional reason may be that the government feels uncomfortable having such a clinic, given that it may be perceived as a symptom of a culture that is against whistleblowers and freedom of speech. The Dutch Whistleblowing Authority provides free psychological care (by one psychologist), which the Israeli Ombudsman is also starting up as part of the development of a more holistic approach to whistleblower protection. While in some other countries (Australia, UK, Republic of Korea), civil society organizations have stepped in to fill that need, whistleblowers in most of the studied countries are referred to general employee assistance programs that are installed to support employees with various kinds of psychosocial needs, like stress and the consequences of harassment or bullying. Some interviewees claim that these programs often cannot meet the particular needs of whistleblowers who have experienced retaliation.

Most governmental whistleblowing agencies in our study provide information to whistleblowers about the procedure (Australia, Belgium, the Netherlands, Israel, OWB in USA) and/or give advice to would-be whistleblowers about their decision to report (Belgium, Israel, the Netherlands, OWB in USA). The OWB of the American SEC, for example, operates a hotline where (would-be) whistleblowers, their attorneys, and other citizens can ask information about the program (e.g., eligibility criteria for awards, confidentiality guarantees, investigative procedure and the appropriateness of the SEC to handle a specific tip, see SEC 2017). Whereas in Israel advice to whistleblowers is not formally a task of the Ombudsman or the State Comptroller, these agencies do inform whistleblowers about the risks of whistleblowing and available reporting channels. Only the Dutch Whistleblowing Authority offers more comprehensive advice. Whistleblowers are given continuous support throughout the entire investigation, for example, in the form of assistance before and during the investigation (including practical help like writing letters to employers) and legal advice during the entire procedure (but not representation in court). This approach is similar to the support and assistance given by some NGOs (Ireland, Republic of Korea, UK, USA and Serbia), although these often also provide legal counselling and representation in court.

3.5. Whistleblowing Agencies and the Prevention of Wrongdoing

Most governmental whistleblowing agencies in our study (Australia, The Netherlands, Republic of Korea, UK, and USA) invest in the prevention of wrongdoing, but the scope of this prevention task differs. Probably at the forefront is the recently established National Guardian Office in the UK, which performs 'speak-up culture audits' of health care organisations and publishes the results thereof in culture review reports (that include recommendations and requirements with a set deadline). In other countries, such a watchdog-like approach is only taken by civil society organisations. The National Guardian Office also provides awareness raising and training, and supports inter-vision between Guardians at Hospital Trust level. In the other four countries, the prevention tasks are not as comprehensive as those of the NHS Guardian. Some whistleblowing agencies train other agencies (e.g., Office of Special Counsel in USA) or public officials (e.g., Australian Ombudsman) on how to implement the whistleblowing legislation. The Dutch Whistleblowing Authority goes a step further by also assisting employers with implementing whistleblowing policy. Moreover, this agency has the ambition to operate as a center of knowledge and expertise for whistleblowing policy and integrity management. Some NGOs, like GAP (USA) and Pistaljka (Serbia), also operate as a knowledge center concerning whistleblowing policy and provide ad hoc advice to employers with questions about whistleblowing legislation. In addition, these NGOs, like Integrity@Work (Ireland) and Public Concern at Work (UK), provide training for agencies (and in the case of Serbia, also judges) involved in whistleblowing protection or investigation.

4. Discussion and Conclusions

We agree with Moberly (2014) that external recipients of whistleblower disclosures are under-studied. Most whistleblowing studies have focused on whistleblowing legislation and the whistleblower: "what makes them report, what they report, how many and how often whistleblowers come forward, and what happens to them" (Lewis et al. 2014, p. 19). While our study did not analyze the effectiveness of external whistleblowing agencies in dealing with whistleblower concerns (Moberly 2014), it lays the groundwork from which further in-depth research can be conducted with reference to the actual role of the recipients in enhancing whistleblowing protection. Our study particularly aimed to gain a greater understanding of the various roles and tasks that external recipients of disclosed concerns (both government agencies and NGOs) have in various countries with whistleblowing legislation. In this study, we have seen two emerging trends concerning whistleblowing protection. First, countries are increasingly installing stand-alone whistleblowing legislations covering both public and private sectors. Whilst stand-alone whistleblowing legislation in itself is not new (Brown et al. 2014; Vandekerckhove 2010), what is new is that one piece of legislation covers both public and private sector whistleblowing. This approach seems, however, to have been more difficult for federal countries (like Australia, Belgium, and USA), which often have a fragmented legislative framework with a variety of whistleblowing statutes at different government levels, and sometimes (in Australia, USA) one or more separate whistleblowing laws for the private sector. On the one hand, this approach lacks coherence and may be confusing for whistleblowers. On the other hand, as one of our interviewees confirmed, one advantage of a fragmented legal framework is that whistleblowers often have different agencies they can go to in the case of reprisal; they thus have different options to seek relief. It remains unclear why a unified legal framework does not necessarily create a more centralized institutional framework. The UK and Ireland are key countries to study this further. Both these countries have a unified whistleblowing legislation, yet a fragmented institutional framework. This institutional framework continues to change, however, with a number of 'new comers' such as Integrity@Work in Ireland, and WhistleblowersUK and the National Guardian Office in the UK. It was clear in our study that institutional actors in all countries were seeking to learn from the Dutch and French institutional experiments with centralized and holistic government agencies.

Second, there is a clear trend to install governmental whistleblowing agencies to implement whistleblowing legislation. The majority of the studied countries already have one or more of these agencies, which often have several tasks in whistleblowing protection. However, the precise combination of tasks differs between the studied countries. The Netherlands stands out with a combination of advisory, preventive, and twofold investigative tasks (wrongdoing and retaliation claims) and psychosocial care in one agency. However, this agency, established in 2016, received severe criticism and negative media attention, because in 2016 and 2017 no investigation had been completed (see, e.g., Rengers 2017; Voskuil 2017). The next years will show whether the agency will be able to make a new start implementing the recommendations of a recent internal investigation (Ruys 2017). The Israeli Ombudsman[9] and the SEC (USA)[10] each combine four of the five tasks of the Dutch Whistleblowing Authority. It seems that the importance of a holistic approach in whistleblowing protection is increasingly emphasized. More and more whistleblowing agencies recognize that whistleblowing protection is not only about responding to retaliation claims of whistleblowers, but also about investigating and trying to stop the wrongdoing, as well as advising would-be whistleblowers about their decision to report. However, research on the effectiveness of less or more holistic ways in which external recipients deal with whistleblower disclosures is lacking (Lewis et al. 2014; Vandekerckhove et al. 2014). More insight is also needed into how easily these tasks can be combined within the same agency or even the same department, and the possible positive or negative effects of such attempts. To what extent is there, for example, a conflict of interest when investigations of wrongdoing and retaliation are combined, and if so, which safeguards are needed to avoid partial investigations? How do advice to (would-be) whistleblowers and an independent investigation of disclosed wrongdoing go together? And what are the consequences of (not) installing 'Chinese walls' between any of these functions?

Despite the trend towards a more holistic approach, our study has also shown that not many countries provide funds for specific psychosocial support adapted to the needs of whistleblowers who have suffered from retaliation. Only the Netherlands and Norway have installed such care and Israel is starting it up. In other countries, whistleblowers who need psychosocial support are referred to general employee assistance systems. Research on the effectiveness of either of these systems is, however, lacking. Previous studies have shown that retaliation is a common (but varying) risk for whistleblowers, and that this may result in various types of 'suffering', such as work-related problems (e.g., demotivation, disengagement, and distrust to coworkers) (Smith 2014) and psychological problems (van der Velden et al. 2018) like "anxiety, depression, irritability or dread, even suicidal thoughts" (Hedin and Månsson 2012, p. 162). However, more research is needed to determine which whistleblowers suffer and how they suffer (particularly outside the USA where most research is conducted) (Smith 2014). Moreover, scholars should also analyze how those who have experienced reprisals have overcome the consequences of it and which support mechanisms are helpful. Such research would be useful for the debate on whether governments should invest in specific tailor-made psychosocial support for whistleblowers or refer those who suffer from retaliation to general employee assistance programs.

Finally, our study shows that a lack of expertise among those who need to implement whistleblowing legislation strongly weakens the position of the whistleblower, as seen in the Australian Commonwealth Ombudsman and the MSPB (USA). This confirms the finding in the Australian WWTW study (Annakin 2011) that insufficient skills of staff results in unsatisfactory assessment and response to whistleblowing disclosures. Therefore, it seems promising that some governmental whistleblowing agencies (e.g., NHS in UK and Australian Ombudsman) and NGOs invest in the training of government officials involved in the implementation of the legislation (e.g., GAP, Integrity@Work, Public Concern at Work) or judges who enforce whistleblowing protection (e.g., Pistaljka). Moberly (2014), referring to Miceli et al. (2009), in the same line argues that recipients of concerns should receive training to deal with whistleblower disclosures, but that research on the effects of such trainings is needed.

In conclusion, this paper aimed to increase our understanding of the role of external recipients of whistleblowing concerns in practice and calls for more such research. This study, however, had some limitations that should be taken into account in further research. First, given time and budget constraints, we were only able to conduct a limited number of interviews in each of the selected

---

9   The Israeli Ombudsman (1) investigates wrongdoing reported by whistleblowers, (2) investigates alleged retaliation against whistleblowers, (3) provides psychosocial support to whistleblowers, and (4) performs prevention tasks in terms of awareness raising via information dissemination campaigns.

10 The SEC combines following tasks: (1) advice to whistleblowers, (2) investigation of alleged wrongdoing, (3) investigation of alleged retaliation, and (4) prevention.

countries. This limitation was to some extent overcome by consulting many documents and reports which offered rich data on the practice of whistleblowing protection. Moreover, the interviewees were all experts on this topic and therefore able to critically assess both the validity of the written information, and strengths and weaknesses of whistleblowing protection in their country. Further research could try to get in contact with more key stakeholders within the studied agencies to gain in-depth knowledge of how they operate in practice. Particularly in countries with limited written information in English (e.g., Norway and Serbia) and data collection by researchers who do not speak the respective languages, thus relying more on interview data, it is advisable to include more interviewees in the study. Second, given the focus on the comparison of differences and similarities between countries, this study can only give an overview of trends and challenges. More detailed case studies should be conducted to further unravel institutional practices and mechanisms of whistleblowing protection in the respective countries, particularly outside USA and UK context, which have already been studied extensively. Third, this study only reports on whistleblowing arrangements in 11 countries. Given the importance of national, legislative, and cultural context for whistleblowing protection, the findings cannot be generalized to countries not included in this study. Nevertheless, given the diversity of countries in the sample (which was deliberately aimed for at the outset of the study), the conclusions could offer useful insights for whistleblowing arrangements in other countries.

Author Contributions: Conceptualization, K.L. and W.V.; Methodology, K.L. and W.V.; Validation, K.L. and W.V.; Formal Analysis, K.L. and W.V.; Investigation, K.L. and W.V.; Resources, K.L. and W.V.; Writing-Original Draft Preparation, K.L. and W.V.; Writing-Review & Editing, K.L. and W.V.; Visualization, W.V.; Supervision, K.L.; Project Administration, K.L.; Funding Acquisition, K.L.

Funding: This research was funded by the Dutch Whistleblowing Authority.

Conflicts of Interest: The authors declare no conflicts of interest.

References

Annakin, Lindy. 2011. In the Public Interest or Out of Desperation? The Experience of Australian Whistleblowers Reporting to Accountability Agencies. Unpublished Ph.D. thesis, University of Sydney, Sydney, Australia. Available online: https://ses.library.usyd.edu.au/bitstream/2123/7904/1/l_annakin_2011_thesis.pdf (accessed on 22 June 2018).

Ayers, Susan, and Steven E. Kaplan. 2005. Wrongdoing by consultants: An examination of employees' reporting intentions. *Journal of Business Ethics* 57: 121–37. [CrossRef]

Bjørkelo, Brita. 2017. Norwegian whistleblowing research: A case of Nordic exceptionalism? In *Selected Papers from the International Whistleblowing Research Network Conference*. Edited by David Lewis and Wim Vandekerckhove. London: International Whistleblowing Research Network, pp. 6–17.

BluePrint for Free Speech. 2015. *Breaking the Silence. Strengths & Weaknesses in G20 Whistleblower Protection Laws.* Melbourne: BluePrint for Free Speech.

Bosua, Rachelle, Simon Milton, Suelette Dreyfus, and Reeva Lederman. 2014. Going public: Researching external whistleblowing in a new media age. In *International Handbook on Whistleblowing Research*. Edited by Alexander Jonathan Brown, David Lewis, Richard E. Moberly and Wim Vandekerckhove. Cheltenham: Edward Elgar Publishing, pp. 250–72.

Brown, A. J., Daniel P. Meyer, Chris Wheeler, and Jason Zuckerman. 2014. Whistleblower Support in Practice: Towards an Integrated Research Model. In *International Handbook on Whistleblowing Research*. Edited by A. J. Brown, David Lewis, Richard E. Moberly and Wim Vandekerckhove. Cheltenham: Edward Elgar Publishing, pp. 457–94.

Commonwealth Ombudsman. 2017. *Annual Report 2016–2017.* Canberra: Commonwealth Ombudsman.

Council of Europe. 2014. *Recommendation CM/Rec(2014)7 of the Committee of Ministers to Member States on the Protection of Whistleblowers.* Strasbourg: Council of Europe.

De Graaf, Gjalt. 2010. A report on reporting: Why peers report integrity and law violations in public organizations. *Public Administration Review* 70: 767–79. [CrossRef]

Devine, Tom. 2015. International best practices for whistleblower statutes. In *Developments in Whistleblowing Research*. Edited by David Lewis and Wim Vandekerckhove. London: International Whistleblowing Research Network, pp. 7–19.

Devine, Tom. 2016. International best practices for whistleblowing policies. In *Checkmate to Corruption: Making the Case for a Wide-Ranging Initiative on Whistleblower Protection*. Edited by Wim Vandekerckhove. Geneva: Public Services International, pp. 23–26.

Devine, Tom. 2017. *Corrected testimony of Thomas Devine. Government Accountability Project before the House Oversight and Government Reform Committee, Subcommittee on Federal Workforce, U.S. Postal Service and the Census on Whistleblower Protection since Passage of the Whistleblower Protection Enhancement Act*. Washington: U.S. Government Publishing Office.

Dworkin, Terry Morehead, and Melissa S. Baucus. 1998. Internal vs. external whistleblowers: A comparison of whistleblowering processes. *Journal of Business Ethics* 17: 1281–98. [CrossRef]

Dworkin, Terry Morehead, and Arthur J. Brown. 2013. The Money or the Media? Lessons from Contrasting Developments in US and Australian Whistleblowing Laws. *Seattle Journal of Social Justice* 11: 653–713.

European Commission. 2018. *Proposal for a Directive of the European Parliament and of the Council Establishing Common Minimum Standards for the Protection of Persons Reporting on Breaches in Specific Union Policy Areas*. Brussels: European Commission, April 23.

Fafo. 2016. *Whistleblowing and Freedom of Speech in Norwegian Working Life 2016*. English Summary of Varsling og Ytringsfrihet i Norsk Arbeidsliv 2016, Fafo-Rapport 2016. Oslo: Fafo, p. 33.

Fasterling, Björn, and David Lewis. 2014. Leaks, legislation and freedom of speech: How can the law effectively promote public-interest whistleblowing? *International Labour Review* 153: 71–92. [CrossRef]

Hedin, Ulla-Carin, and Sven-Axel Månsson. 2012. Whistleblowing processes in Swedish public organisations—Complaints and consequences. *European Journal of Social Work* 15: 151–67. [CrossRef]

Lewis, David, and Sissel Trygstad. 2009. Protecting whistleblowers in Norway and the UK: A case of mix and match? *International Journal of Law and Management* 51: 374–88. [CrossRef]

Lewis, David, Arthur J. Brown, and Richard Moberly. 2014. Whistleblowing, its importance and the state of the research. In *International Handbook on Whistleblowing Research*. Edited by Arthur J. Brown, David Lewis, Richard E. Moberly and Wim Vandekerckhove. Cheltenham: Edward Elgar Publishing, pp. 1–34.

Loyens, Kim. 2012. Integrity Secured. Understanding Ethical Decision Making among Street-Level Bureaucrats in the Belgian Labor Inspection and Federal Police. Ph.D. dissertation, Katholieke Universiteit Leuven, Leuven, Belgium.

Loyens, Kim, and Wim Vandekerckhove. 2018. *The Dutch Whistleblowing Authority in an International Perspective: A Comparative Study*. Utrecht University and University of Greenwich, forthcoming.

Mesmer-Magnus, Jessica R., and Chockalingam Viswesvaran. 2005. Whistleblowing in organizations: An examination of correlates of whistleblowing intentions, actions, and retaliation. *Journal of Business Ethics* 62: 277–97. [CrossRef]

Miceli, Marcia P., and Janet P. Near. 1992. *Blowing the Whistle: The Organizational and Legal Implications for Companies and Employees*. New York: Lexington.

Miceli, Marcia P., and Janet P. Near. 2002. What makes whistle-blowers effective? Three field studies. *Human Relations* 55: 455–79. [CrossRef]

Miceli, Marcia P., Janet P. Near, and Charles R. Schwenk. 1991. Who blows the whistle and why? *Industrial and Labor Relations Review* 45: 113–30. [CrossRef]

Miceli, Marcia P., Janet Pollex Near, and Terry M. Dworkin. 2008. *Whistle-Blowing in Organizations*. New York: Routledge.

Miceli, Marcia P., Janet P. Near, and Terry Morehead Dworkin. 2009. A word to the wise: How managers and policy-makers can encourage employees to report wrongdoing. *Journal of business ethics* 86: 379–96. [CrossRef]

Moberly, Richard. 2014. 'To persons or organizations that may be able to effect action': Whistleblowing recipients. In *International Handbook on Whistleblowing Research*. Edited by A. J. Brown, David Lewis, Richard E. Moberly and Wim Vandekerckhove. Cheltenham: Edward Elgar Publishing, pp. 273–97.

Morvan, Patrick. 2009. A comparison of the freedom of speech of workers in French and American law. *Indiana Law Journal* 84: 1015–46.

Moss, Philip. 2016. *Review of the Public Interest Disclosure Act 2013. An Independent Statutory Review Conducted by Mr. Philip Moss AM*. Canberra: Department of the Prime Minister and Cabinet.

Near, Janet P., and Marcia P. Miceli. 1996. Whistle-blowing: Myth and reality. *Journal of Management* 22: 507–26. [CrossRef]

Near, Janet P., Terry Morehead Dworkin, and Marcia P. Miceli. 1993. Explaining the whistle-blowing process: Suggestions from power theory and justice theory. *Organization Science* 4: 393–411. [CrossRef]

OECD. 2011. *Study on Whistleblower Protection. Frameworks, Compendium of Best Practices and Guiding Principles for Legislation*. Paris: OECD.

Osterhaus, Anja, and Craig Fagan. 2009. Alternative to Silence: Whistleblower Protection in 10 European Countries. Report for Transparency International, November 15. Available online: https://www.transparency. org/whatwedo/publication/alternative_to_silence_whistleblower_protection_in_10_european_countries (accessed on 22 June 2018).

PACE (Parliamentary Assembly of the Council of Europe). 2009. The Protection of Whistleblowers. Report of the Committee of Legal Affairs and Human Rights, Document 12006. September 14. Available online: http://assembly.coe.int/nw/xml/XRef/Xref-XML2HTML-en.asp?fileid=12302 (accessed on 22 June 2018).

Parliamentary Joint Committee on Corporations and Financial Services. 2017. *Whistleblower Protections*. Canberra: Parliamentary Joint Committee on Corporations and Financial Services.

Patton, Michael Quinn. 1990. *Qualitative Evaluation and Research Methods*. Newbury Park: Sage.

Rengers, Merijn. 2017. Crisis in Huis voor Klokkenluiders (Crisis in Dutch House for Whistleblowers). *NRC*, October 19. Available online: https://www.nrc.nl/nieuws/2017/10/19/crisis-in-huis-voor-klokkenluiders-13583268-a1578008 (accessed on 22 June 2018).

Roberts, Peter. 2014. Motivations for whistleblowing: Personal, private and public interests. In *International Handbook on Whistleblowing Research*. Edited by A. J. Brown, David Lewis, Richard E. Moberly and Wim Vandekerckhove. Cheltenham: Edward Elgar Publishing, pp. 207–29.

Roberts, Peter, and A. J. Brown. 2010. The Australian legislative experience. In *A Global Approach to Public Interest Disclosure: What Can We Learn from Existing Whistleblowing Legislation and Research?* Edited by David B. Lewis. Cheltenham: Edward Elgar, pp. 56–73.

Rothschild, Joyce, and Terance D. Miethe. 1999. Whistle-blower disclosures and management retaliation. *Work and Occupations* 26: 107–28. [CrossRef]

Ruys, Maarten. 2017. Advies Voor Een Herstart Voor het Huis Voor Klokkenluiders. Advies, Onafhankelijk Onderzoek en Preventie (Advice for a New Start for the Dutch House for Whistleblowers: Advice, Independent Investigation and Prevention). Available online: https://huisvoorklokkenluiders.nl/wp-content/uploads/2017/12/Advies-voor-een-herstart-voor-het-Huis-voor-klokkenluiders-dec-2017.pdf (accessed on 22 June 2018).

SEC. 2017. *Annual Report to Congress: Whistleblower Program*. Washington: Securities and Exchange Commission.

Smith, Rodney. 2014. Whistleblowing and Suffering. In *International Handbook on Whistleblowing Research*. Edited by Alexander J. Brown, David Lewis, Richard E. Moberly and Wim Vandekerckhove. Cheltenham: Edward Elgar Publishing, pp. 230–49.

UNODC. 2015. *Resource Guide on Good Practices in the Protection of Reporting Persons*. Vienna: UNODC.

van der Velden, Peter G., Mauro Pecoraro, Mijke S. Houwerzijl, and Erik van der Meulen. 2018. Mental health problems among whistleblowers: A comparative study. *Psychological Reports*. [CrossRef] [PubMed]

Vandekerckhove, Wim. 2010. European whistleblowing policies: Tiers or tears? In *A Global Approach to Public Interest Disclosure: What Can We Learn from Existing Whistleblowing LEGISLATION and research?* Edited by David B. Lewis. Cheltenham: Edward Elgar, pp. 15–35.

Vandekerckhove, Wim, Alexander J. Brown, Richard E. Moberly, and David Lewis. 2014. Strategic issues in whistleblowing research. In *International Handbook on Whistleblowing Research*. Edited by Alexander J. Brown, David Lewis, Richard E. Moberly and Wim Vandekerckhove. Cheltenham: Edward Elgar Publishing, pp. 522–30.

Vaughn, Robert G. 2012. *The Successes and Failures of Whistleblower Laws*. Cheltenham: Edward Elgar.

Voskuil, Koen. 2017. Huis voor Klokkenluiders Stort in Elkaar (Dutch House for Whistleblowers Collapses). *AD*, December 14. Available online: https://www.ad.nl/binnenland/huis-voor-klokkenluiders-stort-in-elkaar~a264c38e.X (accessed on 22 June 2018).

administrative sciences

MDPI

Short Note

The Role of Collusive Dynamics in the Occurrence of Organizational Crime: A Psychoanalytically Informed Social Psychological Perspective

Sandra Schruijer

Utrecht University School of Governance, Utrecht University, Bijlhouwerstraat 6, 3511 ZC Utrecht, The Netherlands; s.g.l.schruijer@uu.nl

Received: 30 April 2018; Accepted: 21 June 2018; Published: 27 June 2018

Abstract: This short reflective paper discusses collusion from a psychoanalytically informed social psychological perspective. From this perspective, collusion represents a non-conscious group dynamic in which the participants 'play together' to keep a threatening or painful reality out of awareness. To illustrate the dynamics, two examples from the world of infrastructure and from higher education are provided. Although collusion in itself is not criminal, it may lead to neglectful or criminal behavior. Since it is a system-level phenomenon, holding individuals accountable will not end the dynamics.

Keywords: collusion; group dynamics; psychology; psychoanalysis; systems–psychodynamics

1. Introduction

Corporate or organizational crimes are defined as "illegal or harmful acts, committed by legitimate organizations or their members, for the benefit of these organizations" (Call for Papers). Examples of these crimes include financial manipulation, accounting fraud, cartels, bribery, environmental harms and corporate human rights violations. In this paper, I will focus on the phenomenon of collusion, which refers to a secret agreement between two or more parties to realize a fraudulent or illegal goal (American Dictionary of the English Language). In economic science, collusion represents a secret agreement between companies, which is often unwritten and manifests itself in cartels and implicit price agreements with unfair competition as a consequence (Ayres 1993). In policy sciences, such conspiring involves civil servants committing civil crimes (Van den Heuvel 2005). The phenomenon of collusion that I will be addressing derives from social psychology and from psychoanalysis. This collusion pertains to non-conscious relational dynamics between two or more parties (individuals, groups or organizations) that 'play together' so as to keep a threatening or painful reality out of awareness. Rather than outsiders being unknowing of secretive deals, as in cartels, it are now the protagonists themselves that are unaware of their collusive dynamics. Below, I will first define the concept of collusion from a social psychological and subsequently, a psychoanalytic point of view. After this, I will provide some examples. Finally, I will conclude with some reflections regarding the relationship between collusion and crime.

2. What Is Collusion from a Social Psychological and a Psychoanalytic Perspective?

Collusion is the central theme of social/organizational psychologist Jerry Harvey, who was known for his formulation of the Abilene paradox (Harvey 1988) where groups fail to act in line with the (unanimous yet private) preferences of their group members and even act in the opposite way. In his book entitled *How come everytime I get stabbed in the back my fingerprints are on the knife* (Harvey 1999), Harvey describes how individuals are complicit to their own downfall because they failed to speak out. Human beings need to be in meaningful contact with others and their fear of abandonment and separation form the core of this phenomenon. People tend to remain silent when they imagine that their opinion deviates from those of significant others. They entertain negative fantasies about the consequences especially as they fear rejection. Therefore, it remains untested whether indeed there is a diversity in ideas, preferences, interests and feelings. Since no one speaks out, the group members reinforce one another in their false beliefs, i.e., the beliefs that they incorrectly attribute to the other group members.

Thus, collusion in the psychological sense refers to a hidden dynamic among protagonists. The dynamic involves an implicit and often non-conscious collaboration that is aimed at mutually satisfying hidden needs and/or warding off fears (such as, finding approval, boosting one's self-esteem, avoiding rejection or exclusion, not being confronted with powerlessness or insecurity and so on). Protagonists share a joint desire to avoid a confrontation with a possibly painful or threatening reality. As a consequence, (real or imagined) differences in interests, preferences and identities are neglected or glossed over and parties may arrive at a premature or false consensus (Schruijer 2008a; Gray and Schruijer 2010). Certain contexts are more prone to collusive dynamics than others as they may trigger strong fears of being excluded, such as inreorganization or under fierce performance regimes. As previously mentioned, protagonists are often hardly conscious of their underlying fears. Outsiders see through the collusion faster than the protagonists themselves and they may help expose the collusive dynamics through confrontation. Furthermore, group members who have managed to keep their psychological independence may be capable of breaking through a collusive group dynamic. Once confrontation takes place, group members can become aware of the collusive dynamics.

Collusion is the opposite of task conflict where a diversity of interests, ideas and preferences are openly voiced and proactively worked with (Jehn 1995; Schruijer 2008a). The suppression of diversity is also a key characteristic of conformity and groupthink (Janis 1972), yet the dynamics of the latter two phenomena are different. In conformity and in groupthink, there are pressures from a known majority onto a known differently thinking individual. Thus, there are outside pressures, which in groupthink are also manifested in directive leadership. In collusion, the group members' fears and individual fantasies prevent them from speaking out and from testing reality. Thus, the pressures come from within (although in reality, the pressures from within and without can co-exist). Colluding group members may even privately agree, yet they find it impossible to communicate their agreement: in the Abilene Paradox, group members do just the opposite to what group members individually want to do or believe. Further, collusion in the social psychological sense is different from organizational secrecy (Costas and Grey 2014), which is a phenomenon described as the processes of intentional concealment of information. Collusion is a non-conscious dynamic. Some may see through it faster than others while some may see the contributing acts of others more clearly than how their own behavior reinforces the dynamics.

The term collusion has a long history in psychoanalysis, which pertains to a relationship between individuals who unconsciously confirm one another in one's behavior. Applied to the relationship between a psychoanalyst and an analysand, it has been defined as "a resistance between therapist and patient in which the transference and countertransference become interlocked in a tacit agreement to avoid a mutually fantasized catastrophe" (Karlsson 2004). An example could be a psychoanalyst who has a strong need for admiration and hence, cannot help the analysand to understand the latter's idealization of the analyst in terms of a defense of aggression (Stroeken 2000). Collusion can occur in any type of relationship. In the therapeutic world, couple dysfunction can be understood as projecting intrapsychic difficulties on the other who subsequently may act out some of these projections (e.g., Zeitner 2003).

Understanding collusion as a social defense against anxiety (Menzies-Lyth 1959), which occurs in a larger organizational and societal context, fits a systems–psychodynamic perspective on groups and organizations (Vansina and Vansina-Cobbaert 2008). A systems–psychodynamic perspective works within notions from psychoanalysis and systems theory to understand the (conscious and unconscious) emotional dynamics operating at the level of social systems while also finding ways to work with these. Long, who adopts a systems–psychodynamic perspective, has written about perverse cultures where collusive dynamics are a central feature. These dynamics underlie the manifest corruption in and of organizations. Perverse cultures are characterized by: (1) the realization of individual goals or pleasures at the expense of others; (2) simultaneously seeing while also denying reality; (3) the engagement of others as accomplices in the perversion; (4) turning a blind eye; and (5) a self-reinforcing cycle of perversions (Long 2008, p. 15).

A systems–psychodynamic perspective unearths the unconscious emotional underpinnings of collusion. It uses psychoanalytic understanding while trying to deindividualize collusion (and other) phenomena. Collusion needs to be understood at a social system level and not as individual behavior. The context of the social system is considered to be very important. Harvey also described collusion as a group or social system phenomenon. It is interesting to note that Jerry Harvey, like many of his contemporaries, such as Irving Janis, were familiar with psychoanalytic thinking as (social) psychologists, reflecting the less specialized training at the time as well as the openness to psychoanalysis, which is very different to current times (Schruijer and Curseu 2014).

3. Some Examples

I will present some examples where I was directly involved either as an action researcher or organizational member. Thus, I could sense and experience the dynamics. In my work on interorganizational collaboration (Schruijer 2008b), I have frequently encountered collusive dynamics. In various runs of a two-day simulation involving seven legally autonomous parties working around a regional development issue (Vansina et al. 1998), intended to help participants (managers and other practitioners) to learn about relational dynamics in an experiential way, it often proves increasingly difficult to engage in task conflict, needed to arrive at constructive plans that realize joint goals while also serving one's own interests. Having quite unsuccessfully dealt with the complexities, diversities and ambiguities, the participants instead settle for a vague and untested final deal and quickly wave away any doubt, critical remark or new piece of information that may be uttered during the last meeting. Thus, unrealistic deals are made as any deal is apparently considered better than no deal (although the simulation's instructions make it very clear that no deal is expected), even though this deal serves no one's interests and is based on false and unchecked assumptions. This reality does generally kick in during the one-day review after the actual simulation albeit slowly. Initially, individuals often think they have collaborated very well and seem happy with what they experience as successful agreements. It is only after the feelings of disappointment and/or shame are experienced that the defenses are dropped.

Another example is when I was asked to work with a group of contractors and the principal agent on the redevelopment of a major highway in the Netherlands (Schruijer 2015). Wanting to overcome the traditional win–lose climate, the protagonists had initiated an informal table that met regularly with all stakeholders present. The idea was to discuss the problems, mobilize the constituencies and deal with the concerns before escalation could occur at formal contract tables. It was an innovation for those involved and collaborative relationships were built among the various contractors and the governmental principal. However, as the parties became more and more careful not to destroy the burgeoning collaborative relationships, real concerns and potentially divisive issues disappeared from the discussion. Although parties intended to bring in their concerns, the meetings ended without much tension. For example, there was a growing concern among all stakeholders that they could not meet the deadline which they proudly had moved forward. Rather than addressing the issue and openly discussing the problems and possible solutions at the informal table as they had agreed to do, they acted as if nothing was the matter. The parties seemed satisfied and felt they were collaborating well. As such, these dynamics undermined the raison d'être of the well-intended informal table When interviewing parties afterwards, they were wondering why they had not brought in their pressing concerns. Once the collusive dynamics, which resulted in them not facing their reality, were addressed through outside interventions, the protagonists could recognize the dynamics that kept them trapped and they were able to subsequently deal with the issues. The tendency to collude in keeping important concerns out needs to be seen in light of a threatening context: (a) a major building fraud was still in the back of their minds; (b) a history of win–lose conflict as a consequence of tendering based on the lowest price existed; (c) protagonists, who sincerely wanted to show the world that collaboration between contractors on the one hand and the principal on the other was possible, were confronted with their respective constituencies who did not at all believe so; and finally (d) negative newspaper articles circulated concerning the financial and time excesses of large infrastructural projects.

Collusive dynamics can also be encountered at universities as I once experienced as an external examiner of a PhD committee. My negative assessment was met with hostility by one of the supervisors. I was requested to step down from the committee, which I refused. By then, I had found out that there was an ex-supervisor who had given up on this PhD project as, so I was told, it was doomed to fail. I asked for a response to my assessment from the supervisors, which I did not receive, although I was reassured by mail that an open discussion was to be held on the day of the defense (while the PhD was to be conferred anyhow, in line with the regulations, as all other examiners had approved of the thesis). I asked for the reports of the other examiners, which I did not receive. Furthermore, I requested that my report was to be sent to the other examiners which, as I later learned, never happened. I rang the dean, sharing my view that at least a discussion among committee members was needed. The dean commented that the correct procedure was followed so no intervention was needed. Days before the formal ceremony, I contacted the two other external examiners: one was surprised that he had not received my formal report while also expressing his doubts about the quality of the PhD. After the ceremony, the other examiner whispered in my ear that so much more was wrong with the thesis. No discussion among committee members took place on the day itself as the chair decided there was no time for that. Afterwards, the dean told me that the examination procedure was to be changed while one of the supervisors expressed his frustration over me sending my report to the address provided rather than to the supervisor informally. It struck me how all discussion was avoided during the whole process. Even the assessment procedure (consisting of soliciting only a 'yes, the manuscript can proceed to the formal defense" or "no, it cannot" from the examiners) precludes the sharing and discussion of ideas. Systems, routines, regulations and the decisions of key actors all avoided a platform where opinions and ideas could be shared and reality could be tested. There was no shared interest to do so. I have analyzed this particular experience in more detail (Schruijer 2013) and situated it in a larger university context that implicitly seems to discourage negative assessments (as among other factors, a substantial output bonus for each successfully defended PhD is conferred to the university).

Other examples can be taken from different sectors. A recently published one that explicitly uses the term 'collusive dynamics' pertains to the child protection practice (Revell and Burton 2016), which has been criticized for professional negligence. The latter is attributed to collusive dynamics by Revell and Burton against the background of performance pressures. Practitioners have difficulties discussing the troublesome emotional aspects of their work with their supervisors while the latter fail to explore what makes it difficult to confront actual abuse as this may work against meeting the performance indicators. Well-elaborated examples of collusive dynamics in perverse cultures are provided by Long (e.g., Long Term Capital Management (LTCM) and Parmalat) herself (Long 2008). The consequences of the many examples provided above vary in seriousness. Not all examples result in corruption, although the collective denial of reality and acting upon such delusions can definitely be called perverse.

4. Reflection

The question remains—is collusion criminal? Unlike the general understanding of collusion as fraud or deceit, collusion in the psychological meaning is no crime. However, it is a phenomenon that may result in non-action, neglect, irresponsible, corrupt or other criminal behavior or may result in people collectively choosing the wrong course of action. In reality, individuals are often either held accountable or held culpable for the outcome of collusive dynamics. Individuals under whose jurisdiction the negative consequences occur are often taken off duty or dismissed. Those who are held to be culpable may have indeed acted culpably. Yet, if collusive dynamics are at play, punishing an individual will not change the climate under which culpable behavior may have occurred, although finding a culpable individual (or an innocent scapegoat) may help alleviate feelings of anger, shame and anxiety in the larger system.

Adm. Sci. **2018**, *8*, 24

Pointing out and removing a bad apple may be sensible but it does not address the underlying dynamics that created the bad apple or at least allowed the bad apple to flourish.

Conflicts of Interest: The author declares no conflicts of interest.

References

Ayres, Ian. 1993. How cartels punish: A structural theory of self-enforcing collusion. *Columbia Law Review* 87: 295–323. [CrossRef]

Costas, Jana, and Christopher Grey. 2014. Bringing secrecy into the open: Towards a theorization of the social processes of organizational secrecy. *Organization Studies* 35: 1423–47. [CrossRef]

Gray, Barbara, and Sandra Schruijer. 2010. Integrating multiple voices: Working with collusion. In *Relational Practices, Participative Organizing*. Edited by Chris Steyaert and Bart Van Looy. Emerald: Bingley, pp. 121–35.

Harvey, Jerry B. 1988. *The Abilene Paradox and Other Meditations in Management*. Lexington: Lexington Books.

Harvey, Jerry B. 1999. *How Come Everytime I Get Stabbed in the Back My Fingerprints Are on the Knife*. San Francisco: Jossey-Bass.

Janis, Irving L. 1972. *Victims of Groupthink*. Boston: Houghton Mifflin.

Jehn, Karen A. 1995. A multimethod examination examination of the benefits and detriments of intragroup conflict. *Administrative Science Quarterly* 40: 256–82. [CrossRef]

Karlsson, Roger. 2004. Collusions as interactive resistances and possible stepping-stones out of impasses. *Psychoanalytic Psychology* 21: 567–79. [CrossRef]

Long, Susan. 2008. *The Perverse Organization and Its Deadly Sins*. New York: Routledge.

Menzies-Lyth, Isabel. 1959. The functions of social systems as a defence against anxiety: A report on a study of the nursing service of a general hospital. *Human Relations* 13: 95–121. [CrossRef]

Revell, Lisa, and Victoria Burton. 2016. Supervision and the dynamics of collusion: A rule of optimism? *British Journal of Social Work* 46: 1587–601. [CrossRef]

Schruijer, Sandra. 2008a. *Samenwerking, Collusie en de rol van Devianten*. Utrecht: Utrecht University.

Schruijer, Sandra. 2008b. The psychology of interorganizational relations. In *The Oxford Handbook of Interorganizational Relations*. Edited by Cropper Steve, Mark Ebers, Chris Huxham and Peter Smith Ring. New York: Oxford: Oxford University Press, pp. 417–40.

Schruijer, Sandra. 2013. Venalism in higher education: A systems–psychodynamic perspective. *Organizational and Social Dynamics* 13: 115–26.

Schruijer, Sandra. 2015. Like hedgehogs making love: Ups and downs in the relationship between a public body and private contractors in reconstructing a main Dutch highway. Paper presented at NIG Panel 13: Public Private Partnerships, Nijmegen, The Netherlands, November 5–6.

Schruijer, Sandra, and Petru L. Curseu. 2014. Looking at the gap between the social psychological and psychodynamic perspectives on group dynamics historically. *Journal of Organizational Change Management* 27: 232–45. [CrossRef]

Stroeken, Harry. 2000. *Nieuw Psychoanalytisch Woordenboek*. Meppel: Boom Koninklijke Uitgevers.

Van den Heuvel, Grat. 2005. The parliamentary enquiry on fraud in the Dutch construction industry collusion as concept between corruption and state-corporate crime. *Crime, Law and Social Change* 44: 133–51. [CrossRef]

Vansina, Leopold S., and Marie-Jeanne Vansina-Cobbaert. 2008. *Psychodynamics for Consultants and Managers: From Understanding to Leading Meaningful Change*. London: Wiley.

Vansina, L., T. C. B. Taillieu, S. G. L. Schruijer, W. Pasmore, and R. Woodman. 1998. 'Managing' multiparty issues: Learning from experience. In *Research in Organizational Change and Development*. Edited by William A. Pasmore, Abraham B. Shani and Richard W. Woodman. Greenwich: JAI Press, vol. 11, pp. 159–83.

Zeitner, Richard M. 2003. Obstacles for the psychoanalyst in the practice of couple therapy. *Psychoanalytic Psychotherapy* 20: 348–62. [CrossRef]

MDPI

St. Alban-Anlage 66

4052 Basel

Switzerland

Tel. +41 61 683 77 34

Fax +41 61 302 89 18

www.mdpi.com

Administrative Sciences Editorial Office

E-mail: admsci@mdpi.com

www.mdpi.com/journal/admsci

www.ingramcontent.com/pod-product-compliance
Lightning Source LLC
Chambersburg PA
CBHW051907210326
41597CB00033B/6053